ANCIENT JAPANESE NOBILITY

The *Kabane* Ranking System

BY
RICHARD J. MILLER

University of California Press

ANCIENT JAPANESE NOBILITY
The *Kabane* Ranking System

ANCIENT JAPANESE NOBILITY

The *Kabane* Ranking System

by Richard J. Miller

UNIVERSITY OF CALIFORNIA PRESS
BERKELEY · LOS ANGELES · LONDON
1974

UNIVERSITY OF CALIFORNIA PUBLICATIONS:
OCCASIONAL PAPERS

Number 7: History

Approved for publication January 12, 1973

University of California Press
Berkeley and Los Angeles
California

University of California Press, Ltd.
London, England

ISBN: 0-520-09494-8
Library of Congress Catalog Card Number: 73-620018
© 1974 by The Regents of the University of California
Printed in the United States of America

In memory of
PETER ALEXIS BOODBERG
1903–1972

Acknowledgments

In the preparation of this work during the last six years I have received much help, guidance and encouragement from many colleagues and friends to whom I wish to extend my most sincere thanks. Without their kind consideration on numerous occasions, I very much doubt that this study of ancient Japan would have been published. I am indebted to International Christian University, Tokyo, for use of its library facilities during my years on its faculty prior to 1970. I appreciate the use of the various facilities of the University of California at Berkeley and Davis, also. I wish to express my gratitude to the University of California, Davis, for the provision of Faculty Research Grants during the last three academic years of 1970-73, which facilitated completion of this study.

A number of specialists read all or portions of earlier drafts of the manuscript, and a number of their suggestions were incorporated in two subsequent revisions. They include Professor Kwang-ching Liu, Mr. Key Hiuk Kim and Mr. Shuzō Koyama, my colleagues at the University of California, Davis; Professors Delmer M. Brown, Wolfram Eberhard, William McCullough and Helen McCullough of the University of California, Berkeley; Dr. Felicia G. Bock of Berkeley; Professors J. Edward Kidder and Roger Matthews of International Christian University, Tokyo; and Professor John W. Hall of Yale University. To all of these who have lent a helping hand, I wish to express my indebtedness, but I hasten to add that what inadequacies remain in this present work are my responsibility alone.

My special thanks also goes to Mr. Key Hiuk Kim who kindly provided the calligraphy for this volume. Finally, I wish to express my deep gratitude to Miriam, my wife, for her unfailing encouragement and for her infinite patience and devotion in the typing of the various drafts of the manuscript.

Richard J. Miller

University of California, Davis

Abbreviations

KJK	Kojiki.
KJK I	Donald L. Philippi, tr. Kojiki.
KJK II	Basil Hall Chamberlain, tr. Kojiki or Records of Ancient Matters.
KJK III	Kurano Kenji, Takeda Yūkichi, annotators. Nihon koten bungaku taikei, vol. 1, Kojiki-Norito.
NRD	Kawade Shobō. Nihon rekishi daijiten.
NSK	Nihon Shoki.
NSK I	W. G. Aston, tr. Nihongi, Chronicles of Japan from Earliest Times to A.D. 697.
NSK V	Sakamoto Tarō, Ienaga Saburō, Inoue Mitsusada, Ōno Susumu, annotators. Nihon koten bungaku taikei, vols. 67-68, Nihon Shoki.
SNG	Shoku Nihongi.
SNG I	Saeki Ariyoshi, ed. Zōhō rikkokushi, vols. 3-4, Shoku Nihongi.
SSJR	Shinsen Shōjiroku.
SSJR I	Kurita Hiroshi. Shinsen shōjiroku kōshō.
SSJR II	Saeki Arikiyo. Shinsen shōjiroku no kenkyū, honbunhen.

Contents

Introduction	1
I. Problems and Methodology	18
II. Grants of Muraji to Eighteen Individuals in A.D. 680-681	34
III. Grants of Muraji to Fifty-five Uji in A.D. 682-684	38
IV. Emperor Tenmu's Eight-Rank Kabane System of A.D. 684	52
V. Grants of Mahito to Thirteen Uji in A.D. 684	59
VI. Grants of Asomi to Fifty-Two Uji in A.D. 684	72
VII. Grants of Sukune to Fifty Uji in A.D. 684	84
VIII. Grants of Imiki to Eleven Uji in A.D. 685	94
IX. The Lower Four Grades of Kabane	102
X. Kabane Patterns	108
XI. Sample Analyses	113
A. Lamentations According to Imibe no Hironari	114
B. Graves and Ancestors	124
C. Quantification of Nihon Shoki Activities Categories	127
XII. Conclusions	135
Appendix I: Inventory of Kabane-Bearing Uji and Individuals Noted in the Nihon Shoki from the Beginning of the Reign of Keitai through that of Jitō	147
A. Inventory of Kabane-Bearing Uji and Individuals not Granted Kabane during Tenmu's or Jitō's Reigns	149
B. Inventory of Kabane Grantees during Tenmu's and Jitō's Reigns Grouped by Uji	160
Appendix II: Inventory and Distribution of Kabane listed in the Shinsen Shōjiroku	188

Table I: Chronological Listing of the <u>Kabane</u>-Recipient <u>Uji</u> and Individuals During the Reign of Tenmu	191
Table II: Alphabetical Listing of the <u>Kabane</u>-Recipient <u>Uji</u> and Individuals During Tenmu's and Jitō's Reigns	197
Bibliography	205

Introduction

This monograph is devoted to the investigation and description of a system of noble titles as it existed and functioned in Japan during the pre-Nara period of the sixth and seventh centuries A.D. These titles are known as kabane, a term that appears frequently in both the Kojiki (KJK) and Nihon Shoki (NSK). Briefly defined here, but described in detail in the body of this monograph, kabane were titles of nobility that were hereditary in nature and were borne by all members of a given uji, a term most often translated as "clan" but more accurately rendered as "lineage group."

During the sixth and seventh centuries, before the reign of Emperor Tenmu (A.D. 672-686), the sources refer to approximately thirty different kabane, the number varying as to the limits one wishes to place on his definition of the term. To a far less than absolute degree, and in ways that are not totally clear, the kabane, for the top echelons of the sociopolitical hierarchy in the sixth and seventh centuries, were indicators of a relative-ranking system based largely upon the type of real or fictive ancestry a given lineage group believed it had or was accepted to have had. For the lower echelons of the hierarchy kabane were indicators of status based upon an uncertain combination of various factors including lineage, occupation, and service to the state.

For example, we find that such kabane as kimi, omi, and muraji were traditionally borne by the most prestigious lineage groups because of their relatively close blood relationship with the imperial line; because of the reputed roles their progenitors played in support of the imperial line in mythological times and in the founding of the Japanese state; because of their military, political and economic power and influence in more recent historical times; or because of managerial services performed for the imperial line. By contrast one finds that such _kabane_ as _atahi_, _obito_, _miyatsuko_, _kishi_, _fubito_ and _agatanushi_ were borne by lineage groups because of the managerial service they had traditionally rendered to the imperial line, or because their ancestors had formerly been territorial magnates in regions removed from the court and had, in some way and at some time in the past, been brought into a more direct relationship with the imperial line. It is also in this lower category of _kabane_-bearers that frequently are found incorporated lineage groups of continental or immigrant origin.

Japanese scholars consistently use either the term "_uji-kabane seido_" or "_shisei seido_," which means the _uji-kabane_ system, because of the intimate relationship between lineage groups, or _uji_, and their titles, or _kabane_. For some centuries prior to the Nara period this system constituted a fundamental aspect or, one might well say, the very fabric of the sociopolitical organization of ancient Japan subsequent to the establishment of the Japanese state. It was a system in which social, occupational and political factors and considerations were so interwoven as to be inseparable. A detailed textual analysis of the _NSK_ for the sixth and seventh centuries, the period encompassed by this present study, demonstrates this inseparability: therein any social group identified as an _uji_ bears a _kabane_.

Evolving as early as the fourth or early fifth centuries, but clearly established and functioning by the early sixth century, was this system in which certain lineage groups performed on a hereditary basis specific services or pursued specific occupations for, or on behalf of, the imperial house. While the chieftains of these lineage groups possessed and had control of their own blood-related members as well as of various types of occupational groups (_be_) not related by blood to the lineage groups, they also had gained or were given administrative charge of numerous types of occupational groups of workers belonging to the imperial house.

Not only did this system grow increasingly complex with the passage of time, but there developed marked differences and contrasts in the relative size, influence and strength of the numerous lineage groups participating to one degree or another in services for the imperial line. It is generally agreed by Japanese scholars that certain titles, which from earlier times had merely been used as terms of honor, respect or deference (kaishō), gradually came to be used as designators that reflected the relative and variant ranking and status of these lineage groups within the overall sociopolitical structure of the Japanese state. With this development, the earlier titles of honor and respect may be termed kabane.

There are at least two basic approaches one may take to the study of uji during the two centuries prior to the Nara period. First, one may analyze the internal components of a number of specific uji with the aim of constructing a hypothetical "model" uji, on the basis of the scattered references and rather fragmentary data one finds in the KJK and NSK. This model would include a number of components such as the lineage group's chieftain (uji-no-kami), the group's venerated progenitor or deity (uji-gami), the group's blood-related members (uji-bito), as well as collateral descent groups of varying degrees of subservience and relationship with the main descent group. The model would also include information on the structure and functions of other human components of the uji, such as occupational or workers' groups (be or tomo), which were largely composed of agricultural workers, probably in a state closely resembling serfdom, as well as of other types of more specialized workers and suppliers of goods and services. While not related by blood to the lineage group under whose control they existed, they nevertheless constituted an integral component of the uji and its most basic economic and often military asset.

The second approach that one might pursue in the study of uji involves the broader subject of the functions and the roles they played within the Japanese society. This approach centers attention on the relationships between the various uji and the imperial house, on the interrelationships of the uji themselves, and on their relative ranking within the overall sociopolitical structure of the Japanese state. By the beginning of the sixth century A.D. Japanese society was characterized by a remarkable complex of aristocratic lineage groups, some of which were so powerful economically, militarily and politically, that they were able to vie with one another, as well as with the imperial house, for control of government.

The records provide many indications that by the sixth century a few of the uji were not only very large and controlled substantial numbers of agricultural workers and military forces, but certain of them had also extended the degree of their influence by establishing cooperative relationships with both real and fictive collateral descent groups, groups which we may term sub-uji. A powerful uji in control of such an extended family-like federation, as well as the collateral descent groups so controlled, most often bore their own unique uji surnames, but they all bore the same kabane and claimed descent from the same uji progenitor. Some of these powerful uji claimed descent from kami, while others claimed descent from former emperors. As such, the latter were, or claimed to be, collateral descendants of the reigning sovereign and, in common with the imperial line, direct descendants of the country's most prestigious progenitrix, Amaterasu Ohomikami, the Sun Goddess.

One result of the evolution of such a sociopolitical structure was the great attention paid to genealogical matters by the compilers of the KJK and NSK in the early eighth century. Another result of such a complex social structure was the importance of relative ranking, and it is to this subject as it relates to kabane that the present monograph is primarily devoted. The kabane that were borne by Japan's ancient lineage groups by the sixth and seventh centuries were manifestations of the status differentiations inherent within Japan's nobility system. As such they symbolized many of the status-related values of that ancient society. The analysis of the determinants of kabane ranking is one salient means of increasing our insight into some of the values that influenced the interrelationships and relative standing of aristocratic lineage groups in the several centuries before the Nara period.

The structural characteristics and functional modes of the Yamato state in the sixth century were products of an evolutionary process that had required centuries. By the early part of that century the state was in the control of a few powerful lineage groups. The NSK portrays a situation in which the chieftains of these powerful groups shared in the control of the Yamato state and were technically subservient to a monarch who, because of his preeminent lineage harking back to the Sun Goddess, acted as the chief of chieftains. When the twenty-sixth sovereign, known posthumously in history as Emperor Keitai, came to the throne around A.D. 507 the chieftains of the Ohotomo no Muraji, Mononobe no Muraji and Kose no Omi lineage groups shared with Keitai the control of the state. By the end of the sixth century frequent and violent factional struggles among the chieftains of the most powerful lineage groups had led to the elimination of the Ohotomo, Kose and Mononobe from prime positions of leadership and to the replacement in that position by the chieftain of the Soga lineage group.

In concert with an imperial prince, known posthumously in history as Shōtoku Taishi, Soga no Umako violently eliminated the Mononobe leadership in A.D. 587. The NSK depicts the sixth century as one of great tension and competition between a few extremely powerful uji who competed with one another to share as exclusively as possible the rule of the land with the reigning sovereign, the chieftain of the Sun Line. And by the end of that century we find that the Soga and the imperial house had formed a hegemony which was to be the prototype of the dyarchy that was to characterize Japanese rulership for centuries to come.

In the next half century, prior to A.D. 645, there developed a major power struggle between the imperial house and the Soga, even though the two groups were, to an extraordinary degree, intimately related by blood through intermarriage. In fact, as much Soga as imperial blood flowed in the veins of some of the scions of the Sun Line. It appears from the NSK account for the first half of the seventh century that the over-aggressiveness of the Soga possibly foreshadowed the supreme ambition of the Soga to supplant the chieftain of the imperial line with their own chieftain. But finally, through the stealthy plans of Nakatomi no Kamako (later to be Fujihara no Kamatari), in cooperation with Imperial Prince Naka no Ohoe, the Soga leadership was subjected to bloody extermination in a palace coup in A.D. 645.

At least this is the picture drawn by the NSK, but it must be remembered that the compilers of that work in the early eighth century represented the thinking of some of the very elements that had successfully vanquished the Soga. Even though the probable bias of the NSK may lead one to question certain aspects of its account of the rise and fall of the Soga uji, there can be no doubt but that the sixth century and the first half of the seventh witnessed an important transition in both the components and modes of governance at the highest echelons of state. And yet while that transition involved great change, it is also eminently clear that such change as did occur was basically accomplished within the traditional societal framework of the clan or lineage-group structure which had gradually evolved in preceding centuries. Thus, we find in that period, not the evolution of new governmental institutions, but rather a diminution in the number of lineage groups participating in conjunction with the imperial house in the rule of the country. These changes constituted a continuing trend toward the greater degree of centralization of government that also had started much earlier.

The rise of the Soga uji to paramount position among all other uji contributed positively to another ongoing trend, namely, the enhancement of the power and prestige of the sovereign and the imperial house as a whole, a process which would continue and accelerate throughout the remainder of the seventh century. By the first quarter of the seventh century, the sovereign's position as primus inter pares was decidedly stronger in competition with the Soga than it had been in the early sixth century when the "equals" were numerous and included such powerful lineages as the Kose, Ohotomo,

Mononobe and the Soga.

The half century following the palace coup of A.D. 645 was a period during which the state's new leadership at court made fundamental institutional innovations in a program known under the rubric of the Taika Reform (Taika no kaishin). Within a little more than half a century a central and provincial governmental bureaucracy had been formulated, based largely on organizational adaptations of contemporaneous Chinese models. The central governmental structure was characterized by its eight ministries and a large number of departments, bureaus and offices, each with a Chinese-sounding name, and all symmetrically arranged under the top administrative body known as the Council of State (Daijōkan), which, in turn, was in the charge of a Chancellor (Daijō Daijin), the highest administrative offical below the rank of the emperor. Next in rank within the Council of State were the Ministers of the Left and Right (Sa-U Daijin) and below them numerous other officials in graduated positions. The reform program also included the demarcation of local administrative units within the state, comprising the capital area, the Home Provinces (kinai), provinces (kuni), districts within provinces (kōri), as well as towns, villages, etc. Provisions were made for each administrative unit to be staffed with designated types and numbers of officials.

While these institutional innovations provided for a new central and local governmental structure, other statutes of the reform were aimed at realizing the claim that the emperor and the state should possess absolute supremacy over all other social and political entities of the country. Regulations were issued ordering that private ownership of both land and peoples be placed under the control of the government. And in order eventually to fulfill the aims of these regulations, provisions were also made for the compilation of census and tax records and for the allocation and future periodic reallocation of land.

The objective of the reformers was to bring to an end the traditional clan rule of the state by groups of powerful lineage groups clustered around the imperial house. During the sixth century the highest officals at the court had been known as the ohoomi and ohomuraji, the ohoomi being the most powerful chieftain of lineage groups bearing the kabane of omi and claiming descent from an imperial ancestor, and the ohomuraji being the most powerful chieftain of lineage groups bearing the kabane of muraji and claiming descent from any one of a number of deity (kami) progenitors. Prior to the defeat of the Mononobe by the Soga in A.D. 587 there were normally appointed on the accession of an emperor one ohoomi chieftain and one or two ohomuraji chieftains. For example, the reign of Keitai opened in A.D. 507 with the chieftains of the Ohotomo no Muraji and the Mononobe no Muraji lineage groups being appointed ohomuraji, and the chieftain of the Kose no Omi group being appointed ohoomi. However, from A.D. 587, after the defeat of the Mononobe by the Soga, and until the Taika palace coup of A.D. 645, only one such high post, that of ohoomi, was held by the chieftain of the Soga no Omi lineage group.

The new administrative structure established during the fifty years of the Taika Reform era after A.D. 645 replaced this uji-based central-government structure with the complex bureaucratic hierarchy mentioned above. The reformers' provision of central and provincial bureaucracies of graduated rank and responsibility aimed both at removing the control of the court and government from the one or more powerful uji chieftains who had traditionally clustered around the central clan-dominated power structure, and at removing the control of local government from the numerous, though influential, chieftains of lesser uji, who had traditionally dominated rulership in regions removed from the court. The reformers' abolition of private ownership of land and peoples aimed at destroying the traditional economic based which for centuries had supported and made possible the survival of the clan system of government. In other words, the new system was established on the premise that the central government's control of appointive offices and their emoluments would weaken and perhaps eliminate the traditional preference system that depended on, and had its roots in, clan connections and relationships. But many of these aims of the Taika reformers were not to be realized and were to remain in the realm of theory, for the records clearly demonstrate that traditional *uji* and family-like relationships continued for centuries to dictate position and preferential treatment within the state structure. The power of one's *uji*, precedence, and status based upon lineage considerations continued to provide the criteria of position within government and society. Thus, the political institutional changes that were implemented in the last half of the seventh century were not nearly as revolutionary, nor did they exert as pervasive an influence in the directions one might have anticipated.

While it is undeniable that the imperial institution eventually was elevated by the help of these changes to an unchallengeable and paramount position within the state, it is also true that individuals from many of the same *uji* which had been influential during the sixth and early seventh centuries continued to be appointed to the highest offices in the late seventh and eighth centuries. The Taika reforms implemented substantial innovations in the realms of political structure and theory, but those innovations brought about little change in the types of persons who staffed the positions of leadership within the new political mechanism. While the changes wrought in the political realm had the effect of asserting the social and political paramountcy of the imperial line over all other lineage groups, the concomitant effect was to assert, to a far greater degree than thitherto, the social supremacy of the noble lineage groups that had traditionally functioned near, and had been traditionally identified with, the court and capital over all elements of the provincial aristocracy. The reforms had the effect of further emphasizing the hierarchical structure of society and state by more boldly drawing the lines dividing the imperial line from all other court-oriented noble lineage groups, as well as the lines dividing these noble lineage groups from the regional aristocracy.

In cultures that appear to undergo relatively rapid change, innovation frequently is characterized by mere organizational rearrangements accompanied by terminological changes which mask the continuation in power of the very social groups that have long shared in the control of the state. Fundamental innovation is attained only when such groups adopt new values and modes of operation. However, this type of innovation is usually attained only after a long transitional period of adaptation and accommodation. It is during periods of this sort that one finds innovative administrative experiments and reaffirmations of traditional social values juxtaposed, and Japan in the seventh century was no exception in this regard. In spite of the many organizational changes that were instituted in Japan at that time, an incorrect understanding of the Japanese state and society will result if one ignores the numerous traditional values that continued to influence decision making, and if one is satisfied by merely typifying the era as one of change and innovation. One finds that in such areas as government and society the values of the traditional native cult of Shintō exerted strong influences on many major innovations and continued to coexist with them, sometimes performing the function of a countervail and at other times of a balance. Despite the rapid infiltration of Buddhist thought and the building of temples and monastic structures in the seventh century, the native cult, while certainly at times overshadowed in Japan's surge to match some of the cultural splendors of T'ang China, remained an essential feature of the life and society of the time.

The cultural importations of continental origin that accompanied Buddhism undoubtedly provided new and satisfying aesthetic and religious experiences, but, behind the facade of such importations and their adaptations, the native cult remained in fundamental ways unmoved. It remained unmoved simply because it had for long been inextricably fused with some of the basic considerations that determined the social rank, status and position of the sovereign and the imperial house, and of the many lineage groups that comprised the top strata of Japan's aristocratic society. The pantheon of the native cult provided the majority of such groups with their kami progenitors whose alleged relative ranking in mythological times was a direct reflection of the relative ranking and status of their descendants in the seventh century.

It is therefore not surprising that Shintō was institutionally and prominently grafted to the new government structure that was created on the basis of Chinese models in the second half of the seventh century. The details of that structure were described in the penal and administrative codes of the Taihō era (Taihō Ritsu-Ryō), which were put into effect in A.D. 702. There we find that while the Council of State is designated the highest administrative body in government, the Jingi-kan or Council of Kami Affairs, which was the department in charge of matters relating to the native cult, was not subordinated to it. To the contrary, the relative status of the Jingi-kan is reflected in the fact that it was placed on the same footing as the Council of State and enjoyed precedence over it. Such an arrangement reasserted, as far as the aristocratic lineage groups are concerned, the continuing essential value placed in the native cult, and, of even more importance, it reflected the essential value of the native cult as supportive of the claims of the sovereign and the imperial house to absolute social and political supremacy.

The study of the kabane system as it functioned during the sixth and seventh centuries provides significant insight into some of the traditional values of that period, particularly as they were connected to relative status, prestige and rank of many of the uji that comprised Japan's aristocracy. The starting point of this study is Tenmu's new kabane system that he established in A.D. 684. This new system was an integral phase of that sovereign's many acts aimed at achieving a more highly centralized state under the absolute control of the crown. By that system social ranking of noble lineage groups within the sociopolitical hierarchy was rationalized and made relative to the rank of the then reigning emperor, the chieftain of the lineage group tracing its ancestry back to the Sun Goddess.

Emperor Tenmu (A.D. 673-686) undoubtedly was one of the few vigorous and more independent sovereigns to be found in Japan's long history. His social and political prestige and preeminence, combined with a forceful personality, hastened the formulation of a strong centralized state that had been evolving for decades before his reign. He instituted numerous administrative reforms that contributed directly to the further sinification of the government's bureaucratic structure and control mechanisms. But despite his innovations and bureaucratic reforms, he retained a traditional Japanese mode of distinguishing social differentiation of the aristocracy on the basis of kabane, and he reaffirmed that mode of distinction by instituting an eight-rank kabane system (yakusa no kabane) in A.D. 684. From a study of kabane and their use during his reign, it is apparent that traditional institutions and methods were encouraged to the degree that they enhanced the claims to the prestige and paramount position of the ruling house. While the innovative bureaucratic adaptations from the continent were aimed at providing the sovereign and the most powerful chieftains with a more manageable and centralized government apparatus, the reaffirmation of the kabane system represented a continuing need for a traditional mode of status identification of noble lineage groups.[1] By the reign of Tenmu the reconstitution of the nobility

---

[1] The cap'rank system (kan'i) is an example of a seventh-century innovation that served eventually as another device to enhance the claims made by the imperial house to paramount position within the sociopolitical hierarchy. Established originally in A.D. 603 (Suiko 11/12/5), it consisted of six grades named after as many Confucian virtues, with each grade divided into greater and lesser degrees, resulting in a total of twelve ranks. Each rank within the system was visually distinguished by the color of caps officials were to wear. Six different colors were designated for the six grades, and the greater or lesser degrees of rank within each grade were distinguished by darker and lighter shades of the color. The system was revised and expanded in 647 (Taika 3/12/1) to thirteen ranks, consisting of six grades, each of which was divided into greater and lesser degrees, plus a single initial rank at the bottom. Visual distinction in the various ranks was accomplished by the color of the various caps, the type of material used, and hair ornaments. The system was further expanded in 649 (Taika 5/2/0) to nineteen ranks, and again in 664 (Tenchi 3/2/9) to twenty-six ranks. It is generally accepted that the first three revisions of the cap-rank system were necessary because of the expanding diversification of the duties and numbers of officials following the Taika coup of 645. It is believed that the cap-rank system as originally established in 603, aimed at integrating officials into the court hierarchy on

below the level of the imperial house had become essential, because of many changes and events that had occurred in the previous two centuries.

The use of kabane to signify a vague sort of social ranking system had developed centuries before the reign of Tenmu, but during the long period of their use, the individual import of each of the various traditional kabane became less apparent. In many of the periods covered by the KJK and NSK one finds specific accounts claiming that social relationships had become confused, that imposters took unto themselves kabane inappropriate to their real social standing, and that a rectification of such malpractices was required. Another element of confusion was created by the fact that through the centuries many lineage groups had expanded in size and complexity, and branch lineage groups, or what may be called sub-uji, had separated from their main houses and had established themselves in new geographic locations. When they did so they retained both their traditional kabane titles and claims to the same

---

the basis of ability and merit, rather than primarily on the basis of social considerations. However, the next revision of the system, which occurred in 685 (Tenmu 14/1/2), provided for the creation of certain ranks to be borne exclusively by princes (ō) as distinguished from officials (shin). In doing this, a two-tiered system was established in which twelve ranks in the upper tier were reserved for princes and forty-eight ranks in the lower tier were reserved for officials. The two tiers of ranks differed in terminology, but the twelve ranks reserved for princes and the first sixteen of the forty-eight ranks reserved for officials in general coincided as far as rank alone was concerned. Following the reign of Tenmu, this type of distinction in kind of rank based on social considerations was further delineated in the Taihō Code of 701. There a three-tiered system, differentiated by the terminology used in each tier, provided four ranks for princes of the blood (shinnō) in the top tier, fourteen ranks for other princes (ō) in the middle tier, and thirty ranks for officials in the bottom tier. In this case the top fourteen of the thirty ranks reserved for officials and the fourteen ranks reserved for princes coincided as far as rank alone was concerned. The last revision of this system prior to the middle of the nineteenth century appeared in the Yōrō Administrative Code of 718. That revision reverted to a two-tiered system, the upper tier consisting of the same four ranks reserved for princes of the blood (shinnō), but the lower tier of thirty ranks were reserved for both princes and officials. The conclusion is inescapable that the last three revisions of official ranks were aimed, at least in part, at enhancing within the sociopolitical hierarchy, the special social position and ranking enjoyed by the immediate family members of the sovereign. For succinct explanations of these ranking systems, see "Ikai" and "Kan'i" in NRD, and for one of the most comprehensive studies, see Kida Shinroku, Reisei ni okeru kunshin jōge no chitsujō ni tsuite, 1972.

lineage as their main houses.

As this sort of proliferation accelerated with the passage of time, the power and importance of many sub-uji diminished to the point where they wielded far less influence than their parent uji. In other cases sub-uji surpassed the parent uji in both economic power and political influence. In a society in which relative social rank had traditionally depended on lineage, confusion was the concomitant of these trends.

The situation by the last quarter of the seventh century was further complicated by a number of events and changes of cardinal political importance that had transpired in the previous century and a half. The sixth century opened with the elevation of Wohodo no Sumera Mikoto, posthumously known as Emperor Keitai, to be chieftan of the Sun Line and ruler over the tribal confederation of Yamato. He was a direct descendant in the fifth generation of Homuda no Sumera Mikoto, posthumously known as Emperor Ōjin. Keitai's elevation to the position of emperor represented the coming to power of a cadet branch of the Sun Line, and by the end of the seventh century the descendants of that cadet branch came to constitute a new nobility, occupying the highest echelons of the social hierarchy below the level of the imperial house.

Exerting equal influence on the changing character of the social and political components of the state were the importation from the Asiatic continent of Buddhism, together with other forms of philosophy and ethics, and knowledge of new technologies. During this process significant numbers of immigrant groups from the continent and their descendants found places in the lower strata of Japanese society, by reason of their technically advanced knowledge, training and abilities. They were settled throughout the Home Provinces of Yamato (Kinai), and some of the leaders of these groups attained varying degrees of prominence in economic, political, social and diplomatic affairs. Also of significance were the struggles between native Japanese factions headed by major lineage groups such as the Kose, Ohotomo, Mononobe, Nakatomi and Soga, which led successively to the attainment of paramountcy by the Soga in the late sixth century, to the elimination of the senior line of the Soga uji in the middle of the seventh, and to the rise of the Fujihara branch of the Nakatomi uji in the eighth and ninth centuries. Those struggles ended by eliminating certain lineage groups from the locus of power, while enabling others to take their places.

One last event must be listed here, because its outcome formed the basis for the immediate patterns of loyalty to the crown that were operative during the reign of Tenmu. This event was the Jinshin War (Jinshin no ran) of A.D. 672 in which Tenmu succeeded in defeating the faction of lineage groups supporting his nephew, Imperial Prince Ohotomo, the son and heir of Emperor Tenchi. These affairs and movements fundamentally influenced or altered the traditional social alignments and affected the relative ranking of many lineage groups, whether or not they directly participated in such generative events.

The combined impact of those events of almost two centuries' duration produced changes of a social nature requiring official recognition and symbolization. Emperor Tenmu's eight-rank kabane system represented one means of adjusting status labels of the top echelons of the nobility so as to make them coincide more closely with the values and realities of social ranking as they had evolved by the late seventh century. Through the new system he was able to designate which of the lineage groups of the realm were to be graded components of a new, reorganized nobility, each corporate member of which could lay claim to a specific social status that varied as to lineage, influence or service, or a combination thereof.

The following were the kabane of the new eight-rank system, listed in the order of their importance: mahito, asomi, sukune, imiki, michi-no-shi, omi, muraji and inaki. The top two ranks of mahito and asomi were granted primarily to lineage groups on the basis of the degree of blood relationship with the reigning monarch, and it is for this reason that Japanese scholars term the new ranks of <u>kabane</u> the "system of imperial relatives" or <u>kōshin-sei</u>.

While Tenmu's new system gave precedence to imperial relatives, it did more than that. It also recognized the contributions and influence of other lineage groups not related by blood to the Sun Line, groups which were believed to have been of <u>kami</u> or deity lineage. The most influential of these groups were granted <u>sukune</u> and placed in the next echelon below the imperial line. Lastly, Tenmu granted <u>imiki</u> to a few selected <u>uji</u> and thereby elevated them to the next level of the new nobility. They were selected because of their service to the imperial house and the state, and while such service was a primary criterion for their elevation, it is significant that these lineage groups included a few <u>uji</u> that were descended from immigrants from the Asiatic continent. It is clear that the gradations of rank within the new system varied as to their criteria. While the top two <u>kabane</u> ranks were overwhelmingly granted to lineage groups related by blood to the reigning sovereign, the lower ranking <u>kabane</u> of the new system were intended for <u>uji</u> that represented an uneven amalgam of descent types, degrees of power and influence, and service to the Sun Line and the state in both remote antiquity and more recent times.

The study of early Japanese social organization in general has been neglected by Western scholars. This matter was described by John W. Hall as follows: "One of the most neglected chapters in Western literature on Japanese history is that dealing with the life and institutions of the Japanese people in the centuries prior to the Taika Reform of 645.... But little has as yet appeared in English on the political and social organization of the early Japanese. By contrast, it is precisely these fields which have attracted the most intense interest of Japanese historians, especially in the postwar years."[2] It is hoped that this present mono-

---

[2] John W. Hall, <u>Japanese History, New Dimensions of Approach and Understanding</u> (Washington, 1966) pp. 24-25.

graph will contribute to a better understanding of a number of important aspects of the life and institutions of Japan in those early times, particularly as they relate to kabane borne by aristocratic lineage groups that comprised the most influential social and political components in the state below the level of the Sun Line.

CHAPTER I
Problems and Methodology

Reading through the KJK and NSK one meets with a wide assortment of kabane, but neither source explains in any place the nature and function of the kabane system, and a search of the literature in Western languages will not turn up any detailed study devoted to this system. The subject was touched on in English as early as 1882 when Chamberlain published his translation of the KJK. In his translator's introduction (p. xvii) he states:

> Without forgetting the fact that so-called equivalent terms in two languages rarely quite cover each other, and that it may therefore be necessary in some cases to render one Japanese word by two or three different English words according to the context, the translator has striven to keep such diversity within the narrowest limits, as it tends to give a false impression of the original, implying that it possesses a versatility of thought which is indeed characteristic of Modern Europe, but not at all of Early Japan. With reference to this point a certain class of words must be mentioned, as the English translation is unavoidably defective in their case, owing to the fact of our language not possessing sufficiently close synonyms for them.

While Chamberlain recognized that the various kabane could not be translated, he did decide to use a variety of English terms of noble rank to render specific kabane but at the same time stressing "They are merely, so to speak, labels by which titles that are distinct in the original are sought to be kept distinct in the translation." (p. xviii) The following are a few of his renditions into English: asomi is roughly rendered as "court noble," kimi as "duke," omi as "grandee," muraji as "chief," miyatsuko as "ruler," atahi as "suzerain" and agata-nushi as "department lord."[1] The danger inherent in such an approach can be demonstrated by the fact that asomi and sukune were included in Tenmu's revised kabane system after A.D. 684, but not in the traditional, pre-Tenmu system. Also omi and muraji were used in both the pre-Tenmu and the Tenmu systems, but in the former case they were most often indicators of very high noble rank, and in the latter they were indicators of relatively low rank. The other kabane listed above were not included in Tenmu's revised system of 684. Chamberlain was fully aware of the problem, for he later states (p. 59, n.5) in reference to the rendition of a particular kabane,

> Remember that all the names in this and similar lists are hereditary "gentile names," and that "Duke" and the other titles used in this translation to designate them must only be regarded as approximations towards giving the force of the Japanese originals, which are themselves by no means always clear, either etymologically or historically.

In his translation of the NSK in 1896, Aston wisely transliterated the various kabane, rather than attempt either English renditions or translations. He did try to explain briefly the use and function of kabane when he dealt with a specific uji and kabane early in his translation (vol. I, p. 27, n. 7), as follows:

> Adzumi no Muraji is a title corresponding exactly to such English titles as "Duke of Wellington," Adzumi being the name of a place and Muraji a title of honour. It is derived from mura, a village or assemblage, and ushi, master. The titles, called Uji or Kabane, though Kabane is properly the second or honorary element, were in their origin simply official designations, and in the "Nihongi" we frequently

---

[1] These and subsequent statements are in no way meant as negative criticism of the pioneering and often monumental work of many early Western scholars. Rather, the point being demonstrated is that before kabane can be translated or even satisfactorily defined, their uses within a system or systems of kabane must be clarified.

meet with cases where the office and the title were united in the same person. They were, however, hereditary, and by degrees the mere honorary element prevailed. It too, ultimately vanished, these titles becoming simply surnames to which no particular distinction was attached. Japanese writers, the author of the "Nihongi" with the rest, have, for want of a more appropriate character, identified them with the Chinese 姓 or surname, which is only true of a period later than the time covered by the "Nihongi." There was also a personal name (na), but the ancient Japanese seem to have had no proper surnames, although the Uji answered the same purpose in a rough way.

While this treatment is not too helpful for gaining a satisfactory understanding of kabane, it does lay stress on changes that occurred in the use and implications of kabane with the passage of time. While the original implications of muraji may be reflected in its etymological analysis, those implications were no longer present in the use to which the kabane of muraji was put by the late seventh century following Tenmu's revision of the system in 684.

The most complete presentation in English is found in Asakawa's Early Institutional Life of Japan, first published in 1903. There Asakawa occasionally refers to kabane in general as "an honorary title," and, in most cases of specific kabane, he transliterates rather than attempting a translation or rendition. He explains (p. 62):

> The uji was the clan or family name borne by all the members belonging thereto. The kabane was formerly an honorary title, attached to the uji, and, unless revoked for crime, handed down from generation to generation. It gradually came to be regarded as a part of the clan or family name to which it was suffixed.

For the long time span before the Heian period, the study of kabane may be roughly but conveniently divided into three periods: the archaic, for the long span of time before the sixth century; the pre-Tenmu, for the period from the beginning of Keitai's reign in approximately 507 to the institution of Tenmu's revised kabane system in 684; and the post-Tenmu period, for the span of time from Tenmu's reign through the Nara period to the end of the eighth century. As far as kabane usage is concerned, each of the periods is quite distinct, so that only the most general description would be applicable to more than one of the periods.[2] Western investigators generally agree that originally kabane were indicators of social or occupational status, or both, that they next became hereditary in nature and were borne by all members of a given uji, that they gradually became honorary in nature, and that they subsequently became part of the names of the lineage groups that had originally borne the particular kabane. But it must be stressed these changes occurred very gradually and over a very long period, probably from as early as the formative period of the Yamato state to the late Heian period.[3]

[2] This monograph deals primarily with the second of these three periods.
[3] Some specific examples of definitions and renditions of kabane, which are found in Western languages, are listed below in chronological order:
Papinot's *Historical and Geographical Dictionary of Japan* (1910) p. 240, deals in part with kabane as follows:

A title of dignity or rank. It became a family name. Kabane is different from uji, the real family name. The uji was bestowed by the Emperor according to the merit, the kabane was attached to the function; Nakatomi, Fujiwara, etc., are uji; Omi, Muraji, Ason, Sukune, etc., are kabane. Formerly there were only the uji; but the families increased and the kabane were instituted to distinguish their different branches. The principal kabane met with in history are: Omi, Muraji, Tomo no miyatsuko, Waki, Kimi, Atae, Agata-nushi, Inagi, Suguri, etc. When the functions became hereditary, the uji and the kabane together formed the family name.

Katō and Hoshino in their translation of the Kogoshūi (1926) render the term kabane as either "hereditary title" or "title." In the body of their translation Katō and Hoshino render in several ways references that are composed of both an uji name and a kabane title. Sometimes transliteration is used as in the case of "Sake no Kimi," but one also finds examples such as "the Hata family of Kimi rank."

Jean and Robert Reischauer, in their *Early Japanese History* (1937) v. 2, p. 155, also render the term as "hereditary title." They succinctly define

When brief summaries are made of complex institutions that have evolved over a period of centuries, it is often inevitable that they be either inaccurate or misleading. When it comes to pre-Nara history, in general, and to the uji and kabane systems, in particular, the major factor contributing to such inaccuracy is the fragmentary nature of the available primary source materials. Serious methodological problems for the study of pre-Nara social and political institutions are created by the fact that the only two primary

---

kabane as follows:

> An honorary appellation at first given to the Clan Chieftain (Uji-no-kami) by his clansmen (uji-bito), meaning "lord", "chief", "superior", etc. Later developed into a hereditary title held not only by the Clan Chieftain, but by his close relatives as well. Still later it came to be a kind of official post granted by the Sovereign (Tennō). Finally, in 684 it became a kind of order of nobility with eight ranks or degrees...

Sansom, in his Japan, A Short Cultural History (1943), p. 40, refers to kabane as "titles" and describes them as follows:

> An integral part of the clan system, as would naturally be expected in a society so essentially aristocratic in structure, was the system of titles, or kabane. Originally there existed only clan names, such as Nakatomi and Ōtomo, and personal names such as Maro; but it became the custom to describe the more important members of a clan or a corporation by the name of their hereditary office or by some honorific title granted by the court. Thus we have muraji, which means "leader of a group," and might be translated by "duke," agata-nushi, "estate master" and, though of somewhat later origin, fubito, a scribe. As the clans grew in size, their different branches were distinguished by combining the clan name and the title of the hereditary office, and the latter persisted even when the office had been transferred or abolished.

Joseph M. Goedertier, in his A Dictionary of Japanese History (1968) p. 112, defines kabane as:

> Titles conferred on clans in ancient times in order to indicate the degree of social standing within the aristocratic society. Originally the titles indicated the position within a corporation or an official function in the imperial court, but later, when upper and lower classes came into existence, the title served to describe social rank... All these titles were abolished at the time of the Taika Reform in 646, but in 685 eight titles (YAKUSA NO KABANE) were re-established. They gradually underwent changes.

Incidentally, the statement that the kabane titles were abolished in 646 is incorrect. To my knowledge, such an event is described in neither the NSK, nor in later literature.

Other authorities in recent years, in referring to kabane, have used such terms as Standestitel and Standesnamen (Bruno Lewin, Aya und Hata [1962]), or "hereditary title" (John W. Hall, Government and Local Power in Japan, 500-1700 [1966], and Donald Philippi in his translation of the Kojiki, [1968]).

literary sources for this period are the KJK and NSK, to which may be added a few inscriptions on stone, metal and wood. Since the data regarding any given event or institution in the KJK and NSK are fragmentary at best, and since neither of these works deals systematically or thematically with social and political institutions per se, the investigator, whether Japanese or Western, naturally must carefully select and arrange what data are available in order to develop a theme.

But a problem arises when he tries to reconstruct the structural and functional aspects of any system: the fragmentary nature of the sources and the paucity of data inevitably force the investigator to attempt the reconstruction of some particular social or political institution on the basis of every available scrap of what appears to be pertinent data irrespective of their chronological contexts. The result is just as inevitably a description of some schematic structure that is atypical of any specific time period covered by the sources from which the supporting data were originally extracted. And then, when Western investigators refer to Japanese secondary works of this nature and attempt to summarize such structures, an increase in inexactitude may be anticipated.[4]

Japanese scholars have studied, analyzed and interpreted the kabane system for decades, and in the last twenty-five years in particular, they have produced an impressive literature on this and related subjects. In the postwar period, being freed from the nationalistic restraints imposed on them before and during the war, Japanese scholars have studied all aspects of Japanese history and have given them an array of new and often conflicting interpretations. This phenomenon has been particularly true in the treatment of themes and hypotheses relating to social institutions, which are subjects of special interest to political and economic theorists.

But in addition to the influence of political and economic phi-

---

[4]On the nature of the KJK and NSK, see G. W. Robinson, "Early Japanese Chronicles: The Six National Histories," in W. G. Beasley and E. G. Pulleyblank (eds.), Historians of China and Japan (1961), pp. 211-228.

losophies on the interpretation of ancient Japanese history, the paucity and fragmentary nature of the available primary sources, particularly for the pre-Nara period, have led inevitably to the formulation of varying interpretations relating to the importance and role of kabane in those early times. For example, some hypotheses place primary emphasis on the kabane system as a means of better understanding the dynamics of political organization in that early period. Others downgrade the political implications of kabane for the period before the Taika Reform and emphasize, instead, the use of kabane as a means of overcoming the inadequacies of the ranking systems of the post-Taika period when the new Chinese-style legal and administrative systems gradually were brought into effect.[5] It is not surprising that, while Japanese scholars have published a great deal on the subject of the kabane system in the postwar era, confusion should arise in the mind of the Western investigator who attempts to read these materials and on such a basis gain a clear understanding of the system.

Conflicting interpretations of identical data found in Japanese secondary materials, the use of a wide variety of methodologies and standards of judgement, and the plethora of hypotheses combine to create considerable confusion in attempting to gain an understanding of the kabane system.[6] It became clear to me that, if an accurate understanding of the kabane system were ever to be attained, it would be essential first to undertake an independent analysis of the primary sources, the results of which would provide a basis for assessing apparent conflicts in the many available hypotheses and

---

[5] For examples, see B. Kitamura, "Kabane no seido ni kansuru shinkenkyū josetsu," p. 90 and A. Saeki, Shinsen Shōjiroku no kenkyū, kenkyūhen, p. 533.

[6] The principal specialized books and articles on kabane and related subjects, which have been published by Japanese investigators, are listed in the bibliography. Grateful acknowledgement is hereby made for the many insights and methodological suggestions provided by these works, many of which are not possible to document in this present work. Such insights and suggestions have influenced significantly some of the ways in which the NSK data were extracted and systematized in Appendix I, as well as in the matter of parallels and contrasts that may be drawn between the respective data of the NSK and SSJR. Particular acknowledgement of indebtedness in these regards is made to Ōta Akira's monumental Nihon jōdai shakai soshiki no kenkyū (1955).

theories found in secondary works, both Japanese and Western. This undertaking gradually led to the gathering of an incredible number of details which, if they were ever to be systematized and understood, required the formulation of a methodology, and, for purposes of measurement, the application of that methodology to a specific body of data.[7]

The methodology employed in this monograph has two purposes: first, to assess the validity of existing hypotheses on the basis of systematic application of the methodology to available data; and, second, to formulate and assess additional hypotheses that become indicated by such systematic application. Because of the relative paucity of the data available for the period under study, it will be seen in the following pages that the application of the methodology to the data results at times in indicating that some existing hypotheses are more acceptable than others, and at other times it provides little more than the basis for making a calculated and possibly hazardous guess. But in the process of applying the methodology to the data, it will also be found that there do evolve certain grounds in support of new hypotheses. One important factor, however, must always be kept in mind, namely, that such new hypotheses may well reflect more the nature of the sources employed than the nature of the society those sources are alleged to reflect. For example, numerous references will be found on the following pages to quantitative factors involving the number of references in the NSK to each of the various uji studied. This approach basically yields only indisputable quantitative evidence relating to the NSK, but this evidence leads to the hypothesis that a correlation may have existed between the number of NSK references to a given uji and the relative importance of that uji in Japan's

---

[7] This present work on the kabane system is the result of pursuing such a requirement, but it is feared that the complexity of the details herein presented makes it dull reading at best. One is reminded of J. B. Snellen's remark in reference to his partial translation of the SNG where he writes, "The following pages being dry, all but the most hardened readers are earnestly advised to skip them altogether." Transactions of the Asiatic Society of Japan, 2nd ser., XIV (1937) p. 210.

aristocratic society of the seventh century. This hypothesis is then pursued in considerable detail in this work and provides us with new insights into that society, despite the lack of absolute certainty regarding all uji herein studied. This and other hypotheses will be discussed in the following pertinent chapters of this work.

Methodology requires one to delimit. In this work limitations have been placed on the time span to be covered, on the primary source materials employed, and on the nature of the data extracted from the sources and analyzed. These limitations provide a standard for measuring the relative ranking of a specific uji within a identifiable group of uji, or of a specific group of uji among groups of uji. The time span for this study of the kabane system is limited to the 189-year period from 507 (the first year of the reign of Emperor Keitai) through 697 (the last year of the reign of Empress Jitō). The purpose of this limitation is to achieve a description of the kabane system as it functioned during a specific period of history. One advantage of this limitation is that it permits one to avoid overgeneralization and atypical descriptions that are often inherent in summaries based on a longer time span. Another advantage is that it eliminates at this stage the treatment of the early origins of archaic kabane, together with their etymologies and their subsequent evolution prior to the sixth century, all of which are still subject to much controversy and uncertainty in Japan's academic world.

The next limitation involves the primary source materials employed. The basic body of data used for analysis in this work was assembled from the NSK for the limited time period mentioned above. This assembled data is presented in Appendix I: "Inventory of Kabane-Bearing Uji and Individuals Noted in the Nihon Shoki from the Beginning of the Reign of Keitai Through That of Jitō." A number of advantages accrue from this limitation. First, it is generally accepted that the most historically reliable portion of the NSK is that dealing with the sixth and seventh centuries. For purposes of this study, therefore, the assumption is made that data appearing during and after the reign of Keitai relate to historical facts and events; data relating to earlier periods are treated primarily as traditions which were still remembered by the compilers of the NSK in the early eighth century. Second, by confining oneself to the NSK as the primary source from which to assemble the basic data for analysis, a convenient, if somewhat artificial, "standard kabane system" has been delineated, against which kabane-related data of earlier or later texts may be measured. It should be noted carefully that this limitation does not exclude for general use other pertinent sources; it merely excludes them as sources for the assembly of the basic body of data employed for technical analysis in this present study.

Next, in order to achieve a degree of standardization, a limitation was placed on the edition of the NSK from which the basic data for Appendix I was to be extracted. To this end the Nihon Koten Bungaku Taikei edition of the NSK, which was published by Iwanami in 1965, was selected to act as the standard critical edition for the above-mentioned purpose.[8] This edition was edited and annotated by a committee of distinguished Japanese historians headed by Sakamoto Tarō, Inoue Mitsusada and others. For more general purposes numerous other editions of the NSK were employed as well as Aston's translation. Several advantages accrue from this limitation. First, this edition represents the latest and most reliable product of postwar Japanese historical scholarship relating to the NSK. Second, it provides a standard for the often-confusing variations one finds in the glosses and readings for proper names when more than one edition of the NSK is employed. The romanization of uji names, kabane and personal names throughout the basic body of data in Appendix I, as well as in this present work in general, are direct transliterations of the readings found in the NSK V edition.[9] The principal aim of the approach to romanization is to

[8] Hereinafter abbreviated in this work as NSK V.
[9] The only exceptions are the romanizations of Sino-Japanese readings for names of emperors and others.

provide consistency for the purpose of this work alone and is not intended to represent any attempt to reconstruct the ancient Japanese sound structure.

Next, in order to establish a standard by which to make statistical measurements, limitations were placed on the types of data to be extracted from the NSK for inclusion in the basic data represented by Appendix I. To this end only those NSK quotations were extracted in which a kabane appears in conjunction with both an uji name and a personal name, or with either an uji name or a personal name. Conversely, kabane appearing in isolation, or uji names and/or personal names appearing without a kabane were excluded. This process yielded approximately 1548 separate notations.

The notations extracted from the NSK were next assembled according to lineage groups. For this purpose a number of methods were employed to judge which notations referred to which lineage groups. The most convenient method was to rely upon explicit statements in this regard found in the annotations of the standard critical edition of the NSK, i.e., in NSK V. Occasionally similar explicit statements are found in the body of the NSK itself. Clues are also found in the KJK, the Shoku Nihongi (SNG), or in the Shinsen Shōjiroku (SSJR) and their commentaries. Biographical dictionaries and other standard reference works were consulted, as well as many postwar Japanese monographs. In many cases in the NSK different uji names in reality refer to the same lineage group, due to the fact that either abbreviated notations appear in the NSK or that changes in uji names had occurred. For example, Ahe no Asomi Minushi (GR89) and Fuse no Minushi no Asomi are the same person and refer to the same uji, as do Mononobe no Maro no Asomi (GR94) and Isonokami no Asomi Maro. A good example of the assembly of multiple notations referring to the same uji are drawn from the Miwa lineage group (GR87) as follows:

  Miwa no Kimi Takechimaro
  Niwa no Asomi Takechimaro
  Ohomiwa no Asomi Takechimaro

Miwa no Kimi Sakafu
Ohomiwa no Sakafu no Kimi
Sakafu no Kimi[10]

In many instances far less exact criteria were used, and in others no criteria other than logical ones were the basis for the decision to include a given notation under a particular lineage group. As a result, it is clearly recognized that uncertainty exists regarding a number of the notations listed in Appendix I. In the future, errors will be gradually corrected, but, despite such eventual corrections it is believed that the overall patterns reflected in the present listings of lineage groups in Appendix I will not be substantially altered.

It was next found advisable to establish a simple numerical identification system for the various lineage groups that appear in this work. To this end a "Grant Number" (GR) was assigned to each lineage group, and this grant number coincides with the numerical order in which each lineage group was granted kabane during Tenmu's reign. These assigned grant numbers are to be found below in Table I, "Chronological Listing of the Kabane-Recipient Uji and Individuals During the Reign of Tenmu." Although 201 grants were made during Tenmu's reign, only 177 separate lineage groups were involved, since most of them were granted kabane on more than one occasion. For all cases where a given lineage group was granted kabane on more than one occasion during Tenmu's reign, the reader will find the multiple grant numbers listed in Table I. Next, kabane-related data utilized in this study regarding any given lineage group were assembled and listed in Appendix I under the grant number coinciding chronologically with the last grant of kabane which that lineage group received during that reign. For example, Yamato no Atahi Tatsumaro was granted muraji (GR13) in 681 (Tenmu 10/4/12); then his lineage group, the Yamato no Atahi, was granted

---

[10] The exact citations in the NSK for these notations are all found in Appendix I, Part B, under GR87.

the same kabane (GR20) in 683 (Tenmu 12/9/23); and finally the Yamato no Muraji lineage group was granted Imiki (GR189) in 685 (Tenmu 14/6/20).[11] In Appendix I, all NSK references made to this lineage group during the approximate 200-year period covered by this study are listed under Grant Number 189. The procedures described above for the extraction and assembly of kabane-related NSK notations yield a relatively standardized arrangement of data for analytic and comparative studies.[12]

A better understanding of the relative ranking of kabane-bearing lineage groups has been facilitated by the study of the Shinsen Shōjiroku (SSJR) or "The New Compilation of the Register of Families," an important genealogical work of the early ninth century. Any investigation of uji and kabane, of genealogical matters, or of lineage-group classification in the pre-Heian period must include reference to the SSJR. The value of this work lies in its classification of uji into three types of lineage. These three types are lineage groups descending from emperors (kōbetsu), those descending from various kami or deities of heaven and earth (shinbetsu), and those descending from aliens, that is, from ancestors of non-Japanese extraction (shoban).[13] Within the three

[11] The reader will find in this work many notations for dates such as "Tenmu 10/4/12" which stands for "the tenth year, fourth month, twelfth day of the reign of Tenmu." It is recognized that this form of notation is awkward but it has the advantage of indicating in any edition of the NSK the exact location of any reference, thereby obviating multitudes of page references to just one or two selected editions of that work. For additional comments on this problem of dating, please refer to the introductory note to Appendix I, below.

[12] This set of basic data presented in Appendix I has been subjected to various methods of measurement in the preparation of this present study, but it is anticipated that it will be helpful for any future revision of the English translation of the NSK. As notable and valuable a contribution as was Aston's translation of the NSK at the time of its publication in 1896, it now does require extensive revision in the light of modern scholarship, and particularly in relation to the standardization of uji and kabane notations. This is one of the reasons for including in Appendix I the page references to Aston's translation.

[13] The term shoban is used by the SSJR itself for this category of lineage groups, although one will more frequently see in secondary works this category referred to as banbetsu. For example, see Reischauer, Early Japanese History, v. 2, p. 100. It appears, however, that this latter term has been commonly used by Japanese scholars only since the Tokugawa period.

major lineage classifications mentioned above, the SSJR briefly lists the ancestries of each of 1182 uji which are grouped geographically into seven subcategories comprising the left and right sectors of the capital plus the Five Home Provinces of the Kinai. Although the technical terms of kōbetsu, shinbetsu and shoban used in the SSJR are not to be found anywhere in the NSK, the general features of the stratification of noble society as reflected in the SSJR are virtually identical with those that were prevalent at the end of the seventh century as reflected in the NSK. For this reason the relative-ranking patterns of lineage groups noted in the SSJR are of value when used to compare with those of the NSK. In order to compare the NSK and SSJR there was compiled Appendix II, entitled, "Inventory and Distribution of Kabane Listed in the Shinsen Shōjiroku." This inventory is composed of three parts to show the numerical distribution of uji within the forty subsections of the SSJR, the numerical distribution of uji by kabane, and the numerical distribution of uji in the seven geographical subcategories.[14]

For convenience in analyzing and calibrating the relative ranking and status of kabane-bearing groups of uji, a few special approaches and terms have been employed in this monograph, and it would be useful to mention them briefly now. It is assumed that any separately identifiable group of uji possessed unique factors or characteristics that set the group apart from others and determined its ranking within the social order. To identify and describe these factors or characteristics, a relatively analytic approach has been employed to the degree that the nature of the pertinent data extracted from the source materials permits. The approach involves analyses of specific components that comprise what may be called the "profile" of any given group of uji. What

---

[14] A valuable translation of the preface to the SSJR is found in Ryusaku Tsunoda (ed.), Sources of the Japanese Tradition, pp. 87-90. Of great use is the latest critical edition of the SSJR by Saeki Arikiyo and entitled Shinsen Shōjiroku no Kenkyū, Honbunhen (Tokyo, 1966); hereafter abbreviated in this work as SSJR II.

this present monograph basically consists of are analyses of the profile components of those groups of uji that were granted kabane during the reign of Tenmu. For a given group of uji, all of which were granted the same kabane, the profile components of the group consist of the following: the nature and implications of the particular kabane granted; the nature and implications of the prior and/or original kabane (singular or plural) that had been borne by the various uji constituting the group; the types of lineage and ancestry represented in the group; and the number of times the uji constituents are referred to in the NSK. This last profile component is referred to as "NSK reference frequency."

The various ways in which these components are analyzed and compared will be self-evident from a reading of the following chapters of this monograph. However, it will be seen that only certain of these components—sometimes only one—seem to reflect and apparently constitute the unique character of a given group of uji. For example, the type of ancestry was the sole determinant of status at the highest echelon of the nobility and was progressively less so at each successive lower echelon. While kabane-recipient groups of uji are the primary object of this present study, the same methodological approach may be used in analyzing the profile components of any group of uji, and the results are often valuable and informative. Examples of applications of this approach to other types of group-related problems are presented below in Chapter XI in two essays entitled, "Lamentations According to Imibe no Hironari," and "Graves and Ancestors."[15]

In preparing this monograph I made use of many of the splendid products of Japanese scholarship, but I want to stress that the unique contribution of this present monograph is the analysis of kabane on the basis of NSK data relating only to the sixth and seventh centuries and the way in which these data have been quanti-

---

[15] In order to gain a better understanding of the methodology employed throughout the balance of this monograph, the reader is urged to acquaint himself first with the content and form of the two appendices and two tables to be found at the back of this work.

tatively analyzed. The quantitative approach is of value because it provides conclusive indications of the degree of balance that existed between lineage and power considerations in the determination of kabane-ranking in Tenmu's new system. Certainly, this quantitative approach leaves much to be desired, but it must be recognized at the same time that the fragmentary nature of the NSK impels one to use all available analytic approaches, even though some of them may be less than fully satisfactory. While the quantitative approach involving NSK reference frequency may be faulty in reflecting accurately many aspects of Japan's social history of the sixth and seventh centuries, the approach does produce an accurate analysis of aspects of the NSK text itself; and in the present absence of sufficient supporting data from other sources, the NSK text and the history of the sixth and seventh centuries will remain for us essentially one and the same thing.

CHAPTER II
Grants of *Muraji*
to Eighteen Individuals in A.D. 680–681

On the eighth day of the first month in the ninth year of the reign of Emperor Tenmu (A.D. 680) the NSK records that the emperor granted the kabane of muraji to Imibe no Obito Kobito. This represented the first of four occasions on which the emperor granted muraji to eighteen individuals in approximately the next two years. For these eighteen grants, the NSK registers the name of the individual's uji, the kabane he bore prior to being granted muraji, and his personal name (na). These eighteen individuals represent fourteen different uji since in three instances the grants were made to more than one individual belonging to the same uji.[1]

For purposes of analysis it is assumed here that any separately identifiable group of uji that was granted kabane during Tenmu's reign possessed unique factors or characteristics that set the group apart from others and contributed to its ranking within the social order of the time. On the basis of kabane grants alone, these eighteen individuals, representing fourteen different uji, fall into four separate groupings as follows:

1. Six uji represented by seven individuals who were granted muraji but whose uji as a whole are not recorded in the NSK as later being granted muraji or any other kabane.

2. Four uji represented by seven individuals who were granted muraji and whose uji as a whole were later granted muraji but were not then subsequently granted any other kabane.

---

[1] In order better to follow the discussion in this and the next chapter, the reader should refer to Appendix I, Part B, GR1 through GR73 and to Table I, Parts A and B.

3. One uji represented by one individual who was granted muraji and whose uji as a whole was later granted the kabane of sukune.
4. Three uji represented by three individuals who were granted muraji and whose uji as a whole were later granted muraji and subsequently granted the kabane of imiki.

In this chapter I will deal with only the first of these four groups. The second, concerning the grants of muraji to uji rather than to individuals will be dealt with in Chapter III; the third concerning uji that were granted sukune will be dealt with in Chapter VII; and the fourth, concerning uji that were granted imiki will be dealt with in Chapter VIII.

The first group consists of the following seven individuals representing six uji:

GR4	Tawi no Atahi Yoshimaro
GR5	Sukita no Kurahito Mukutari
GR6	Sukita no Kurahito Ishikatsu
GR7	Kafuchi no Atahi Agata
GR15	Shishihito no Miyatsuko Okina
GR16	Yamashiro no Koma Ikamaro[2]
GR17	Toneri no Miyatsuko Nukamushi

It should be stated that this very small grouping as presented here in this study of kabane is more of a device than anything else. But this device is used solely for the purpose of facilitating the analysis of groups of uji in terms of the ranking of the ultimate rather than that of the initial kabane granted them during Tenmu's reign. With so few uji to deal with in this particular group and with so few data concerning them in the NSK, SNG and SSJR, the following comments serve merely as groundwork for the next chapter concerning a much larger grouping of uji about which considerably

---

[2] Of the 201 kabane grants made during Tenmu's reign, this is the only recipient whose prior or original kabane is not recorded. There are numerous citations of similar cases recorded in the SNG for the Nara period.

more data are available in the sources. It is only in this light that the following brief description takes on any meaning whatever.

Virtually nothing is known about five of these six uji, because, from the reign of Keitai in the early sixth century through the reign of Jitō at the end of the seventh, the NSK contains only eight references to them, six of which merely record the granting of the kabane of muraji. The only one of the six about which something is known is the Kafuchi no Atahi uji (GR7) to which Agata belonged. Even in this case, however, our information is far from satisfactory. Between the second and fifth years of Kinmei's reign (i.e., 540-543) the NSK contains a dozen or more references to the role played by a member of this uji as the Japanese representative in Ara in Korea. The next reference is not until 669 when a member of this uji was sent on a mission to T'ang China. In all of the Nara period covered by the SNG, only one other member of this uji is mentioned and then only once. In the early ninth century the SSJR informs us that the uji was of foreign origin and derived from Paekche.[3]

Some authorities have reasoned that Tenmu granted kabane to certain individuals as a means of rewarding them for meritorious services rendered to the crown, especially for parts they played in supporting Tenmu in the civil disturbance known as the Jinshin War of 672.[4] And indeed there was one individual among these seven to receive muraji who had supported Tenmu at that time in his struggle with his nephew, Prince Ohotomo, posthumously known as Emperor Kōbun. He was Toneri no Miyatsuko Nukamushi (GR17), who was granted a higher cap rank on Tenmu 11/1/9, and when he died on Tenmu 11/2/0, the NSK records that he was granted a posthumous cap rank specifically as a reward for meritorious services rendered during that conflict. This grant of a cap rank for meritorious service to the crown is really the only piece of evidence available concerning the possible reason for the granting of muraji to the other five

[3] SSJR II, pp. 326-327.
[4] For example, see Ōta, Nihon jōdai shakai soshiki no kenkyū, pp. 563-564.

uji in this group of six; however, even here, questions arise. First of all, kabane and cap rank functioned quite differently. Kabane most usually were corporate in nature and were borne by all members of a given lineage group or uji, whereas, cap ranks were never corporate in nature.[5] They were granted as appropriate rewards for an individual's merit and were held only by individuals and not by the members of his uji. Additionally, the NSK, during the reigns of Tenmu and Jitō, never specifies a reason or reasons for the 202 kabane grants made during those reigns. One can only conjecture in the absence of information to the contrary that meritorious service to the crown may have been, at least in part, the basis for the grant of muraji to the seven individuals in this particular group of six uji.

One additional comment needs to be made, namely, that during the sixth and seventh centuries, before the reign of Tenmu, the kabane of muraji was borne by some of Japan's most powerful and influential lineage groups, groups whose activities one will find most often cited in the NSK. By contrast, the seven individuals presently under discussion, who were granted muraji by Tenmu in 680 and 681, certainly may not be classified as either powerful or influential on the basis of available evidence. It can be said with some certainty, consequently, that the ranking of uji granted muraji during and after Tenmu's reign represented a considerably lower sociopolitical stratum of society than that of uji that had borne the pre-Tenmu muraji. This small group of seven individuals drawn from six uji perhaps represented the most humble stratum of the newly organized system of nobility based on kabane ranking that was formally instituted later in 684.[6]

[5] See ch. III, sec. F, below, for a discussion of the corporate nature of kabane grants. The term "cap ranks" is a rendition of kan'i 冠位 and refers to that system of ranking that was closely copied after continental models and first instituted in Japan in Suiko 11 (603). It was altered and made progressively more complex on four occasions before Tenmu 14 (685). After the implementation of the Taihō Legal Code of Taihō 1 (701), this system was abandoned and a system of court ranks (kan'i 官位) was thereafter employed. See Introduction, n. 1, above.

[6] See ch. IV, below, for a discussion of the formal institution of Tenmu's eight-rank kabane system.

CHAPTER III
Grants of *Muraji* to Fifty-Five *Uji* in A.D. 682–684

A. INTRODUCTION

   The kabane of muraji was next awarded to fifty-five uji on four occasions between A.D. 682 and 684, on Tenmu 11/5/12, 12/9/23, 12/10/5 and 13/1/17. For purposes of analysis, this figure of fifty-five is reduced to forty-two, because, after the establishment of Tenmu's eight-rank kabane system in the tenth month of 684, three of the fifty-five were granted the kabane of sukune, and ten, the kabane of imiki. These uji will be analyzed in future chapters dealing with the highest kabane they were later awarded, either sukune or imiki. The forty-two uji here analyzed include four of the members who were among the eighteen individuals who had been earlier granted muraji. For purposes of analysis a distinction is drawn here between those that were granted muraji and were not later granted a higher kabane, and those that were first granted muraji and were then later granted sukune or imiki. Only the former are dealt with here. The following table will clarify these figures:

	No. of Awards	No. of Individuals	No. of Uji not given further Awards
	18	18	6
	55	0	42
Totals	73	18	48

B. ANALYSIS BASED ON ORIGINAL KABANE

   The following table shows the distribution of forty-two muraji-recipient uji in terms of the kabane they bore prior to being awarded muraji.

	Muraji Recipients
miyatsuko	33
obito	3
fubito	3
agata-nushi	3
Total	42

A number of observations are here possible. First, by far the largest single group of uji granted muraji had previously borne the kabane of miyatsuko, which was the traditional kabane of the tomo no miyatsuko, or what we may refer to as a class of royal managers under the direct control of the imperial line and the court. The fact that the large majority of thirty-three uji in this group had formerly borne the kabane of miyatsuko makes it clear that muraji by the 680s was an indicator of the social rank of uji that had traditionally functioned as royal managers under the direction of the central government. It is also clear that the kabane of muraji at this time was an indicator of a considerably lower sociopolitical order than it had been during the pre-Tenmu period. The uji bearing the kabane of miyatsuko prior to being awarded muraji served as local officials in the Home Provinces or as managers in charge of namesake and child-substitute groups (minashiro-be and mikoshiro-be), or in charge of other kinds of occupational groups (be) and groups of immigrant workers. Ōta Akira has compiled the following occupational distribution for these forty-two uji:[1]

---

[1] Ōta, Nihon jōdai shakai soshiki no kenkyū, p. 565. Unfortunately, Ōta does not cite the sources of this information. Ōta's figures are used by Takeuchi, "Tenmu 'hassei' seitei no igi," Shien, 43, p. 38. See also Ueda, Nihon kodai kokka seiritsu shi no kenkyū, p. 266. See Table I, Part B, for details concerning the grantees in this group.

Occupation	No. of Uji
1. Local officials in the Home Provinces	5
2. Tomo no Miyatsuko in charge of namesake and child substitute groups	11
3. Tomo no Miyatsuko in charge of occupational be	20
4. Tomo no Miyatsuko in charge of immigrant groups	5
5. Unknown	1
Total	42

As valuable and interesting as this information is, it should be pointed out that one must avoid the questionable assumption that such an occupational distribution for these forty-two uji is accurately descriptive of the situation that existed in the last quarter of the seventh century when Tenmu granted these uji the kabane of muraji. It is feared that this classification of occupation is based on assumptions derived from implications conveyed by the names of some of these uji or is based on information drawn from the KJK and NSK for the period prior to the sixth century. A search of the NSK reveals that virtually nothing is known about the sixth and seventh-century activities of a large number of these particular uji. Just because the name of the uji mentioned by the NSK during the seventh century is the name of an occupation does not automatically mean more than that the uji in question may have been, in much earlier times, traditionally so occupied. In fact, there are extremely few references in the NSK in the sixth and seventh centuries to individuals engaged in an activity the name of which coincides with the name of their uji. To cite a random sample, the reader will have noticed above that one authority claims that five of these forty-two muraji-recipient uji were local officials in the Home Provinces. The following is a list of these five, with the figure after the name of each representing the total number of NSK references to each uji during the 189-year period of this study.

Grants of Muraji to Fifty-Five Uji

GR No.	Uji	NSK References
GR21	Kurukuma no Obito	2
GR65	Yoshino no Obito	1
GR69	Takechi no Agatanushi	2
GR70	Shiki no Agatanushi	1
GR72	Mino no Agatanushi	1

It is well known that before the end of the seventh century, the kabane of obito and agatanushi were traditionally borne by local officials. However, for these five uji we have only seven references in the NSK, five of which are mere listings of the grant of the kabane of muraji during Tenmu's reign. That leaves only two references, one of which refers to Kurukuma no Obito Tokomaro (GR21) on Tenchi 7/2/23, where we are informed that this man's daughter was a consort of Tenchi. The other reference is to Takechi no Agatanushi Kome (GR69) on Tenmu 1/7/0, where we are informed that this man was the chief official in charge of the District of Takechi (Takechi no Kōri), a district known to have been in the Province of Yamato. While this single reference tells us that the one member of the five uji in question was indeed a local official in one of the Home Provinces, we have no information from the NSK about members of the other four uji holding public office. In fact, it would seem to me that having a daughter who became the consort of an emperor would be more justification and reason for an uji being awarded a kabane than that one of an uji's members was a local official.

It is entirely possible that these uji as a group were awarded muraji because by the time of Tenmu, that kabane, rather than being an indicator of rank reflecting their occupations, was more accurately an indication of their relatively low position in the sociopolitical hierarchy.

One gains the impression that the fifty-five uji that were recipients of muraji must have attained their relative ranking in the sociopolitical hierarchy of the time on some basis other than traditional occupations. If one employs the argument that such occupations formed the basis for the muraji grants to these fifty-five uji, then one must expand the argument to explain why thirteen of these uji were later in Tenmu's reign granted the new and higher kabane of sukune and imiki. The subsequent award of sukune or imiki to those thirteen uji after 684 may have represented the award of new kabane that coincided with the relatively higher sociopolitical ranking of that particular group of uji based upon service to the crown. The grants of sukune and imiki were far more reflective of this consideration than that such higher kabane coincided with their traditional occupational statuses.

C. ANALYSIS BASED ON SSJR CATEGORIES

In analyzing the composition of any given group of uji, the categories of the SSJR often prove to be of considerable value. The application of these categories, for example, to the groups of uji that were awarded mahito, asomi and sukune later in Tenmu's reign provide considerable insight into their respective group compositions. Unfortunately, a similar application to the forty-two that were granted muraji provides one with very little new, positive insight. Nevertheless, the distribution of this group of uji in terms of the SSJR categories is as follows:[2]

kōbetsu, or "imperial" uji	2*
shinbetsu, or "deity" uji	16
shoban, or non-Japanese uji	8
unknown	16
Total	42

*One uncertain

One of the very few observations that can be made is that the count of those uji in the kōbetsu (or "imperial") category is considerably lower than those of the shinbetsu (or "deity") and shoban

[2] Figures adapted from Ōta, Nihon jōdai shakai soshiki no kenkyū, pp. 565-66 and Takeuchi, "Tenmu 'hassei' seitei no igi," Shien, 43, p. 38.

(non-Japanese) categories, and that the shinbetsu category is the most prominent of the three. If this observation means anything at all, it is that while this group of forty-two muraji-recipient uji may have functioned as managers and local officials for the crown, they were not, by and large, related by blood to the imperial line. It should not be surprising that the analysis of this group of uji by the genealogical categories of the SSJR yields so little new insight; the reason is simply that blood relationship with the imperial line or with the more powerful uji in the Home Provinces was not a fundamental criterion for this group of forty-two uji being elevated by Tenmu to the lower levels of his new aristocracy.

A more important feature of the genealogical distribution of these forty-two uji outlined above is the presence of an estimated eight uji classified as shoban, that is, of non-Japanese extraction. A study of muraji grants as recorded in the SNG and Nihonkōki, which cover the period 697 to 791 and 792 to 833, respectively, may be schematized as follows:

Original Kabane	No. of Muraji Awards	No. of Non-Japanese Stock
miyatsuko	13	11
fubito, suguri,[3] omi,[4] kusushi and eshi	20	20
atahi and obito	8	2[5]

It will be seen that, just as in the case of the forty-two muraji grants made during Tenmu's reign, there remained among the uji granted muraji in the eighth and early ninth centuries a significant percentage that were classified as being of non-Japanese extraction.

---

[3] 村主 According to the SSJR, a kabane confined exclusively to uji of non-Japanese lineage. See suguri in Appendix II, Part B.

[4] 使主 Not to be confused with the far more common omi of 臣. This kabane appears just five times in the SSJR, once for an uji of shinbetsu lineage and four times for uji of shoban lineage. See omi in Appendix II, Part B.

[5] Data adapted from Ueda, Nihon kodai kokka seiritsu shi no kenkyū, p. 267.

D. NSK REFERENCE FREQUENCY

As one works through the various data regarding individuals and uji in the NSK, it becomes increasingly apparent that, in general, there is a relationship between the importance of certain groups of uji and the large number of NSK textual references to them and their members. At least this hypothesis provides one with an additional means of analyzing NSK data for possible further elucidation of the relative importance of two or more identifiable groups of uji. For example, this group of fifty-five uji (GR19 through GR73) were granted the kabane of muraji, but subsequently thirteen of them were granted higher kabane in Tenmu's new eight-rank system, three being granted sukune and ten being granted imiki. The first thing that strikes an observer of the forty-two uji not later awarded sukune or imiki during Tenmu's reign is that very few of them played anything approaching a prominent role in the pages of the NSK in the sixth and seventh centuries.[6] Additionally, as one might well expect, there is a rather marked difference in the respective prominence of these forty-two uji and the thirteen uji that were later awarded either sukune or imiki:

	NSK Reference Frequencies	Average References per uji
The 42 uji not later granted higher kabane	99	2.3
The 13 uji later granted sukune or imiki	147	11.3
Total	246	

The sharp contrast between these two groups is shown by the average of only 2.3 references per uji for the group of forty-two uji and the average of 11.3 per uji for the group of thirteen.

The relative distribution by frequency of the uji in these two

---

[6] In the analyses in this monograph the words "prominence" and "prominent" are used in a special sense to refer to the number of references in the NSK to a given uji or a given group of uji for the period of this study from the beginning of Keitai's reign through Jitō's.

groups expresses a similar sharp contrast:

No. of NSK References	The 42 Uji	The 13 Uji
1	27	
2	6	1
3	1	1
4	2	4
5	1	1
6	1	2
7	1	1
8	1	
10	1	
13	1	
14		1
31		1
57		1

This relative distribution table, besides demonstrating the differences in prominence, reveals that for twenty-seven of the group of forty-two uji virtually no information concerning their activities is contained in the NSK for the sixth and seventh centuries. Those twenty-seven references are the mere listing of the receipt of the kabane of muraji that distinguishes these uji as a group.

A search of the SNG likewise yields no convincing evidence that this group of forty-two muraji-recipient uji played any notable role during the Nara period. Quite to the contrary, the evidence points to only two and possibly three of these uji being worthy of more than just a few citations in the SNG. Thirty of these uji are not mentioned even once in the pages of that record, and seven of them enjoy only one reference each. The SNG reference distribution for this group of uji is as follows:

No. of References	No. of Uji
0	30
1	7

3	1
4	2
9	1
16	<u>1</u>
Total	42

Although dealing with a period later than the body of this present study, this negative evidence of the SNG demonstrates again the relatively low status of the muraji-recipient uji that were not granted the higher kabane of sukune or imiki later in Tenmu's reign. One wonders what Tenmu's intention was in distinguishing this particular group of uji with the grants of muraji. If the members of this group were of sufficient service to the crown and thus were important or influential enough to be so honored, it is indeed curious that the activities of so many of them are recorded in neither the NSK or the SNG. One can only conjecture that their services to the crown were of sufficient importance to be distinguished by the grant of muraji, but that their services were of the variety not usually recorded in the NSK. As is often the case when services are essential but commonplace, they are not "newsworthy" and are seldom described in the documents of antiquity. Another explanation may be that the nature of the services rendered by the members of this group of uji to the court seldom brought them into close personal contact with those court officials and scribes who recorded the "remarkable" for posterity.

F. THE CORPORATE NATURE OF KABANE

It is now possible to undertake a discussion of the corporate versus the individual character of the muraji grants made to the two groups of recipients already discussed, the first composed of eighteen named individuals and the second composed of fifty-five uji. These two groups of muraji grants have aroused discussion in Japanese historical literature, with some authorities claiming that the first eighteen grants of muraji to eighteen individuals were confined to those persons alone. Others claim that the kabane of muraji in those eighteen cases were limited in their application to just the direct descendants of the recipient, and others claim that such muraji grants were fully corporate in nature and could be borne by all members of the uji to which the individual belonged.[7]

Some authorities claim that the first eighteen grants to individuals were corporate in nature, but the evidence in support of this hypothesis is far from convincing. The following indirect evidence in support of this fully corporate theory of the first eighteen grants may be cited: on the occasion of the muraji grant on Tenmu 9/1/8 (680) to Imibe no Obito Kobito (GR1) the NSK informs us that Kobito "presented [at court] his joyful acknowledgment along with his younger brother Shikobuchi."[8] Such a notation would seem to indicate that Shikobuchi shared in the benefits of the muraji grant that had been made to Kobito. At no place does the NSK specifically note that the grant of muraji applied to the entire Imibe uji, but the term "Imibe no Muraji" in its corporate sense is used by the NSK considerably later, on Tenmu 13/12/2 (684), when we find the kabane of sukune being granted to the entire uji (cf. GR142).[9]

The nature of this evidence does not permit one with certainty to claim that these first grants of muraji to eighteen individuals constituted a corporate grant to all members of the fourteen uji represented. In fact, a review of all NSK and SNG references to individuals belonging to these uji reveals no single clear-cut example of two members of any one of them bearing the kabane of muraji.

While the indirect evidence cited above may lend a little support to the corporate-character theory of all of these first eigh-

---

[7]Compare Ōta, Nihon jōdai shakai soshiki no kenkyū, p. 564, Ueda, Nihon kodai kokka seiritsu shi no kenkyū, p. 265, and Abe, Uji-Kabane, p. 69.

[8]NSK I, v. 2, p. 345; NSK V, v. 2, p. 439.

[9]We then later find Shikobuchi bearing sukune during the following reign in 690 (Jito 4/1/1) when he played an important role in the enthronement ceremonies of the Empress Jitō. He is also referred to once in the SNG in 702 (Taihō 2/3/11) on the occasion of his death, at which time he is also listed as bearing the kabane of sukune.

teen muraji grants, there is available equally indirect evidence to support the thesis that the first muraji grants were confined to the eighteen listed individuals and were not applicable to their respective uji. First, as was mentioned above, these eighteen individuals represent fourteen different uji. It seems unlikely that if these muraji grants were intended to be corporate in nature it would have been necessary to award muraji to more than one individual belonging to the same uji as was done in the cases of two members of the Sukita uji (GR6 and GR7), to three individuals of the Oshinumi uji (GR8, GR9 and GR10) and to the two individuals of the Ohokoma uji (GR10 and GR11). Additionally, if these first eighteen grants were intended to be corporate in nature it is difficult to explain why two of these particular three uji, the Oshinumi no Miyatsuko uji (GR52) and the Ohokoma no Miyatsuko uji (GR39) were later granted muraji on Tenmu 12/9/23. There are five additional examples listed in the NSK of individuals being granted muraji, only to have their uji later granted muraji as well. The examples are as follows:

			Dates of Grants
1.	GR2	Kusakabe no Kishi Ohokata granted muraji	Tenmu 10/1/7
	GR59	Kusakabe no Kishi granted muraji	" 12/10/5
2.	GR3	Nishikori no Miyatsuko Wokida granted muraji	" 10/4/12
	GR34	Nishikori no Miyatsuko granted muraji	" 12/9/23
3.	GR13	Yamato no Atahi Tatsumaro granted muraji	" 10/4/12
	GR20	Yamato no Atahi granted muraji	" 12/9/23
4.	GR14	Kadobe no Atahi Ohoshima granted muraji	" 10/4/12
	GR33	Kadobe no Atahi granted muraji	" 12/9/23
5.	GR18	Fumi no Atahi Chitoko granted muraji	" 10/12/10
	GR19	Yamato no Aya no Atahi granted muraji[10]	" 11/5/12

[10] These two, GR18 and GR19, refer to the same uji, the full name of which

If Kusakabe no Kishi Ohokata (GR2) was granted muraji on Tenmu 10/1/7, and if that grant was corporate in its application, then why was it necessary to grant muraji almost three years later to the Kusakabe no Kishi uji (GR59)? The same question may be asked for each of the five examples listed above. In view of this indirect evidence, all that can be said is that the first eighteen grants were very probably not corporate in nature.

Although questions linger as to the individual versus the corporate nature of the first eighteen grants of muraji, the available data indicate that the fifty-five grants of muraji made between 682 and 684 (Tenmu 9/1/8 and 10/12/29) were corporate in nature and applied to the members of the recipient uji. The clearest supporting illustration is found in the NSK references to the Kifumi no Miyatsuko uji (GR44), which was granted muraji on Tenmu 12/9/23. Within that uji were two individuals named Ohotomo and Honjitchi. Their names both appear in the NSK with the kabane of miyatsuko before their uji was granted muraji. After that grant, both of their names appear in the NSK with the kabane of muraji, demonstrating that the grant was applicable to more than just one member of the uji. The following references in the NSK arranged in chronological order support this conclusion:

GR44	Kifumi no Miyatsuko Honjitchi	Tenchi 10/3/3 (671)
	Kifumi no Miyatsuko Ohotomo	Tenmu 1/6/24 (672)
	Kifumi no Miyatsuko	Tenmu 12/9/23 (683) (Granted muraji)

is the Yamato no Aya no Fumi no Atahi uji. See GR195c in Appendix I. This uji appears as Yamato no Aya no Muraji in GR195 at which time the uji was granted imiki. The NSK is far from uniform in its mode of notation when it comes to complex combinations containing an uji name, the personal name (na), and kabane. Support for treating these particular notations as representing the same uji is based in part on the following variety of NSK references.

Fumi no Atahi Agata (Jomei 11/7/0)
Yamato no Aya no Fumi no Atahi Agata (Kōgyoku 1/2/2)
Yamato no Aya no Atahi Agata (Hakuchi 1/10/0)
Fumi no Atahi Maro (Hakuchi 5/2/0)
Yamato no Aya no Fumi no Atahi Maro (Taika 1/9/3)

Kifumi no Muraji Ohotomo   Jitō 1/8/28 (687)
Kifumi no Muraji Honjitchi   Jitō 8/3/2   (694)

Additionally, Ohotomo and Honjitchi, as well as seven other members of that uji, appear in the SNG bearing the kabane of muraji.[11]

G. THE RELATIVE RANKING OF THE KABANE OF MURAJI

The reader will have noticed several passing references in this and the preceding chapter to the kabane of muraji as an indicator of relative rank that varied as between the pre-Tenmu period, on the one hand, and the Tenmu and post-Tenmu periods, on the other. For purposes of clarification, it is necessary at this point to anticipate some of the discussion in the next and subsequent chapters dealing with the details of the institution and implementation of Tenmu's new eight-rank kabane system from 684. Muraji in the pre-Tenmu period was borne by many lineage groups, including some of ancient Japan's most illustrious, which one finds most frequently cited in the NSK. Nevertheless, when Tenmu's new eight-rank system was instituted in 684 we find that muraji ranked seventh. It would appear from the available evidence cited above that the ranking of the muraji grants made to eighteen individuals (as already discussed in Chapter II) and to fifty-five uji (as discussed in this chapter) coincided far more with the seventh rank in Tenmu's new system than with that of the muraji of the pre-

---

[11] For Ohotomo, see SNG, Taihō 1/7/21, Taihō 3/7/5; for Honjitchi, see SNG, Taihō 2/12/23 and Keiun 4/6/16. Additional evidence in support of the corporate nature of these muraji grants may be found in the SNG as follows:

GR52 Oshinumi no Miyatsuko uji: 3 individuals bearing muraji
GR61 Fune no Fubito uji: 16 individuals bearing muraji
GR62 Iki no Fubito uji: 4 individuals bearing muraji
GR69 Takechi no Agatanushi uji: 4 individuals bearing muraji

Additionally, there is some indirect evidence provided by the NSK pointing to the corporate nature of these muraji grants. For example, the NSK records the grant of muraji to the Yamato no Aya no Atahi uji (GR19) on Tenmu 11/5/12, and then notes that on the 27th day of the same month, "The Yamato no Aya Atahi, male and female all presented themselves. They rejoiced at the grant of the kabane, and paid their respects to the Emperor." Aston's translation with slight changes. See NSK I, v. 2, p. 355. For the original text, see NSK V, v. 2, p. 452.

Tenmu period. But one of the problems that Japanese historians have wrestled with arises from the fact that Tenmu's grants of muraji to those eighteen individuals and fifty-five uji were made in the approximate four-year period prior to the institution of his new eight-rank system. In 685 and 686, after the establishment of the new eight-rank system, grants of muraji were made but then only to two obscure individuals. During his entire reign Tenmu made a total of 201 kabane grants involving 177 uji, and the uji that had not been granted one of the new kabane during that reign continued to bear their traditional pre-Tenmu kabane. Consequently, the problem arises as to the relationship, as far as relative ranking is concerned, between the pre-Tenmu kabane of muraji and that of the Tenmu and post-Tenmu periods.

By way of summary and in anticipation of the more detailed discussions that are presented in the following pages, it will be helpful to point out here that the granting of various kabane to those 177 uji during Tenmu's reign represented a readjustment of the relative ranking only of selected uji that were either powerful and influential or that were most closely associated with the imperial line by reason of lineage or service. To mention just one example of this readjustment as it relates to muraji, the coexistence of the new and traditional systems reflects the fact that Tenmu elevated a selected few of the uji that had borne the traditional kabane of muraji to the third rank of sukune in his new system (as discussed in Chapter VII, below). The result of this action appears to have afforded the uji that were granted muraji earlier in his reign with the same relative rank within the new sociopolitical hierarchy as that enjoyed by the bearers of the traditional kabane during that reign. It is this factor which makes more significant the discussions contained in this and the preceding chapters, but it is a significance that will not be wholly clear until one progresses through the balance of this study.

八色姓

CHAPTER IV
Emperor Tenmu's Eight-Rank *Kabane* System of A.D. 684

A. INTRODUCTION

On the first day of the tenth month in the thirteenth year of the reign of Emperor Tenmu (A.D. 684) the following edict was promulgated:

> The kabane of various uji are again modified and kabane of eight ranks [yakusa no kabane] are [hereby] constituted. By this means the multitude of kabane of the empire will be integrated. The first [rank] is called mahito; the second, asomi; the third, sukune; the fourth, imiki; the fifth, michi-no-shi; the sixth, omi; the seventh, muraji; and the eight, inaki.[1]

In the social and political history of Japan in the pre-Nara period this edict is of great importance, because it is the first clear presentation anywhere in the KJK or NSK of a precise relative ranking system for kabane. As has already been mentioned, many kabane had been in use for centuries prior to Tenmu; but with regard to their relative ranking and importance, modern scholarship has so far been able to elucidate little more than that a few of the kabane were superior in rank to others. For example, one frequently sees mentioned in the literature that the kabane of omi and muraji were the two most important and numerous in that early period before the institution of Tenmu's eight-rank system.[2] This

---

[1]Compare Aston's translation, NSK I, v. 2, pp. 364-365. For Japanese text, see NSK V, v. 2, p. 465.
詔曰更改諸氏之族姓,作八色之姓,以混天下萬姓.一曰真人.二曰朝臣.三曰宿禰.四曰忌寸.五曰道師.六曰臣.七曰連.八曰稲置.

[2]In some cases, misleading English renditions have been applied to these two kabane. For example, one finds "Imperial Chieftain" as the rendition for

statement is true in so far as it goes, but provides no clarification of the nature or relative standing of the many other kabane one finds in the pages of the primary sources.

Precisely for such reasons Tenmu's edict is valuable to the historian in a number of ways. First, it provides a means by which to determine in part the relative ranking of the lineage groups that were granted these kabane of the new eight-rank system during Tenmu's reign. Second, it provides a useful tool for extrapolating in order to gain a better understanding of the relative sociopolitical ranking of many lineage groups mentioned in the NSK for the period before the reign of Tenmu. Third, it provides a ranking system affixed to a point in time which is useful in measuring the degree of upward or downward sociopolitical mobility of many lineage groups both before and after the establishment of Tenmu's new eight-rank kabane system. Fourth, the new kabane system presented in the edict provides the investigator with a valuable starting point for measuring some of the interplay in the last half of the seventh century between Japan's traditional sociopolitical system and the new Chinese-style systems gradually adapted to Japanese needs in the forty years from the beginning of the Taika Reform movement to 684.

---

omi and "Deity Chieftain" as the rendition for muraji. This terminology is based on that of the categories of the SSJR of the early ninth century, but in actuality there are many examples in both the NSK and the SSJR of omi-bearing lineage groups being classified as of other than kōbetsu or "imperial" lineage and also of muraji-bearing lineage groups being classified as of other than shinbetsu or "deity" lineage. A review of the distribution of these two kabane in the SSJR demonstrates merely that the majority but not all of omi-bearing lineage groups fall into the category of kōbetsu or "imperial" groups and that the majority but not all of muraji-bearing lineage groups fall into the category of shinbetsu or "deity" groups. The following table is based on Appendix II, Part B, Distribution of Uji by Kabane in the SSJR:

	No. of Omi References	No. of Muraji References
kōbetsu or "imperial" uji	47	19
shinbetsu or "deity" uji	12	154
shoban or uji of foreign descent	0	74
unauthenticated	4	11
	63	258

B. TENMU'S EDICT

The edict of Tenmu 13/10/1 does not appear at first reading to be more than a simple statement of fact. Nevertheless, the terminology employed in this edict has been the subject of considerable debate, investigation and interpretation. The result has often been confusion and misinterpretation in Western literature. The edict begins by stating that the kabane of the uji were to be modified again or reformed, that the kabane in what was presumably to be an eight-rank system was established, and that these actions in some way would affect the kabane of the entire country. However, a number of specific problems relating to the language of this edict require investigation, as follows: One, what is the meaning of the phrase "again modified"? Two, were the kabane of all uji or were just certain ones to be affected by the modification? Three, what is the meaning of "will be integrated"? Let us deal with each of these three questions separately.

The first predicate of this edict, "again modified," a translation of 更改 , presents a problem, because there is serious question that the kabane system as a rational, identifiable system had ever been modified at some earlier date. One does not know with certainty to what particular earlier event, if any, this phrase refers. The words "again modified" are a construction that appears in only three other places in the NSK where it may mean: (1) to do something again; (2) to do something again but in a somewhat different manner than before; or (3) to reform (i.e., to change or modify again the form of) an established system.[3] It is doubtless

---

[3]The example for the first meaning appears in Nintoku 53/5/0 (traditional date, 365) where an official was sent to Silla, but on his way he found a white deer, which was considered to be a good omen. He thereupon interrupted his journey, returned to the court and presented the white deer to the emperor. He then "again selected an [auspicious] day [for his departure] and left" on his original mission. 更改日而行 (NSK V, v. 1, p. 411). The example for the second meaning appears in the first year of Empress Jingū's regency (traditional date, 201) when the bodies of two Shintō priests (hafuri) were disinterred from their common grave, placed in coffins again and separately reinterred. 更改棺櫬．各異以埋之 (NSK V, v. 1, p. 347). The third example appears to have a direct bearing on the present problem and is found in Tenmu

in this last and third sense that the term in Tenmu's edict is to be taken.

The question then arises that if the kabane of the uji were indeed "again modified" by Tenmu, when and in what way or ways were they modified earlier? The only possible answer seems to be a story that appears in the KJK, in the NSK and in the preface of the SSJR regarding the rectification of uji names and kabane in the fourth year of the reign of Emperor Ingyō (traditional date 415). While one may well question the historical reliability of the KJK and NSK for the reign of Ingyō, it is certain that the account of this rectification program was remembered as an important event in the social history of Japan in the early eighth century when the KJK and NSK were compiled, as well as in the early ninth century when the SSJR was compiled. This event is cited today by Japanese authorities as possibly being the previous modification to which Tenmu's edict refers, even though such authorities are unlikely to accept the historicity of the event itself. The most complete account of the event is contained in the NSK which reads as follows:

> 4th year, Autumn, 9th month, 9th day. The Emperor made a decree, saying:--"In the most ancient times, good government consisted in the subjects having each one his proper place, and in names [kabane] being correct. It is now four years since we entered on the auspicious office. Superiors and inferiors dispute with one another: the hundred surnames are not at peace. Some by mischance lose their proper surnames [kabane]; others purposely lay claim to high family [uji]. This is perhaps the reason why good government is not attained to. Deficient in wisdom although We are, how can We omit to rectify these irregularities? Let the Ministers take counsel, and inform me of their determination." All the Ministers said:--"If Your Majesty, re-

---

(14/1/21 (684). It is there stated that "the appellations of court ranks were again modified and the grades were increased [in number]. 更改爵位之號. 仍增加階級 There is little question but that this action refers to an earlier revision in the cap-rank system that had been made on Tenchi 3/2/9 (664), a system that had evolved, in turn, from earlier systems.

storing that which is lost and correcting that which is perverted, will thus determine Houses and surnames [i.e., <u>uji</u> and <u>kabane</u>] your servants will stake their lives in recommending the adoption of such a measure."

28th day. The Emperor made a decree, saying:--"The ministers, functionaries, and the Miyakko of the various provinces [i.e., <u>Kuni no miyatsuko</u>] each and all describe themselves, some as descendants of Emperors, others attributing to their race a miraculous origin, and saying that their ancestors came down from Heaven. However, since the three Powers of Nature assumed distinct forms, many tens of thousands of years have elapsed, so that single Houses [<u>uji</u>] have multiplied and have formed anew ten thousand surnames [<u>kabane</u>] of doubtful authenticity. Therefore let the people of the various Houses and surnames [<u>uji</u> and <u>kabane</u>] wash themselves and practise abstinence, and let them, each one calling the Gods to witness, plunge their hands in boiling water." . . .Therefore those who had falsified their titles were afraid, and slipping away beforehand, did not come forward. From this time forward the Houses and surnames [<u>uji</u> and <u>kabane</u>] were spontaneously ordered, and there was no longer any one who falsified them.[4]

---

[4]Aston's translation (v. 1, pp. 316-317). The brackets are mine and represent the glosses found in the most recent edition of the <u>NSK</u> in the <u>Nihon Koten Bungaku Taikei</u> series. This same event is also referred to twice in the <u>KJK</u>, first in the preface and second in the account of the reign of Emperor Ingyō. In Philippi's translation of the <u>KJK</u>, the first reference (p. 39) reads as follows: "and the titles [<u>kabane</u>] were corrected and the clan-names [<u>uji</u>] selected during the rule of TOPO-TU-ASUKA [Ingyō]." The brackets are mine. For the Japanese text see <u>KJK III</u>, pp. 42-43. The second reference in the same translation (p. 332) reads as follows: "At this time the emperor, deploring that the families [<u>uji</u>], and titles [<u>kabane</u>] of the various families [<u>uji</u>], and names [<u>na</u>] of the people of the kingdom had become confused, placed <u>kukabe</u> [perhaps cauldrons used for a kind of ordeal in which the hand is plunged into hot water] before (the deity) KOTO-YASO-MAGA-TU-PI of AMA-KASI, and established the families and ranks of the myriad corporation-heads of the kingdom." The brackets are mine. For the Japanese text, see <u>KJK III</u>, pp. 290-292. The following is a translation of the pertinent passage in the preface of the <u>SSJR</u>: "During the reign of Ingyō, however, family relations were in great confusion. An edict was accordingly issued, ordering that oaths be tested by the trial of boiling water. Those whose oaths were true remained unscathed, while the perjurers were harmed. From this time onwards the clans

When Tenmu's edict uses the terms "again modified" perhaps some other event is alluded to, but modern scholarship has not identified any other event with any more certainty than this one recorded in the reign of Ingyō.

The second question regarding the edict is whether all or just some of the kabane were to be included in the modification represented by the establishment of Tenmu's eight-rank system. This question seems to be confined more to Western scholars and their interpretation of the grammar and word usage in Tenmu's edict. For example, Aston translates the opening sentence of the edict as follows: "The hereditary titles of all the families are again re-formed, and eight titles of eight classes instituted."[5] (Emphasis mine.) This problem centers on the elucidation of the two-character compound 諸氏 as used in the edict of Tenmu 13/10/1. The character 諸 is nonspecific, and depending on its textual context and one's interpretation, it may mean "many," "all," "some," or "various." This particular two-character compound cited above is found in only five NSK references prior to its use in the text in question, but contextual and grammatical analysis of these five references does not lead to any certain decision that would aid interpretation.[6] Tenmu's edict may have been referring to either "all" or "some" of the uji, but from the way in which the edict was later implemented, it is certain that the kabane of "various" but not "all" uji were to be "again modified."

This conclusion is closely related to the third of the specific problems relating to Tenmu's edict, namely, what is the meaning of the sentence that reads, "By this means the multitude of kabane of the empire will be integrated?" The available data drawn from

---

[uji] and families [kabane] were established and there were no imposters. Rivers ran in their proper courses." Translation taken from Tsunoda, Sources of Japanese Tradition, p. 89, with only one suggestion that the word "families" in this translation be changed to "kabane." The brackets are mine.

[5]NSK I, v. 2, pp. 364-365.

[6]The five examples are found under the following dates: Ingyō 4/9/9 (NSK V, v. 1, p. 439); Tenmu 4/2/15 (NSK V, v. 2, p. 417); Tenmu 8/8/1 (NSK V, v.2, p. 437); Tenmu 10/9/8 (NSK V, v. 2, p. 449), and Tenmu 11/12/3 (NSK V, v. 2, p. 457).

sources up to the early ninth century, primarily from the SNG and the SSJR, amply demonstrate that Tenmu's new eight-rank kabane system supplemented rather than replaced the traditional system. The new system was not intended completely to replace the older one; rather, it was merely placed above the old system. The old kabane continued to be used in the eighth century, but the bearers were either of relatively low status or were purposely overlooked.[7] The study of kaban usage in the century following Tenmu's reign demonstrates that his new system coexisted with the earlier pre-Tenmu system, and it is therefore possible to interpret that such coexistence represented what was meant in the edict's statement that the institution of the new system would bring about an integration of the multitude of kabane of the empire.

From the time Tenmu's new system was established in 684 until the year before Tenmu's death in 686, one hundred and twenty-six grants of the first four grades of the new system were made to as many different uji in the following ratios: thirteen grants of mahito, fifty-two grants of asomi, fifty grants of sukune, and eleven grants of imiki. The grants of the final four grades of the new system largely remain a problem, because grants of the new kabane of the fifth grade, michi-no-shi, as well as of the sixth grade of omi, and of the eighth grade of inaki were not made during the balance of Tenmu's reign nor in the following reign of Jitō, and the SNG likewise remains silent on the matter. (This problem is treated in some detail in Chapter IX, below.) Let us first turn to the analyses of the 126 grants of the first four grades of the new eight-rank kabane system before going on to the various hypotheses that have evolved out of what appears to have been an interruption in the full implementation of the new system.

---

[7] For many examples of such coexistence, refer to Appendix I, Part A: "Inventory of Kabane-Bearing Uji and Individuals not Granted Kabane During Tenmu's and Jitō's Reigns." Note in particular that the Soga uji was not a recipient of one of Tenmu's new kabane. See also Appendix II, Part B, "Distribution of Uji by Kabane in the SSJR," where one will find many of the traditional pre-Tenmu kabane that were still in use in the early ninth century. One will also find numerous references to such kabane in the standard index of the SNG entitled Shoku Nihongi Sakuin, v. 2 in Rikkokushi Sakuin, 4 vols. (1963-69).

真人

CHAPTER V
Grants of *Mahito* to Thirteen *Uji* in A.D. 684

A. INTRODUCTION

The NSK informs us that on the same day that Tenmu issued his edict establishing the new eight-rank kabane system, mahito, the highest of the eight ranks, was granted to thirteen different uji.[1] In anticipation of the following analysis a few introductory comments may be appropriate here. Of first importance is the fact that, as a group, these thirteen uji ranked very high in the sixth and seventh centuries in the overall social hierarchy of Japan. It is equally important to stress that the available data, as reflected in the NSK, indicate that these few uji enjoyed great social distinction despite the fact that they are mentioned surprisingly few times in the NSK. Additionally, it is clear from references to them in the SNG that they achieved positions of high political importance during the eighth century. Their social position is also given top ranking by the SSJR in the early ninth century.

Because their primary importance lay in who they were by reason of their lineage, genealogical data concerning them is more abundant than any other type available. Since their high social position was based on ascription rather than achievement, it is natural that the records should plentifully contain data that stresses such a basis of rank. As dull as these data may be for readers now, they must be presented at least in part because they reflect an important aspect of the values system which was being imposed on lineage groups in Japan during the seventh century when the paramountcy of the imperial line was sharply ascending. And when that

---

[1] For additional details, see Appendix I, Part B from GR74 through GR86, as well as Table I, Part C.

paramountcy became fully accepted in theory in the following century, social ranking within the realm was made relative to the paramount social ranking of the reigning sovereign.

B. ANALYSIS ON THE BASIS OF ORIGINAL KABANE

All Thirteen uji, which were granted mahito on Tenmu 13/10/1, had borne earlier the kabane of kimi. This kabane appears frequently in both the KJK and NSK. However, in the KJK it is written with the character 君 whereas in the NSK it is written with either the character 君 kun or with the character 公 kō, to use these two characters' Sino-Japanese readings.² One wonders why this distinction between what appear to be two different types of kabane of kimi was maintained by the compilers of the NSK, but it is obvious that this distinction was meaningful to them. It may even be that such a distinction was an invention of those compilers; and the available evidence does indicate that, if this distinction was indeed an invention, its aim probably was to place uji bearing the kabane of kimi (kō) apart from and above uji bearing kimi (kun). Most Japanese authorities agree that both kun and kō were read kimi and that, on the basis of evidence in the KJK, NSK and SSJR, no substantive difference originally existed between the two. It is very likely that the use of two different characters for rendering kimi was a device that was in current use by Tenmu's reign and that the basic purpose, as stated above, was to give preferential treatment to uji that bore the kabane of kimi (kō) and that were alleged to have been rather more closely related by blood to the imperial line than other uji.³

Any distinction that may have been maintained until the mid-eighth century was rendered markedly less explicit in A.D. 759 (Tempyō Hōji 3) when the SNG records that the bearers of the kabane

---

²I have maintained the same distinction by rendering the one as "kimi (kō)" and the other as "kimi (kun)".

³K. Iwahashi, Jōdai kanshoku seido no kenkyū, pp. 16-19; T. Abe, Uji-Kabane, pp. 35-37. See also, "Kimi" in NRD, v. 3, p. 475.

of kimi (kun) would henceforth use the character kimi (kō) in rendering their kabane in writing.[4]

By the early ninth century we find that this distinction was virtually lost and that the majority of kimi-bearing uji listed in the SSJR were of the kimi (kō) variety. The following table presents the SSJR distribution of the two varieties of kimi:

SSJR Categories	Kimi (kō)	Kimi (kun)
kōbetsu: "imperial" uji	41	3
shinbetsu: "deity" uji	3	1
shoban: non-Japanese uji	9	0
Totals	53	4

Perhaps the most important observation that can be made regarding the thirteen mahito-recipient uji is that they all originally bore the same kabane of kimi. In this respect, among many others, this group of uji stands in sharp contrast with the muraji recipients which were discussed above in Chapter III. There it was demonstrated that the seventy-three individuals and uji that were granted muraji between 680 and 684 had originally borne a wide variety of kabane including the following: obito, kishi, miyatsuko, atahi, kurahito, fuhito and agata-nushi. Whereas the muraji recipients had been representative of differing backgrounds, as demonstrated by the wide variety of their original kabane, the mahito recipients reflected a uniform background, namely, their relatively close blood relationship with the imperial line.

C. ANALYSIS BASED ON SSJR CATEGORIES

It must be remembered that any discussion of the relative ranking of kabane-bearing uji within the overall sociopolitical hierarchy of the late seventh century must include consideration of at least three other major social segments: first, the members of the imperial house; second, uji that were not granted new kabane

---

[4] See Shoku Nihongi, Asahi Shinbun (1939) v. 2, p. 30, (hereinafter abbreviated as SNG I, v. 2); K. Iwahashi, Jōdai kanshoku seido no kenkyū, p. 18.

by Tenmu but continued to bear their traditional pre-Tenmu kabane; and, third, commoners composed of families and individuals that bore no kabane. A significant negative characteristic of kabane is that they were not borne by members of the imperial house. The members of the imperial house functioned within a relative-ranking system possessing its own distinctive status symbols and titles. Tenmu's eight-rank kabane system, therefore, is subject to the interpretation that in one way it functioned indirectly to differentiate the bearers of Tenmu's new kabane from the members of the imperial house ranking above them, as well as from both the bearers of traditional kabane and the commoners without kabane ranking below them.

The available genealogical data of the KJK, NSK and SSJR indicate that the uji granted mahito on Tenmu 13/10/1 occupied the top echelon of the nobility, below the level of the imperial family. For at least eleven of these thirteen uji granted mahito, evidence of the distinctive nature of their lineages is to be found in the SSJR, much of which is supported by the KJK and NSK as well.

It seems desirable at this point to present some rationale for using the data found in the SSJR, which was composed in the early ninth century, in analyzing the composition of lineage groups of the seventh and earlier centuries.[5] Because it is well known that a number of changes occurred during the eighth century in both the application and implication of some kabane, it may seem to be of questionable value to rely on the SSJR of the early ninth century in analyzing patterns of more than a century earlier. But some Japanese scholars have pointed out that the SSJR is indeed useful for such purpose, because, in general, it does present a classification system of uji types based on lineage that is similar to the system reflected in the NSK account for the reign of Tenmu.[6]

---

[5]This matter is presented here rather than in Chapter III, Section C, above, because in analyzing the mahito recipients, lineage is the prime determinant of their relative ranking, whereas, in the case of the muraji recipients, lineage is either of very minor importance or of none whatever.

[6]For example, see K. Iwahashi, Jōdai kanshoku seido no kenkyū, p. 31.

Book I of the SSJR records the alleged ancestry of 335 uji, which it classifies as kōbetsu or "imperial" uji, meaning uji that claimed to be direct descendants of emperors.[7] While no longer considered to be members of the imperial family, these uji did claim to have a common ancestry with the Sun Line, and many of them claimed to be collaterally closely related to sovereigns who reigned in the sixth and seventh centuries. These 335 uji are listed as residing in any one or more of fourteen geographical subdivisions within the capital and in the five Home Provinces. As a clue to the theme of relative ranking, it is of significance that the ancestries of eleven of the above-mentioned thirteen mahito-recipient uji are listed in the first five geographic categories. Furthermore, they are all placed either at the top or very near the top of the list of uji included under each of the five geographical categories. The following table gives the eleven uji in the order in which they appear in SSJR, and it is assumed that the order in which uji are listed in the SSJR reflects to a considerable degree the relative ranking of uji as it existed during the latter part of the seventh century, during the eighth, and during the early ninth century. If this assumption is accepted, then the superior relative ranking and status of these eleven uji in the early ninth century is well attested.

Book I of SSJR Geographical Subdivision	Number of Uji listed	Genealogical References to 11 of the 13 Uji[8]
1. Sakyō (Left Capital)	30	6 listed within first 7 places
2. Ukyō (Right Capital)	11	6 listed within first 9 places
3. Yamashiro Province	1	1 "
4. Yamato Province	1	1 "
5. Settsu Province	1	1 "
(6-14 not applicable)	291	0 "
Totals	335	15[9]

[7] See Appendix II, Part A.
[8] The genealogies of two of the thirteen uji are not found in the SSJR and are otherwise unknown.
[9] It should be noted that in the SSJR a given uji is often listed under more than one geographical subdivision, and if the identical ancestry is indicated in each listing, it is assumed that such multiple listings represent geographically separated sub-uji of a single, extended uji.

The table above shows that the first five geographic subdivisions of Book I of the SSJR lists 30, 11, 1, 1, and 1 uji respectively. In the first geographic subdivision, Sakyō Kōbetsu (Left Capital, Imperial Uji) listing thirty uji, six of the eleven uji (Okinaga GR84, Yamaji GR86, Hata GR83, Mikuni GR77, Michi GR75, Moriyama GR74) are included, and the sequence in which they are listed ranges between first and seventh place out of a possible thirty places. In the second geographical subdivision, Ukyō Kōbetsu (Right Capital, Imperial Uji) listing eleven uji, six of the eleven mahito-recipient uji (Yamaji GR86, Mikuni GR77, Sakata GR82, Tajihi GR80, Wina GR81, Tagima GR78) are included, and the sequence in which they are listed ranges between first and ninth places out of a possible eleven places. The third through the fifth geographical subdivisions each contains a single uji among which are found three of the eleven uji (Wina GR81, Tagima GR78, Sakahito GR85). When one considers that the SSJR contains ancestral references for a total of 1182 uji, the very high relative ranking of this group of eleven mahito-recipient uji--measured on the basis of relative sequence of their SSJR ancestral listings--is better appreciated.

From ways in which the listings of the SSJR are arranged, it is clear that the uji occupying top place in the social hierarchy, below the level of members of the imperial family between the seventh and the ninth centuries, were those that traced their descent from the Ōjin-Keitai-Tenmu imperial line. In support of this thesis is the fact that the SSJR first cites in Book I, under the first five geographical subdivisions the imperial ancestors of forty-four mahito-bearing kōbetsu uji. Their ancestors range between Ōjin and Tenmu. However, emperors who reigned prior to Ōjin, or emperors who descended in the line of Nintoku (son of Ōjin) that ended with Buretsu, are not listed as ancestors of any of these forty-four uji. Even within this category, the uji listed as descending from Keitai are much more numerous than those listed as descending from Ōjin. Only six of the forty-four uji trace their ancestry to Ōjin, whereas the balance of thirty-eight trace theirs either to Keitai or to emperors descending from Keitai.[10]

D. NSK REFERENCE FREQUENCY

Japanese scholars have often referred to this group of thirteen uji as "the long-silent relatives of the emperor," meaning, of course, that the NSK contains so few references to them. In the 165-year period prior to the reign of Tenmu, that is from the beginning of Keitai's reign in 507 to the end of Tenchi's reign in 671, only twelve references to the members of this particular group

---

[10] The close tie between the descent of an uji from Keitai or from one of his immediate ancestors, on the one hand, and the award of mahito by Tenmu, on the other, is supported by additional evidence. The three uji descending from Ōjin and awarded mahito by Tenmu were Okinaga GR84, Yamaji GR86, and Hata GR83. The SSJR lists all three of these as descending from Ōjin's son, Imperial Prince Waka-nu-ke-futa-mata, the great-great grandfather of Keitai (SSJR I, pp. 59-65; SSJR II, pp. 149-50; KJK I, pp. 272, 297; NSK I, v. 1, p. 255; NSK V, v. 1, p. 364). A number of other mahito-bearing uji are listed in the SSJR as descending from Ōjin but only these three descending from Ōjin's son, Waka-nu-ke-futa-mata, the direct ancestor of Keitai, were awarded mahito by Tenmu. The reason seems more than likely explained by the fact that they were closely related to Keitai, rather than that they traced their ancestry to Ōjin.

The KJK and NSK contain twelve genealogical references to nine of the thirteen uji awarded mahito by Tenmu. Genealogical references to four of the thirteen uji are lacking in both the KJK and NSK (Moriyama GR74, Michi GR75, Takahashi GR76, and Umaraki GR79). For three of the thirteen such references appear only in the KJK (Hata GR83, Okinaga GR84, and Yamaji GR86), and for another three (Tagima GR87, Sakata GR82, and Sakahito GR85) such references appear only in the NSK. Three of the uji enjoy genealogical references in both the KJK and NSK (Mikuni GR77, Tajihi GR80, and Wina GR81). In all cases but one, these genealogical references in the KJK and NSK provide the same ancestry as found in the SSJR. That one exception is found in the case of the Mikuni uji GR77. The genealogical references in the NSK and SSJR agree that Keitai was the ancestor of the Mikuni, but the KJK claims it to be Ōjin. This conflict is explained by Motoori in his Kojikiden as arising over a confusion in names of similar pronunciation. The KJK claims the Mikuni uji's ancestor was the grandson of Ōjin, Oho-hodo-no-Miko (KJK I, p. 297), and Motoori explains that this name was confusedly taken for Keitai's which was Wo-hodo-no Mikoto (KJK I, p. 384). The NSK claims for the Mikuni uji descent from the son of Keitai, Mariko (sometimes read Maroko-no-Miko; NSK I, v. 2, p. 6; NSK II, v. 2, p. 24). Philippi indicates that the KJK text is corrupt where it details the Mikuni uji's ancestry (KJK I, p. 297, n. 5). The fact that the Keitai ancestry for the Mikuni is listed in three different places in the SSJR (Sakyō, Ukyō, and Yamashiro; Cf. SSJR I, pp. 65, 92, 102) lends support to the correctness of Motoori's explanation. Keitai is now generally accepted as the ancestor of the Mikuni uji. (SSJR I, p. 65; SSJR II, p. 150; A. Ōta, Seishi kakei daijiten, p. 5758; A. Ōta, Nihon jōdai shakai soshiki no kenkyū, p. 570; T. Abe, Uji-Kabane, p. 33.)

of uji appear in the NSK, whereas, in the following twenty-five year period, encompassing the reigns of Tenmu and Jitō (672-696), there appear but forty-nine references. There are long periods of total silence when none of these uji, nor their members, is mentioned even once. For example, not a single reference is made to any activities of this group of uji during the crucial fifty-four year period between 586 (the second year of Yōmei) and 641 (the thirteenth year of Jomei), a period of momentous events including the Sogas' rise to greatest influence, the importation of Buddhism, the work of Shōtoku Taishi, and other events culminating in the Taika palace coup in 645.

This silence is indeed a mystery, and the paucity of NSK references prevents us from attaining anything approaching a full picture of the roles they played in society and government before Tenmu's reign. Is it possible to assume that "nonactivity" was a seventh-century characteristic of this group, which perhaps was imposed on it by more powerful forces? It is not until the reigns of Tenmu and Jitō that we are able to attain anything like an understanding of the administrative function of the members belonging to this group of uji. Even for those reigns the number of NSK references is not plentiful. However, the ones that are available indicate that the members of at least three of these thirteen uji granted mahito were appointed to some of the most important administrative posts. It would appear that by the time of Tenmu's reign, the crown had become powerful enough to place a few of its close collateral relations in key positions. But if such was not the reason, at the very least it can be said that from the beginning of that reign a definite policy was implemented to achieve a greater degree of balance in administrative posts and assignments by appointing representatives of the long-standing powerful uji as well as those of uji which were collaterally closely related to the imperial family.

In all of the sixth and seventh centuries, from the first year of Keitai in 507 through the reign of Jitō to 697, the NSK contains

only sixty-one references to the members of this group of thirteen
<u>mahito</u>-recipient <u>uji</u>. Thirteen of these references merely record
Tenmu's grant of the kabane of <u>mahito</u>, eight record genealogical
matters and seven record appointments to administrative positions.
It is this last small group of references that supplies us with
clues as to the importance of these <u>uji</u> in the last quarter of the
seventh century, despite the relative silence of the <u>NSK</u> for earlier periods.

The administrative posts and positions given to some of the members of these <u>mahito</u>-recipient <u>uji</u> may be conveniently subdivided
into matters relating to territorial control on the one hand and
to matters relating to the court and the imperial family on the
other. Under the former of these two subdivisions, four positions
of great importance are mentioned in the <u>NSK</u>. The following discussion is presented in the chronological order in which these
four posts are referred to in that source.

On Tenmu 1/6/26 (672) Tagima no Kimi Hiroshima (GR78) is mentioned as being the <u>Kibi no Kuni no Kami</u>,[11] a title that appears
to mean a person who was in charge of the Province of Kibi, probably something in the order of a governor.[12] Presumably a person
who held such a post in an area as economically prosperous and
strategically located as Kibi no Kuni would be counted as one of
the most influential of court-appointed officials in the provinces.

On Tenmu 6/10/14 (677) the <u>NSK</u> records that Tajihi no Kimi Maro
(GR80) was appointed <u>Settsu no Tsukasa no Kami</u>,[13] a term or office
indicating that he was placed in administrative control of the
Province of Settsu, one of the five Home Provinces. The most important functions and responsibilities inherent in that post were

---

[11]吉備國守 The reading <u>Kibi no Kuni no Kami</u> based on the gloss of <u>NSK V</u>,
v. 2, p. 391.

[12]<u>NSK V</u>, p. 391, n. 41 and p. 434, n. 12. See J. Hall, <u>Government and
Local Power in Japan 500 to 1700</u>, regarding the administration of this area
in the pre-Nara period.

[13]攝津職大夫 The reading <u>Settsu no Tsukasa no Kami</u> based on the gloss of
<u>NSK V</u>, v. 2, p. 430.

68   Ancient Japanese Nobility

the administration and control of the strategic area around the city and port of Naniha, which was from very early times the port of entry for the Home Provinces.[14] There was also a close relationship between administrative positions in Naniha and foreign affairs. It was to the port of Naniha, for example, that foreign emissaries from China and the kingdoms of Korea came throughout Japan's pre-Nara history. It was there that they were frequently received, housed and entertained before and after proceeding to the court.[15]

The third such reference to high territorial office was also held by a member of the Tajihi uji, an important personage by the name of Tajihi no Mahito Shima (GR80). Under the date of Tenmu 11/4/21 (682) in the NSK he is referred to as the Tsukushi no Ohomikotomochi.[16] This post was also of great strategic importance from very early times. References to it appear in the NSK quite often in the sixth and seventh centuries as a government organization in control of a broad area in what is present-day northern Kyushu. From very early times the official in charge of Tsukushi performed important functions of a diplomatic and military nature relating to Japanese interests in Korea. During the seventh century the official in charge of the Tsukushi area was appointed by, and was under the control of, the central government.[17]

The fourth important reference is the one made by the NSK to Michi no Mahito Tomi (GR75) on Tenmu 14/9/15 (685), when he was appointed the Minami no Michi no Tsukahi, a term which Aston translates as "the Commissioner for the Nan-kai-do."[18] He was sent on

---

[14] NSK V, v. 2, p. 430, n. 1.
[15] See the many references listed in Appendix I, Part B, under GR193 regarding diplomatic matters in which the Naniha no Kishi uji participated.
[16] 筑紫大宰 The reading Tsukushi no Ohomikotomochi based on the gloss of NSK V, v. 2, p. 452. It should be pointed out that this uji did not receive the kabane of mahito until 684. It is thought that the use of the term mahito here for an event of 682 is an anachronistic notation added by the compilers of the NSK.
[17] See NSK V, v. 2, p. 574, Supplementary Note 25-29.
[18] 南海使者 NSK I, v. 2, pp. 370-371. The reading Minami no Michi no Tsukahi based on the gloss of NSK V, v. 2, p. 470.

a tour of Nankaidō, which included the old provinces of Kii, Awaji, Awa, Sanuki, Iyo and Tosa, to inspect the provincial governors, district supervisors and the conditions of the common people. While this appointment was probably of only temporary duration, its importance, historically speaking, is that the court by that time was powerful enough to exercise inspectional rights over governors and other local officials along broad areas facing the Inland Sea.

When we turn to appointments to offices relating to the imperial family or to the central administration of the government, there are also just a few NSK references, but the extraordinary nature of these few references indicates that at least select members of the thirteen mahito-recipient uji attained some of the top positions closest to the sovereign during the reigns of Jitō and Mommu (697-707). Again approaching these references chronologically, we find that Tajihi no Shima no Mahito (GR80), already mentioned above as earlier holding the post of Tsukushi no Ohomikotomochi, was appointed Udaijin or Great Minister of the Right in 690 (Jitō 4/7/5), at a time when it appears that a major overhaul of the new Chinese-style bureaucratic system of government was undertaken.[19] Shima held this important position for ten years, during which time he was the second most important administrator in the Council of State (Daijōkan), the highest administrative body of the central government after the introduction of a Chinese-style bureaucracy. In that post he ranked above all but the Chancellor of the Council of State (Daijōdaijin). Ordinarily he also would have ranked after the Great Minister of the Left (Sadaijin), but for the fact that that office was not filled during his ten-year term as Great Minister of the Right. Shima was then promoted to this position of Great Minister of the Left in 700 (Mommu 4/8/?). Another measure of Shima's importance is found in 691 (Jitō 5/1/13) where we are told he was granted a higher court rank plus an increment of three-hundred households to hold in fief, thus bringing his

---

[19] See NSK V, v. 2, p. 503, nn. 28 and 29.

holdings up to five-hundred. This grant was a form of emolument that accompanied his high office. In 697 (Jitō 11/2/28), just before the retirement of Empress Jitō, Michi no Mahito Tomi (GR75), already mentioned above in connection with his appointment as the Minami no Michi no Tsukahi, was appointed as Officer-in-Charge of the Heir Apparent's Palace (Miko no Miya no Tsukasa no Kami),[20] and on the same day Tagima no Mahito Kunimi (GR78) was appointed the Chief Tutor for the Heir Apparent (Miko no Miya no Ohokikashi-zuki).[21] We find also that another member of the Tagima no Mahito uji by the name of Tate, who had been sent as a junior envoy to Silla in 681, was appointed in 704 (Keiun 2/11) to the very important position of Saigū no Kami, or Chief of the Bureau of the Consecrated Imperial Princess.[22]

E. SUMMARY

The available evidence indicates that by reason of their particular imperial ancestry the thirteen uji awarded mahito enjoyed a paramount position within the kabane relative-ranking system that prevailed from the last quarter of the seventh century. That position within the system began to develop at the earliest from the sixth century and continued to be attested by the SSJR in the early ninth century. From the mode of presentation of genealogical material concerning all mahito-bearing uji in the SSJR, it is clear that by the early ninth century top ranking in the sociopolitical hierarchy, below the ranking of members of the imperial family, was enjoyed by uji claiming descent from emperors who, with the exception of Ōjin, reigned in the sixth and seventh centuries. With Tenmu's grant of mahito to thirteen uji in 684 it became unquestion-

---

[20] 春宮大夫 The reading Miko no Miya no Tsukasa no Kami based on the gloss of NSK V, v. 2, p. 532.

[21] 東宮傅 The reading Miko no Miya no Ohokikashizuki based on the gloss of NSK V, v. 2, p. 532.

[22] 齋宮頭 See F. Bock, Engi-shiki, Procedures of the Engi Era, p. 150, as well as the Glossary and Key of that work for many other references to this office.

able that ascription was primary to achievement in the placement of these lineage groups near the pinnacle of the social hierarchy below the level of the imperial family.[23] It is certain that for centuries before Tenmu's reign, high social rank and blood relationship with the imperial house went hand in hand; however, Tenmu's grants of the new top-ranking kabane of mahito to these particular thirteen uji clearly and officially raised their social ranking above that of all other types of lineage groups. While these recipients of mahito were placed socially above all other types of kōbetsu lineage groups, it is perhaps of more importance to note that they were also placed socially above all shinbetsu lineage groups. And it is meaningful in this regard to remember that many of the shinbetsu groups enjoyed control over very substantial power bases encompassing long-established economic, military and political resources.

[23] See T. Abe, Uji-Kabane, p. 41.

朝臣

CHAPTER VI
Grants of *Asomi* to Fifty-Two *Uji* in A.D. 684

A. INTRODUCTION

On Tenmu 13/11/1 (684) the kabane of asomi, the second highest within Tenmu's new eight-rank system, was granted to fifty-two uji.[1] Some of the general characteristics of these grants and the grantees are in sharp contrast with those of the mahito grants discussed in the previous chapter. The sharpest difference between the two groups of grants is that there were many more uji involved in the asomi than in the mahito grants. In addition, it will be found that more space in the NSK is devoted to recording the activities of these uji and their members than is devoted to any other comparable group of kabane recipients. In one respect, however, this group of uji is similar to the group of mahito recipients in that many of them too are alleged to have been collateral descendants of the imperial line, but in their case they descended from emperors who reigned much earlier than those who are claimed as ancestors of the lineage groups that were granted mahito.

Let us proceed to the analysis of the data relating to these grantees in much the same order as in the case of that of the mahito grantees above. Whereas the emphasis in the mahito analysis had to be placed on lineage because of the nature of the uji concerned, it will be found in the case of the asomi recipients lineage considerations are of lesser importance. Traditional power and authority exercised by certain of the asomi-recipient uji during the sixth and seventh centuries were probably of more importance.

---

[1] See Appendix I, Part B, from GR87 through GR138, as well as Table I, Part D.

B. ANALYSIS BASED ON ORIGINAL KABANE

Unlike the group of thirteen uji that were granted mahito, which had all previously borne the kabane of kimi (kō), this present group of fifty-two asomi recipients had previously borne one of three possible kabane, as follows: two had previously borne muraji, eleven had borne kimi (kun), and thirty-nine had borne omi. This is the first occasion since Tenmu began to make numerous kabane grants four years previously in 680 that grants were made to uji that had previously borne muraji, kimi (kun) or omi. The only two muraji uji in this group of fifty-two are the Mononobe no Muraji (GR94) and the Nakatomi no Muraji (GR97), two lineage groups which had long been counted among the most prominent in early Japanese history, and they had borne the muraji kabane for centuries. Muraji was their fixed kabane in all of the many references made to them in both the KJK and the NSK for the two centuries prior to Tenmu's reign, the essential period of this study, but it is important for purposes of this analysis to point out that the muraji borne by these two uji that were granted asomi was completely different and of very much higher status in quality and rank than the kabane of muraji that was granted to the eighteen individuals and fifty-five uji between 680 and 684, described in Chapters II and III, above. As is well known, omi and muraji are not only the two most numerous kabane found in the KJK and in the NSK before Tenmu's reign, but they were also borne by the lineage groups with the most power and influence. However, there were many different strata among the holders of both omi and muraji before Tenmu's new system was instituted, and what Tenmu's new eight-rank kabane system basically accomplished was to grant to the most important omi and muraji-bearing uji one of the new kabane that was more commensurate with their real standing or ranking within the overall sociopolitical hierarchy of the late seventh century.

The omi-bearing uji such as the Kose and the Soga (the latter of which, incidentally, was not granted one of Tenmu's new kabane and virtually ceased to exist by the eighth century) as well as such <u>muraji</u>-bearing <u>uji</u> as the Ohotomo and the Mononobe, had acquired so much power and influence by the fifth century that their chieftains were often designated as the <u>Ohoomi</u> (the Great <u>Omi</u> Chieftain) and the <u>Ohomuraji</u> (The Great <u>Muraji</u> Chieftain). The most cursory review of the <u>NSK</u> for the period prior to the Taika coup of 645 will demonstrate that the most influential individuals, both socially and politically, were those who held the titles of <u>ohomuraji</u> and <u>ohoomi</u>. Their key positions of power and influence are indicated by the fact that their appointments or reconfirmations to those posts are almost always carefully noted in the <u>NSK</u> account of the first months in the first year of the reign of a new emperor or just prior to that in the sections usually referred to as the "Account Before Accession." When one of these officials dies during the course of a given reign, the appointment of his successor is not indicated in the <u>NSK</u> until the beginning of the following reign, but of course this does not necessarily indicate that a successor did not function as such a high official prior to his announced appointment in the <u>NSK</u>.

It is also to be noted that the appointment of an individual who served as either <u>ohomuraji</u> or <u>ohoomi</u> during more than one reign was reconfirmed at the beginning of the next reign and of each successive reign thereafter. There are two possible explanations: one, that the initial appointment to one or the other position at the beginning of a reign did not imply tenure to that office beyond that reign; second, that the appointments and reconfirmations of individuals to these offices ranked perhaps second in importance to the enthronement of a new sovereign.

The following is a list of the powerful individuals of these <u>uji</u> who were either appointed to or reconfirmed in these offices at the beginning of the reigns of sixth- and seventh-century sovereigns:

    Keitai, 1/2/4 (507)

        Ohotomo no Kanamura no Ohomuraji (GR139)

        Kose no Wohito no Ohoomi (GR90)

Mononobe no Arakahi no Ohomuraji (GR94)
Ankan, BA/2/0 (533)
    Ohotomo no Kanamura no Ohomuraji (GR139)
    Mononobe no Arakahi no Ohomuraji (GR94)
Senka, 1/2/1 (536)
    Ohotomo no Kanamura no Ohomuraji (GR139)
    Mononobe no Arakahi no Ohomuraji (GR94)
    Soga no Iname no Sukune no Ohoomi (GRzero)
Kinmei, BA/12/5 (539)
    Ohotomo no Kanamura no Ohomuraji (GR139)
    Mononobe no Wokoshi no Ohomuraji (GR94)
    Soga no Iname no Sukune no Ohoomi (GRzero)
Bidatsu, 1/4/0 (572)
    Mononobe no Yuge no Moriya no Ohomuraji (GR94)
    Soga no Umako no Sukune no Ohoomi (GRzero)
Yōmei, BA/9/5 (585)
    Mononobe no Yuge no Moriya no Muraji (GR94)
    Soga no Umako no Sukune no Ohoomi (GRzero)
Sushun, BA/6/7 (587)
    Soga no Umako no Sukune no Ohoomi (GRzero)
Suiko, (593)
    Notation lacking.
Jomei, (629)
    Notation lacking.
Kōgyoku, 1/1/15 (642)
    Soga no Emishi no Ohoomi (GRzero)

The above data reflects some of the major political shifts from the reign of Keitai until the Taika period. These positions were of vital importance in the administration of the country prior to the gradual institution of a Chinese-style bureaucracy after 645, but they did not represent hereditary posts held in perpetuity by the head of a given powerful *uji*. Rather, they were more like prizes which were first acquired and then held by *uji* chieftains who were powerful and influential enough to do so. In spite of the traditional interpretation that these posts were hereditary, it is apparent that appointments or reconfirmations to these posts were due to other factors. The list above demonstrates the declining power first of the Kose uji, then of the Ohotomo, then of the Mononobe and finally of the rise to paramount position by the chieftain of the Soga uji to the exclusion of all the others.

It can be seen that in the sixth and seventh centuries no rigid organizational pattern was adhered to; it was possible to have two ohomuraji and one ohoomi at a single time, or to have just one ohoomi and no ohomuraji at all.

It was mentioned above that eleven of the fifty-two asomi-recipient uji had originally borne the kabane of kimi (kun), and it was also mentioned in the previous chapter dealing with the mahito-recipient uji that some authorities believe there was originally no substantial difference between the two forms of this kabane, namely, between kimi (kō) and kimi (kun). But the fact remains that the SSJR does preserve certain basic differences in the genealogical data it provides for the uji that originally had one or the other form of the kabane of kimi, a matter which is described in the following section.

C. ANALYSIS BASED ON SSJR CATEGORIES

Using the categories and the vocabulary of the SSJR to analyze the fifty-two asomi-recipient uji reveals that the characteristics of this group of uji sharply contrast with those of the mahito group described in the previous chapter. First, we find that mahito was granted exclusively to uji that claimed descent from some imperial ancestor; or to use the vocabulary of the SSJR, mahito was granted exclusively to uji that were classified as kōbetsu, that is, as "imperial" uji. By contrast, we find that asomi was granted primarily, but not exclusively, to uji of this classification.

The table below showing the profile of the fifty-two asomi-recipient uji on the basis of lineage and original kabane will assist in understanding the following analysis:

Grants of Asomi to Fifty-Two Uji

	Original Kabane			
SSJR Categories	Omi	Kimi (kun)	Muraji	Totals
kōbetsu: "imperial" uji	36	8	0	44
shinbetsu: "deity" uji	2	3	2	7
shoban: non-Japanese uji	0	0	0	0
unknown	1	0	0	1
Sub-Totals	39	11	2	
Total				52

Of the fifty-two uji granted asomi, forty-four fall into the kōbetsu category, thirty-six of which previously had borne the kabane of omi and eight that of kimi (kun). Seven of the asomi recipients are classified as being of shinbetsu stock, and while in numbers they represent a minority of the group, their presence is sufficient evidence to demonstrate that as a group, these fifty-two uji granted asomi were not homogeneous in background as in the case of the mahito recipients.[2] They were homogeneous in neither type of claimed lineage nor in the original kabane they bore before being granted asomi.

While it is true that the majority of these lineage groups claimed descent from emperors, as a group this majority was more distantly related to the imperial line than the mahito lineage groups. By this it is meant that their imperial ancestors were earlier, more remote emperors than those of the mahito groups, which were not earlier than Ōjin (Emperor no. 15). According to data drawn from the KJK, NSK and SSJR, the imperial ancestors of the forty-four asomi-recipient uji in the kōbetsu category range from Jinmu (Emperor no. 1) through Keikō (Emperor no. 12). The data

---

[2] A survey of the SSJR demonstrates that asomi-bearing uji in the early ninth century also were not homogeneous in terms of their ancestral categories. For example, the SSJR lists a total of 108 asomi-bearing uji of which 79 are classified as kōbetsu, 19 as shinbetsu and 10 as shoban. By contrast, the SSJR lists 44 mahito-bearing uji, all of which are of kōbetsu origin. In fact, of the approximate 23 different kabane listed in that work and borne by 1065 uji listed in the first three books of the SSJR (i.e., exclusive of the 117 unauthenticated lineages), the mahito-bearing uji are the only ones confined exclusively to the kōbetsu category. See Appendix II, Part B.

also indicate that a difference in the degree of remoteness existed as between the imperial ancestors of the uji that originally bore omi and those that originally bore kimi (kun), the former being listed in the sources mentioned as possessing more remote imperial ancestors than the latter. For example, the thirty-six uji that had formerly borne omi claimed imperial ancestors ranging from Jinmu (Emperor no. 1) through Kaika (Emperor no. 9), whereas the eight that had formerly borne kimi (kun) claimed imperial ancestors ranging from Sujin (Emperor no. 10) through Keikō (Emperor no. 12). The following table schematizes, in terms of their original kabane, the known imperial ancestors of the mahito-recipient lineage group as well as of the asomi-recipient groups, all of which were of kōbetsu classification.

Reign No.	Emperor	Original Kabane		
		Omi	Kimi (Kun)	Kimi (Kō)
1	Jinmu	1		
5	Kōshō	6		
7	Kōrei	2		
8	Kōgen	26		
9	Kaika	1		
10	Sujin		6	
12	Keikō		2	
15	Ōjin			3
26	Keitai			3
28	Senka			2
30	Bidatsu			2
31	Yōmei	—	—	1
Totals		36	8	11

Based on this ancestral distribution pattern for mahito and asomi grantees, it appears that there was operative in the last quarter of the seventh century a fairly well-defined relative-ranking system of lineage groups that were collaterally related to the imperial family. The highest stratum was composed of uji that were, exclusive of the members of the imperial family itself, the closest collateral relatives of the reigning monarch and that bore the kabane of kimi (kō). These were uji that claimed imperial ancestors from or after Ōjin (Emperor no. 15); to these the kabane of mahito was granted. The next lower stratum was composed of uji that bore the kabane of kimi (kun) and which claimed slightly more remote imperial ancestry; and the next stratum was composed of uji that bore the kabane of omi and that claimed even more remote imperial ancestors. In Tenmu's new system, these two groups of uji, the ones that formerly bore kimi (kun) and those that formerly bore omi, were joined into a single social stratum and granted asomi.

Just a word or two is here required regarding the two asomi-recipient uji that originally bore the kabane of muraji. These are the Mononobe no Muraji uji (GR94) and the Nakatomi no Muraji uji (GR97), who were awarded the very high rank of asomi in Tenmu's new system because of their power, influence and service rather than because of their lineage. In both cases these uji are classified as shinbetsu or "deity" lineage groups. Because their inclusion in the asomi group was not on the basis of lineage, they are more appropriately discussed in the following section of this chapter dealing with NSK reference frequency.

D. NSK REFERENCE FREQUENCY

In the last chapter I mentioned that the mahito-recipient uji have often been called by Japanese scholars "the long-silent relatives of the imperial family," and that this description arose because the activities of the members of those uji appear so infrequently in the sources. However, it was also mentioned that, despite the relative silence of the NSK regarding the activities of those lineage groups in the sixth and seventh centuries, fewer than ten NSK references to official appointments of some of their members during the reigns of Tenmu and Jitō seem to point to the fact that by the end of the seventh century the selected members of some of those uji were among the most important officials at court. Certainly this situation demonstrates that in the case of the mahito-recipient uji there was little or no relationship between their importance in government and the number of NSK references to the activities of their members. When we turn to the present group of fifty-two uji that were granted asomi, and to data available concerning them, we find that, proportionately, a great deal more NSK information is available than in the case of the mahito recipients. In fact, there is a total of 508 NSK references to the asomi-recipient uji and their members during the 189-year period between the beginning of Keitai's reign in 507 to the end of Jitō's in 697.

While the NSK contains more references to this group of uji than to any other identifiable group, and while there is no question but that some of these uji and their members played top political roles in the pre-Nara history of Japan back to the early sixth century, the proposition cannot be accepted that all asomi-recipient lineage groups were, from a political point of view, anywhere near being equally important. In other words, the available evidence indicates that important social ranking of any particular uji within Tenmu's revised kabane system did not necessarily guarantee that its members played an important political role at court. Let us review the available data in support of these conclusions.

The following table details, for the period covered by this study, the general distribution of the fifty-two asomi-recipient uji in terms of the number of NSK references per uji classed in units of ten:

No. of NSK References	No. of Uji
1-10	42
11-20	2
21-30	3
31-40	1
41-50	1
51-60	3
Total	52

Grants of Asomi *to Fifty-Two* Uji   81

It is revealing to note that only ten of these fifty-two uji have more than ten NSK references each. Of a total of 508 NSK references to this group of fifty-two uji during the 189-year period under study, 348 refer to the members of the ten uji enjoying eleven or more NSK references. These higher-frequency uji average 34.8 NSK references each, as compared with the forty-two lower-frequency ones which average only 3.8 each. The following is a list of the ten asomi-recipient uji enjoying the largest number of NSK references:

	Uji	No. of NSK References
GR97	Nakatomi no Muraji	60
GR89	Ahe no Omi	56
GR94	Mononobe no Muraji	53
GR90	Kose no Omi	44
GR87	Ohomiwa no Kimi (kun)	32
GR92	Ki no Omi	28
GR109	Kahahe no Omi	26
GR105	Hozumi no Omi	22
GR91	Kashihade no Omi	16
GR103	Tanaka no Omi	11
	Total	348

It may be of passing interest and of some significance to note that these ten higher-frequency uji are listed within the first twenty-three places in the list of fifty-two asomi-recipients in the NSK on Tenmu 13/11/1. In fact, it appears that in the listing of these fifty-two uji in the NSK there exists a correlation between prominence based on NSK reference frequency and list sequence. For example, if one divides this list into four groups of thirteen uji each, it will be found that there are 317 references to the first group, 103 to the second group, 55 to the third group, and only 33 to the fourth group. Expressed in averages, each uji in the first group of thirteen uji averages 24.4 references, in contrast to 7.9 references for those in the second group, 4.2 references for those in the third group, and only 2.5 for those in the fourth.³

There is evidence available to support the proposition that imperial ancestry was not necessarily the most important criterion for selecting uji to be recipients of the asomi grants. While the data of the KJK, NSK and SSJR demonstrate that the majority of the fifty-two asomi-recipient uji were of imperial lineage, it is revealing to make the following correlations between types of lineage and NSK reference frequency for the ten highest-count uji in this group.

		No. of NSK References	Kōbetsu Lineage	Shinbetsu Lineage
GR97	Nakatomi no Muraji	60		X
GR89	Ahe no Omi	56	X	
GR94	Mononobe no Muraji	53		X
GR90	Kose no Omi	44	X	
GR87	Ohomiwa no Kimi (kun)	32		X
GR92	Ki no Omi	28	X	
GR109	Kahahe no Omi	26	X	
GR105	Hozumi no Omi	22		X
GR91	Kashihade no Omi	16	X	
GR103	Tanaka no Omi	11	X	

If one can accept the proposition that the ten uji with the highest NSK reference frequency listed above were socially and politically the most prominent in the list of fifty-two asomi-recipient uji, it is then of interest to note that lineages of only six out of the ten fall into the kōbetsu or "imperial" category, while the remaining four fall into the shinbetsu or "deity" category.

If, within this category of the ten highest-frequency uji one separates the six kōbetsu uji from the four shinbetsu, it is found that the former group averages only 30.1 references per uji by con-

---

³A similar pattern is observed in Chapter VII, below, concerning the sukune-recipient uji.

trast with an average of 41.7 references for the latter group. Thus, while the majority of _uji_ granted _asomi_ were of _kōbetsu_ lineage, a few very prominent and powerful _shinbetsu_ _uji_ were also included. This evidence at least permits the conjecture, or at most supports the conclusion, that a minimum of two criteria were used in 684 in selecting the fifty-two _uji_ to be granted _asomi_: the _uji_ concerned either had to possess a certain type of imperial lineage and/or they had to be influential and powerful in the political arena.

宿禰

CHAPTER VII

Grants of *Sukune* to Fifty *Uji* in A.D. 684

A. INTRODUCTION

On Tenmu 13/12/2 (684), one month and a day after the award of asomi to fifty-two uji, the third highest rank of kabane within the new eight-rank system was awarded to fifty uji.[1] The analysis of these sukune grants proceeds along lines similar to those followed for the asomi grants presented in the previous chapter. It will be found that the few similarities and the many contrasts between these two categories provide a convenient means of understanding some of the respective, salient characteristics of each of these two groups of uji. In terms of the various categories used in this present work for analyzing the available data, there seem to be many more contrasts than similarities between the asomi-recipient and sukune-recipient lineage groups.

One obvious but not necessarily very significant similarity is that in the former case fifty-five uji received the asomi grants and in the latter case fifty received the sukune grants. But marked contrasts exist in regard to such matters as the respective original kabane of the two groups, and in the types of their respective lineages as recorded in the KJK, NSK and the SSJR. Also the NSK, for the approximate two-hundred-year period of this study, contains nearly twice as many references to the asomi-recipient uji and their members as to the sukune recipients. A significant feature of this analysis of sukune-recipient uji relates to the fact that a sizable number of them that are classified as being of "deity" lineage (shinbetsu) may be grouped according to common kami an-

---

[1] See Appendix I, Part B from GR139 through GR188 as well as Table I, Part E.

cestry. The resulting groupings of uji of claimed common lineage may represent family-like power clusters for a few of the more powerful uji.

B. ANALYSIS BASED ON ORIGINAL KABANE

Forty-nine of these fifty sukune-recipient uji bore the kabane of muraji and one bore the kabane of omi just prior to being granted sukune. In this respect this group of fifty uji is similar to the fifty-five uji that were granted asomi: a preponderant number of uji in both groups had previously borne a single kabane, omi in the case of the asomi recipients and muraji in the case of the sukune recipients. However, in actuality this similarity is less striking than it might otherwise appear, because four of these forty-nine muraji-bearing uji had earlier in Tenmu's reign been granted that kabane between 680 (Tenmu 9/1/8) and 683 (Tenmu 12/10/5), and therefore originally had borne other kabane. The kabane of two of these uji originally had been obito, one had been miyatsuko and the fourth had been kishi. This situation may be conveniently summarized as follows:

	Prior Kabane	Original Kabane
muraji	49	45
omi	1	1
obito		2
miyatsuko		1
kishi	—	1
	50 uji	50 uji

While four is not a significant number in itself, their presence among these fifty lineage groups indicates that sukune of the new system was less homogeneous in constitution than either of the two groups that earlier had been granted mahito and asomi. It would appear that each progressively lower rank within the new Tenmu system tolerated the presence of lineage groups representing a broader, less restricted ranking spectrum within the pre-Tenmu system.

It will be noted that the Moroahi no Omi <u>uji</u> (GR187) is the only one of the fifty <u>sukune</u>-recipient <u>uji</u> to have originally borne the <u>kabane</u> of <u>omi</u>. The significance of this exception escapes us, because nothing more is known about this <u>uji</u>. It is not mentioned anywhere else in the <u>KJK</u>, <u>NSK</u> or <u>SSJR</u>.

C. ANALYSIS BASED ON <u>SSJR</u> CATEGORIES

In terms of the categories, vocabulary and data of the <u>SSJR</u>, thirty-seven of the fifty <u>sukune</u>-recipient <u>uji</u> were of <u>shinbetsu</u> or "deity" lineage, seven were of <u>kōbetsu</u> or "imperial" lineage, and one of <u>shoban</u> or non-Japanese lineage. For the balance of five <u>uji</u> no certain information is available.[2] The following observations and comparisons may be made regarding this distribution of <u>SSJR</u>-type lineage groups. First, with regard to the ratio of "imperial" to "deity" lineage groups, the <u>asomi</u> and <u>sukune</u> groups are opposites. Within the fifty-two <u>asomi</u>-recipient <u>uji</u>, forty-four were counted as being of "imperial" lineage and seven were counted as being of "deity" lineage; but in the case of the present fifty <u>sukune</u> recipients, the ratio is the reverse in that only seven <u>uji</u> are counted as being of "imperial" lineage, while thirty-seven are of "deity" lineage. From this it is clear that <u>sukune</u> was primarily, though not exclusively, designed for <u>uji</u> of "deity" lineage, just as <u>asomi</u> was primarily, but not exclusively, designed for <u>uji</u> of "imperial" lineage. Second, it follows that in the relative ranking system in the last quarter of the seventh century, as represented by Tenmu's eight-rank <u>kabane</u> system, groups tracing their origins to imperial antecedents ranked socially above those that traced theirs to deities.

The seven <u>uji</u> of "imperial" lineage among these fifty <u>sukune</u>-recipient <u>uji</u> must have had approximately the same degree of col-

---

[2]Some of the information on ancestry contained in Table I, Part E, is not wholly certain and is likely subject to adjustment, but it is felt that the general patterns of the data will be but slightly altered. The information was compiled from <u>NSK V</u>, <u>SSJR II</u> and A. Ōta, <u>Nihon jōdai shakai soshiki no kenkyū</u>.

lateral relationship with the imperial family as the group of "imperial" uji that had been granted asomi the preceding month. According to the SSJR, the seven uji with "imperial" lineages within the sukune group trace their ancestry to emperors ranging from Jinmu (Emperor no. 1) to Chūai (Emperor no. 14), which is similar to the case of the "imperial" lineages of the asomi group, which ranged between Jinmu (Emperor no. 1) and Keikō (Emperor no. 12).

The inclusion among the sukune-recipient uji of one that was classified as shoban, that is, as being of non-Japanese origin, represents another feature distinguishing the sukune group from both the mahito and asomi groups. Unfortunately, the significance of the inclusion of this single uji, Miyake no Muraji (GR154), of non-Japanese lineage is not apparent from the only five references to it contained in the NSK for the period of this study, except perhaps for one member, Ihatoko, who had been of assistance to Tenmu in the Jinshin War of 672.

The importance of genealogy in early Japanese history can hardly be overemphasized and some authorities go so far as to claim that originally the KJK and the first half of the NSK were primarily collections of genealogical data to which descriptions of other events had been added. The many references to ancestry, ancestral claims and genealogical records in the KJK, NSK, SNG, and the SSJR all seem to support such an interpretation of those sources. The stress placed on genealogical matters in Japan's early records more than likely resulted from the concern of aristocratic lineage groups to preserve or enhance their traditional social and political positions of preference and prestige based upon various types of lineage considerations. Of considerable interest is the fact that in a number of cases two or more lineage groups made identical ancestral claims. The question arises as to whether such cases represented clusters of uji that may have functioned cooperatively for the attainment of common causes. The available data indicate that these clusters may have been collaterally related by either real or fictive blood relationships. Whether these relationships were real or fictive cannot, of course, be proven by the available sources, but even if that situation were different, proof of the real or fictive nature of these relationships would be of lesser significance then the fact that such loosely affiliated lineage groups can be identified in the patterns of early Japanese sociopolitical life during the same period that the imperial line was apparently successfully imposing its paramountcy over the same groupings of *uji*.

When the *SSJR* was compiled in the early ninth century, the *shinbetsu* category provided a means of classifying into a single broad group all those lineage groups that claimed to be of indigenous Japanese stock but were not of "imperial" descent. The *uji* within this broad classification traced their ancestry back to a select group of *kami* who were of service to the imperial line during the mythological formation of Japan as an inhabitable land and as an organized state. Thus, *uji* in the *shinbetsu* category ranked socially after those in the *kōbetsu* category. A study of the *SSJR* ancestry patterns demonstrates that not all the *uji* in the *shinbetsu* category traced their ancestry to different *kami*; a number of *uji* claim common *kami* ancestry. It is entirely possible that a group of two or more *uji* claiming a common *kami* ancestor represented an affiliation of sorts. The genesis of such affiliations is, by reason of the nature of the sources, almost impossible to verify, but it is possible that small groups of *uji*, which were of lesser power or influence, affiliated with a stronger *uji*, and in the process adopted as their own the ancestry of the *uji* with which they had affiliated.

Book II of the *SSJR* presents ancestral information on 404 *shinbetsu* lineage groups, and the *kami* ancestors of these lineage groups are divided into three categories, namely, the deities of heaven (*ama-tsu-kami*), the heavenly grandson (*ten-son*, i.e., Ho-no-ninigi-no-mikoto), and the deities of earth (*kuni-tsu-kami* or *chigi*). For each lineage group the *SSJR* lists a specific *kami* as its ancestor, or else it states that a given *uji* has the same ancestry as some other *uji* that is listed elsewhere in the work.

If the proposition is accepted that two or more lineage groups claiming a common kami ancestor possibly represent some form of affiliation, it is of special interest to note that there are six such affiliations composed of thirty-three of the uji that were granted either asomi or sukune. These thirty-three uji consist of seven uji of shinbetsu classification that were granted asomi and twenty-six of similar classification that were awarded sukune. These six major groupings of uji by common kami ancestor are listed in the table below.³

It will be noted in the table that five of the six groupings of uji are each clustered around one of the most prominent lineage groups in the history of pre-Nara Japan, the Ohomiwa, Mononobe, Nakatomi, Ohotomo and the Azumi. Only the Wohari uji played a relatively minor role in that period. The first three groups are led by uji that were among the only six uji of shinbetsu classification to have been granted asomi: Ohomiwa uji (GR87), Mononobe uji (GR94) and Nakatomi uji (GR97). The second three groups are led by uji of shinbetsu classification that were granted sukune: Ohotomo uji (GR139), Azumi uji (GR141) and Wohari uji (GR143). This rather remarkable clustering of so many uji on the basis of alleged common kami ancestry may possibly represent an echo of real blood relationship in which kami have been substituted for real common ancestors, but what seems more likely, is that it represents a very early trend of weaker lineage groups to establish fictive blood relationship with more powerful ones.⁴

---

³See Ōta, Nihon jōdai shakai soshiki no kenkyū, pp. 589-590 for a similar treatment of the subject.

⁴In addition to the following examples of uji of shinbetsu classification clustered on the basis of common ancestry, there is one interesting example of a cluster of uji of kōbetsu classification claiming the same imperial ancestry as that of the Soga no Omi uji. While the main trunk of the Soga uji was eliminated in the palace coup of 645, closely related elements of that uji, such as Soga no Ishikaha no Maro and Soga no Akae, remained close to the victors until their respective eliminations in 649 and 672. After that time references to the Soga name virtually disappear from the pages of history. Nevertheless, no fewer than nineteen of the fifty-two uji granted asomi by Tenmu in 684 claimed common ancestry with the Soga no Omi uji. The ancestries of seventeen of the nineteen are recorded in the SSJR and two in the NSK. They are as follows:

GROUPINGS OF <u>ASOMI</u> AND <u>SUKUNE</u>-RECIPIENT <u>UJI</u>
GROUPED ON THE BASIS OF COMMON <u>KAMI</u> ANCESTRY

	NSK Ref. Frequency	Granted Asomi	Granted Sukune
I. Ohomiwa-Related Lineage Groups			
GR87 Ohomiwa	32	X	
GR107 Kamo	4	X	
GR123 Munakata	2	X	
II. Mononobe/Isonokami – Related Lineage Groups			
GR94 Mononobe	53	X	
GR102 Uneme	8	X	
GR105 Hozumi	22	X	
GR151 Kamunakibe	1		X
GR160 Wakayuwe	1		X
GR161 Yuge	1		X
GR170 Hi	4		X
GR173 Yatsume	1		X
GR174 Sawi	4		X
GR176 Ato	4		X
GR180 Uji	1		X
GR181 Woharida	1		X
GR185 Tsukiyone	1		X

GR No.	Uji	NSK Ref. Frequency
GR90	Kose	44
GR92	Ki	28
GR93	Hata	4
GR95	Heguri	5
GR96	Sazakibe	1
GR100	Ishikaha	3
GR101	Sakurawi	8
GR103	Tanaka	11
GR104	Woharida	4
GR109	Kahahe	26
GR112	Karube	2
GR114	Kishita	3
GR115	Takamuku	8
GR120	Tsuno	4
GR121	Hoshikaha	2
GR129	Hayashi	1
GR130	Hami	1
GR135	Sakamoto	9
GR137	Tamate	1

This list was suggested by Shigeo Kitayama's <u>Asuka Chō</u> (pp. 95-96) in <u>Kokumin no Rekishi</u>, v. 3.

III. Nakatomi/Fujihara -
Related Lineage Groups
GR97   Nakatomi   60   X
GR145 Nakatomi no
       Sakahito   1   X

IV. Ohotomo-Related
Lineage Groups
GR139 Ohotomo   83   X
GR140 Saheki   20   X
GR167 Tamanoya   1   X

V. Azumi-Related
Lineage Groups
GR141 Azumi   15   X
GR171 Ohoshiama   2   X
GR183 Ama no Inukai   2   X

VI. Wohari-Related
Lineage Groups
GR143 Wohari   4   X
GR144 Kura   1   X
GR148 Sakahibe   16   X
GR150 Ihokibe   2   X
GR155 Kobe   1   X
GR156 Tasuki no Tajihi   1   X
GR157 Yuki no Tajihi   1   X
GR164 Tsumori   14   X
GR166 Wakainukahi   5   X

D. NSK REFERENCE FREQUENCY

Solely in terms of the number of references in the NSK it can be said that the sukune recipients played a less prominent role than the asomi recipients. During the 189-year period of this study, from the first year of Keitai to the last year of Jitō, the NSK contains approximately 508 references to the members of the lineage groups that were granted asomi, but it contains only approximately 277 references to the members of the fifty uji that were granted sukune. The distribution is as follows:

No. of References	No. of Uji
1-10	44
11-20	4
21-30	1
31-40	0

41–50	0
51–60	0
61–70	0
71–80	0
81–90	1
Total	50

In the case of the fifty-two asomi recipients, ten of them had more than ten NSK references each, the range falling between a low of eleven and a high of sixty. But it will be seen that in the case of these fifty sukune recipients, only six of the uji have more than ten NSK references, the range being unevenly distributed between a low of fourteen and a high of eighty-three. As similarly illustrated in the case of the asomi recipients, which was described in the preceding chapter, we find that just a handful of the sukune-recipient uji possess more than a few passing references in the NSK. And even among this handful of uji just one of them, the Ohotomo no Muraji uji (GR139), towers above all the rest with eighty-three references. The following table illustrates the reference frequencies for these six uji possessing more than ten NSK references.

	Uji	No. of NSK References
GR139	Ohotomo	83
GR146	Haji	21
GR140	Saheki	20
GR148	Sakahibe	16
GR141	Azumi	15
GR164	Tsumori	14
	Total	169

Of the total of 277 NSK references made in the post-Keitai period of the NSK to the sukune-recipient lineage groups, 169 belong to the six groups possessing more than ten references each. In other words, 60 percent of the NSK references to the fifty sukune-recipient lineage groups are made to these six. The average number of references per uji for these six is 28.1, as compared to an average of 45.5 references for the comparable group of the six highest uji among the asomi recipients. The average reference frequency for the forty lower frequency lineage groups among the sukune recipients is only 2.7 references.

For these fifty sukune recipients, just as in the case of the fifty-five asomi recipients, a correlation exists between prominence based on reference frequency and list sequence. In addition to the uji with the single highest reference frequency appearing first on the list (Ohotomo no Muraji GR139), we find that the five uji with the highest NSK frequency are listed among the first ten in the list of fifty uji. The following data likewise supports the claim that, by and large, the more important uji are listed first: If the fifty sukune-recipient uji are divided into four groups of 12, 13, 12, 13 uji, respectively, in the sequence in which they are listed in the NSK, we find that the average reference frequency per uji in these groups would be 15.2, 2.1, 3.9 and 2.0, respectively, demonstrating clearly that the more prominent an uji, the more likely it will be found listed above those of lesser prominence.

忌寸

CHAPTER VIII

Grants of *Imiki* to Eleven *Uji* in A.D. 685

A. INTRODUCTION

On Tenmu 14/6/20 (685) the kabane of imiki, the fourth highest grade within Tenmu's new eight-rank system, was granted to eleven uji. The grant of imiki to so few uji, to which the NSK refers fewer than 140 times in the sixth and seventh centuries, constitutes a far less satisfactory core of data for statistical analysis than in the cases of the grants of asomi and sukune, which together involved 102 uji and almost 800 NSK references. Nevertheless, just as was described in the case of the thirteen mahito recipients involving only approximately sixty references, the imiki-recipient uji played important roles and occupied positions of significance in the sociopolitical hierarchy during the approximate two-century period to which this study is devoted. The special characteristics of this group underline how indispensable these lineage groups were by the late seventh century in the functions that supported the viability of a centralized state.[1]

B. ANALYSIS BASED ON ORIGINAL KABANE

Ten of the eleven imiki-recipient uji bore the kabane of muraji just prior to the receipt of imiki, and only one bore atahi. It is significant, however, that these ten muraji-bearing uji originally had all borne other kabane which were changed when they were granted muraji at various times between 680 (Tenmu 10/1/7) and 682 (Tenmu 12/10/5). Seven of these had originally borne the kabane of atahi and one each had borne obito, kishi and miyatsuko. Thus, the

___
[1] For detailed references to the imiki-recipient groups, see Appendix I, Part B, from GR189 through GR199, and Table I, Part F.

Grants of Imiki to Eleven Uji

original composition of this group of eleven lineage groups, in terms of prior and original kabane, was as follows:

	Prior Kabane	Original kabane
muraji	10	
atahi	1	8
obito		1
kishi		1
miyatsuko	—	1
	11 uji	11 uji

Although very different in terms of the number of uji involved, there is here a similarity between the imiki and sukune recipients. It will be recalled that of the forty-nine muraji-bearing uji that were granted sukune two had originally borne obito and one each had borne kishi and miyatsuko. By contrast, none of the recipients of either mahito or asomi had originally borne kabane that were changed to muraji and then later changed to either mahito or asomi.[2]

The kabane of atahi in the pre-Tenmu period was the most common but not the exclusive kabane borne by various kuni no miyatsuko, an official equivalent to a provincial governor before the Taika Reform, but it was also a title held by a kind of official responsible to the court and in charge at the local level of property and affairs pertaining to the court. Of the eight atahi uji in this present list it is possible that only five were actually kuni no miyatsuko as follows:

	Kuni no Miyatsuko of:
GR189 Yamato no Atahi	Yamato no Kuni
GR190 Kazuraki no Atahi	Kazuraki no Kuni
GR191 Ohoshi Kafuchi no Atahi	Kafuchi no Kuni
GR192 Yamashiro no Atahi	Yamashiro no Kuni
GR198 Ohosumi no Atahi	Ohosumi no Kuni in Saikaidō ?

[2]See ch. X, below, Kabane Patterns, Chart A.

Even within this group there is uncertainty regarding the last, Ohosumi no Atahi (GR198), because of the lack of NSK data. Its inclusion here is purely hypothetical, being based on the facts that its kabane was atahi and that in southern Kyūshū there was an Ohosumi no Kuni. Nevertheless, what little evidence is available on these five uji permit the generalization that almost half of the imiki-recipient uji were probably managers of geographic areas under the control of the court in the last quarter of the seventh century. It is generally accepted that uji bearing the title of kuni no miyatsuko were local influential family-like groupings which, through one means or another, had gradually been brought within the control of the court and central government by the early seventh century.[3]

The second major category among the imiki recipients is represented by the four, and possible five, immigrant uji, as follows:

	Original kabane
GR193 Naniha no Muraji (?)[4]	kishi
GR195 Yamato no Aya no Muraji	atahi
GR196 Kafuchi no Aya no Muraji	atahi
GR197 Hada no Muraji	miyatsuko
GR199 Fumi no Muraji	obito

---

[3]See R. Reischauer, Early Japanese History, v. 2, p. 173, and J. Geodertier, A Dictionary of Japanese History, pp. 165-166. For a convenient table of kuni no miyatsuko of this period, arranged geographically, see NRD, v. 4, pp. 76-77.

[4]There is here a most confusing problem relating to the Naniha no Muraji uji (GR193). This uji first appears in the NSK as the Kusakabe no Kishi uji, and then in 681 (Tenmu 10/1/7) Kusakabe no Kishi Ohokata (GR2) was granted the kabane of Naniha no Muraji. Two years later in 683 (Tenmu 12/10/5) the Kusakabe no Kishi uji (GR59) was granted the kabane of muraji. Care must be taken at this juncture, because there was another Kusakabe no Muraji uji (GR153) that was awarded sukune in 684 (Tenmu 13/12/2), and was not related to the Kusakabe no Kishi/Naniha no Muraji uji (GR2, GR59) mentioned above. See NSK V, v. 2, p. 466, n. 41. Some investigators believe, however, that the Kusakabe no Sukune uji represented the senior branch and that the Naniha no Imiki uji represented the cadet branch of the same extended lineage group. See NRD, v. 4, p. 19. This confusing situation is exacerbated by the lack of standardized notations in the NSK relating to this uji. The ways in which NSK refers to individuals and uji may be illustrated by the following groups of notations, each group referring to just one person:

One frequently sees in secondary materials on Japanese social organization in the pre-Nara period the hypothesis that the kabane of imiki was created by Tenmu primarily to be granted to uji of shoban classification, that is, of non-Japanese origin.[5] As a consequence most analyses of the imiki-recipient uji are highly influenced by this hypothesis. However, the relatively few data contained in the NSK regarding these eleven imiki-recipient groups do not clearly support this hypothesis: only five, or possible six, of the eleven were of immigrant origin. It is likely that the five uji that originally bore the kabane of atahi (and that were probably kuni no miyatsuko) were of approximately the same rank within the late seventh century sociopolitical hierarchy as the five uji of immigrant origin, and for that reason both groups were granted the same kabane of imiki. The hypothesis that imiki was primarily intended for immigrant uji is only supported by data drawn from the SNG for the following century of the Nara period. The SNG records grants to uji that are classified as being of shinbetsu or "deity" origin and that had earlier borne the kabane of imiki; whereas, in the same period, there are many instances of imiki being granted to branch uji that were descendants of the immigrant uji of Hada (GR197) and Aya (GR195 and GR196), two uji that had been earlier granted imiki by Tenmu. During the Nara period, approximately 150 uji bearing imiki can be identified, of which more than 100 are known to have been of immigrant origin.[6]

1. Kusakabe no Kishi Ohokata (Tenmu 10/1/7)
   Naniha no Muraji Ohokata   (Tenmu 12/10/5)

2. Kusakabe no Kishi Ihakane (Kōgyoku 1/2/2)
   Naniha no Kishi Ihakane   (Suiko 6/4/9)
   Kishi no Ihakane   (Suiko 5/11/22)

3. Naniha no Kishi Itabi   (Bidatsu 13/2/8)
   Kishi no Itabi   (Bidatsu 4/4/2)

4. Naniha no Kishi Kunikatsu (Saimei 2/0/0)
   Kunikatsu no Kishi Kuhina (Kōgyoku 1/2/22)

[5] For example, see K. Iwahashi, Jōdai kanshoku seido no kenkyū, p. 31.

[6] See A. Ōta, Nihon jōdai shakai soshiki no kenkyū, pp. 599-600 and "Imiki" (by Naoki Kōjirō) in NRD, v. 1, pp. 438-439.

C. ANALYSIS BASED ON SSJR CATEGORIES

According to the SSJR, the lineages of this group of eleven uji are almost evenly divided between those of shinbetsu or "deity" origin and those of shoban or non-Japanese origin. Five are of shinbetsu classification, with considerable uncertainty relating to one of them, and five are of shoban classification, also with considerable uncertainty relating to one. The ancestry of one is unknown.[7]

Although it appears that imiki was not originally intended as a kabane to be borne primarily by immigrant lineage groups, it had become so by the early ninth century when the majority of the imiki-bearing lineage groups noted in the SSJR were listed as being of immigrant origin. Of the forty-eight imiki-bearing uji listed in the SSJR, only one is classified as of kōbetsu or "imperial" origin, while six are classified as of shinbetsu or "deity" origin. By contrast, forty-one of these forty-eight uji are classified as being of shoban or immigrant origin.[8]

While this evidence supports the thesis that imiki was commonly borne by immigrant groups, particularly during the Nara period, the specific immigrant groups that were granted imiki during Tenmu's reign undoubtedly possessed unusual and important qualifications. They performed a wide variety of indispensable and technologically-advanced services both on behalf of the imperial family and on behalf of some of the uji that were the most powerful in their own right and most influential in policy formulation at court. Consequently, by the seventh century they had become firmly established and broadly scattered in strategic areas throughout the Home Provinces (kinai). A glance at the many sixth- and seventh-century NSK references to the Yamato no Aya no Atahi uji (GR195), which are listed in Appendix I, demonstrates clearly that this lineage group is represented by a minimum of fourteen sub-uji for the period of this study, and we know that this number had expanded to

---

[7] See Table I, Part F for details.
[8] See Appendix II, Part B.

twenty-five by the early ninth century when the SSJR was compiled.[9]

The specialized and technical knowledge of continental origin, which was possessed by the earlier generations of immigrants in the fourth and fifth centuries, and for which there was a demand, greatly facilitated the original integration of such non-Japanese groups into the social and political fabric of pre-Nara Japan. Later generations of these groups in the sixth and seventh centuries continued to perform a variety of technical services, some of which had become hereditary in nature and doubtless dated back to the services their ancestors had rendered soon after their first settlement in Japan. Such a conclusion, for example, is unavoidable from a study of the NSK references to the Naniha no Kishi/Kusakabe no Kishi uji (GR193).

The tradition of immigrants possessing technological know-how is clearly reflected by the SSJR in the early ninth century. There we find, for example, immigrant uji listed in the SSJR as either the exclusive or predominant bearers of certain kabane which were originally merely designations descriptive of their occupations or of specialized services rendered by them. These are wosa (interpreter), eshi (painter or artist), kusushi (medic), fuhito (scribe), miyatsuko (in control of occupational groups such as be or tomo). The numbers of these and their ratio within the three books of the SSJR may be charted as follows:

	wosa	eshi	kusushi	fuhito	miyatsuko
kobetsu or "imperial" uji	0	0	0	3	6
shinbetsu or "deity" uji	0	0	0	0	25
shoban or non-Japanese uji	4	2	1	23	41

D. NSK REFERENCE FREQUENCY

In analyzing this group of imiki-recipient uji on the basis of

---

[9]For an informative account of the roles played by, and the broad distribution of, the Hada and Aya groups, see Otto Lewin, Aya und Hata. See also Seki Akira, Kikajin: kodai no seiji, keizai, bunka o kataru (1956) and Ueda Masaaki, Kikajin, kodai kokka no seiritsu o megutte (1965).

NSK reference frequency, we are faced with the same unsatisfactory situation that pertained to the similar analysis of the mahito recipients; there are too few NSK references to this group. For the period of this study during the sixth and seventh centuries, the NSK contains approximately 136 references for the eleven uji involved. Thus, the average number of references per uji is 12.3, a figure that does not tell us very much. However, more interesting information is obtained by comparing the respective NSK reference frequencies of the two distinctive groups of uji comprising the imiki recipients. These two groups of uji, which were described in the preceding section, are composed of one group of five uji whose original kabane was atahi and another group, also of five uji, whose original kabane were kishi, atahi, miyatsuko or obito. The SSJR classifies all of the first group of uji as being of shinbetsu or "deity" ancestry, while the other group of five uji with various original kabane are classified by the SSJR as being shoban or of immigrant stock. The average number of NSK references per uji for the first group is 4.2, while that of the second is more than five times as great, standing at 22.6.

With so few data available here one would not want to imply that one group of uji was five times as important as the other. In fact, it may well be that what appears to be a marked difference between these two groups has, in reality, very little to do with their relative importance. It is possible, for example, that the uji of non-Japanese ancestry were more frequently mentioned in the NSK, because of the more innovative nature of their activities. Perhaps the group of uji that were of kuni no miyatsuko status in the Home Provinces may have been of equal or of more importance to the court but the routine nature of their administrative responsibilities were not considered to be so remarkable as to rate frequent notation in the NSK.

E. SUMMARY

Despite the paucity of data regarding the imiki-recipient uji, as a group they constituted an important and unique stage in the ranking system reflected in Tenmu's new eight-rank _kabane_ system. First of all, the granting of the fourth grade of _imiki_ to five lineage groups of non-Japanese ancestry represented an important departure: only one lineage group of non-Japanese origin was included among the numerous recipients of the first three grades of Tenmu's _kabane_ system. The award of _imiki_ to two distinctive groups composed of five lineage groups, one group of _shinbetsu_ or of "deity" ancestry and the other of _shoban_ or of non-Japanese ancestry, is a clear demonstration that _uji_ of foreign extraction were recognized by the last quarter of the seventh century as being full and integral members of Japan's noble hierarchy. Symbolically this development also meant that the services to the court of these lineage groups of foreign extraction and of those rendered by the other group composed of _kuni no miyatsuko_ were of at least equal value and importance.

道師臣連稲置

CHAPTER IX

The Lower Four Grades of *Kabane*

From a reading of the edict of A.D. 684 (Tenmu 13/10/1), which was discussed in Chapter IV, above, and from the orderly way in which the top four grades of mahito, asomi, sukune and imiki in Tenmu's new eight-rank system were awarded during the following year and a half, one would have expected the last four grades of michi-no-shi, omi, muraji and inaki to be granted in similar orderly manner to selected lineage groups. But contrary to such expectations, at no time during the remaining year of Tenmu's reign until his death in 686 (Shuchō 1/9/9), nor during the subsequent eleven years of the reign of Empress Jitō until her abdication in 697 (Jitō 11/8/1), does the NSK record grants representing such a methodic completion of the new kabane system. Rather, during the period following the grants of imiki in 685 (Tenmu 14/6/20) until the year before Jitō's abdication, only two grants of muraji and one of imiki were made, and those were made to individuals. The question is whether these three grants fit into the patterns of kabane grants, which were established during Tenmu's reign.

The first of these three grants (GR200) was made to Kuhahara no Suguri Katsu on Shuchō 1/4/8 (685), when he was also awarded a court rank. The NSK describes him as a physician-in-waiting to Tenmu. There is some uncertainty about the reliability of this reference, because the SNG records in 699 (Mommu 3/1/27) that this same person was granted muraji in recognition of the public services rendered by him.[1] There are no other references to this person in the NSK, but there is one reference to a certain Kuhahara no Muraji Hitotari who may have been of the same lineage group and

---

[1] NSK V, v. 2, pp. 476-77 and SNG I, v. 1, p. 9.

who was sent as a junior envoy to Korea in 684 (Tenmu 13/5/28). The SSJR lists a Kuhahara no Suguri uji of shoban or non-Japanese lineage.[2]

The second of these three grants (GR201) was made to Tsukinomoto no Suguri Kachimaro on Shuchō 1/6/1 (685), where the NSK records that he was granted a court rank and twenty households in fief. Nothing more is known about this person or his uji, but one authority, relying upon a Shoku Nihonkōki notation of 837, believes that the Tsukinomoto uji was also of immigrant lineage.[3] These two muraji grants were the first made to uji or individuals whose prior kabane was suguri, a kabane which was almost exclusively borne by lineage groups of immigrant origin. In fact, the SSJR lists seventeen uji bearing this kabane, all of which are so classified. In Chapters II and III, above, which describe the seventy-three muraji grants made earlier in Tenmu's reign, it was pointed out that a number of uji of non-Japanese lineage were granted that kabane. In this respect then the two muraji grants to Kuhahara no Suguri Katsu and Tsukinomoto no Suguri Kachimaro fit into that particular established pattern for muraji recipients.

The last of the three grants was one of imiki which was made to Hada no Miyatsuko Tsunade (GR202) on Jitō 10/5/3 (696). For several reasons this grant is unusual. First, it is the only posthumous kabane grant recorded since the beginning of Tenmu's reign. The NSK records that Tsunade died in 680 (Tenmu 9/5/21), at which time he was granted a posthumous cap rank because of the services he had rendered the crown in the Jinshin War of 672. The NSK, however, does not inform us as to what those services were. Second, a grant of imiki to a person or uji bearing the prior kabane of miyatsuko without first being granted muraji appears to represent an exception to the pattern reflected in the eleven imiki grants that were made in 685 (Tenmu 14/6/20). Third, there is a question of how this grant relates to the fact that the Hada no Miyatsuko

[2] SSJR II, p. 284.
[3] NSK V, v. 2, p. 477, n. 29.

uji was granted muraji (GR40) in 683 (Tenmu 12/9/23) and was later granted imiki (GR197) in 685 (Tenmu 14/6/20).

Some authorities theorize that Hada no Miyatsuko Tsunade may have belonged to a branch of the Hada no Miyatsuko uji that did not share in the grant of muraji in 683 or in that of imiki of 685.[4] A more likely explanation is that the grant of imiki was made in 696 as a special honor to Tsunade personally in order to endow him with a kabane appropriate to the social ranking of his uji, even though it was done posthumously. Tsunade is referred to as bearing the kabane of miyatsuko in 696 when granted imiki because that was the kabane that he and the other members of his lineage group had borne at the time of his death in 680. It is not the usual practice of the NSK compilers to attribute anachronistic kabane rank to uji or individuals.[5] If the grant of imiki to Hada no Miyatsuko Tsunade was made in order to bring his posthumous social ranking up to the standard of the surviving members of his lineage group, it may not have been considered proper to first grant him muraji. By 696 muraji was the indicator of a considerably lower status than it had been in the traditional pre-Tenmu system. If these interpretations are accepted, the posthumous grant of imiki satisfactorily fits the pattern of the imiki grants made during Tenmu's reign in 685.

Of more serious import is the problem of the relative-ranking status of the two muraji grants described just above, as well as of the seventy-three muraji grants made earlier between 680 and 684, just before the promulgation of Tenmu's edict announcing the establishment of his eight-rank kabane system. The question concerns whether the kabane of muraji that were granted during Tenmu's reign represented the seventh grade of the new system established

---

[4]For example, see NSK V, v. 2, p. 530, n. 16.
[5]For example, see references to Haji no Muraji Hodo (GR146) and Hi no Muraji Okina (GR170) in the NSK in 690 (Jitō 4/10/22), even though their respective uji had been granted sukune in 684. The reason why this notation of 690 uses the kabane of muraji is that the event described under the 690 date occurred fifteen years before their respective uji had been granted sukune.

in 684. Let it first be said here that there does not appear to be any final and generally accepted answer to this question. Some authorities claim that these muraji grants were more representative of the muraji in the traditional, pre-Tenmu kabane system than in the new eight-rank system.[6] Others disagree and claim that the grants of muraji made during Tenmu's reign were representative of the seventh rank of the new system, even though many of those grants were made in the years just prior to the official establishment of the new system.[7]

In the absence of any clear statement in the primary sources that would elucidate this problem, there are available in secondary materials a number of hypotheses supporting one side or the other of the argument. The following factors are most frequently set forth in support of the claim that Tenmu's muraji grants did not represent the seventh grade of his new system. First, the NSK systematically records the grants of only the top four grades of Tenmu's new system (mahito, asomi, sukune and imiki) and then appears to leave in limbo the balance of the system represented by the bottom four grades (michi-no-shi, omi, muraji and inaki). Second, if Tenmu's muraji grants were representative of grade seven of the new system, then why were grants of the fifth grade of michi-no-shi, the sixth grade of omi and the eighth grade of inaki never made? Third, some authorities conjecture that the fundamental purpose of Tenmu's new eight-rank kabane system was to establish what they call the kōshin-sei or "the system of imperial relatives," meaning a sociopolitical system which gives top ranking to close relatives of the imperial house. The new kabane system made it possible for Tenmu to elevate, within a number of gradations, the social status of noble lineage groups related within certain degrees to the imperial house. The conjecture continues that once the stabilization of the system of imperial relatives was achieved

---

[6]For example, see T. Abe, Uji-Kabane, p. 69.
[7]For example, see M. Ueda, Nihon kodai kokka seiritsu shi no kenkyū, pp. 265-266.

by the grants of the top four grades of kabane in the new system, it was not important for further stabilization to grant the kabane of the bottom four grades.

Perhaps the weakest point of this conjecture is that imiki was granted systematically to eleven uji, but lineage considerations were definitely secondary in their case. Additionally, those uji were not of kōbetsu stock and were therefore not related to the imperial house. Therefore it follows that if the purpose of the new eight-rank system was only to stabilize the system of imperial relatives, then Tenmu might well have terminated his kabane grants after granting just the three top grades of mahito, asomi and sukune, because the recipients of each of these grades included uji of "imperial" or kōbetsu lineage.

The following factors are often cited in support of the opposite claim, namely, that Tenmu's muraji grants, both before and after the establishment of his new eight-rank system, represented grade seven of the new system. First, the general profile of the group of uji granted muraji indicates that it was representative of a lower social stratum than that of those groups of uji that were granted the top four grades of the new system. In the matter of occupations and types of original kabane, there are marked similarities between those granted muraji before Tenmu instituted his new system and those granted muraji in the following century during the Nara period.[8] Second, the kabane of omi and muraji of the traditional system were borne by some of the most powerful and influential lineage groups whose activities are recorded in the NSK. By contrast the lineage groups that were granted muraji during Tenmu's reign are referred to relatively infrequently in the NSK where, as a group, they occupy far less significant positions. Their social and political status coincided far more closely with the grade of kabane that was seventh from the top in Tenmu's new system than with that which was second from the top in the tradi-

---

[8]See related discussion in ch. VIII, sec. C, above.

tional system. In the light of available data it may never be possible to decide precisely what ranking was conveyed by the _kabane_ of _muraji_ granted during Tenmu's reign; it can only be said with confidence, at this stage, that the lineage groups which were granted _muraji_ during Tenmu's reign and were not subsequently granted the higher _kabane_ of _sukune_ or _imiki_ represented the lowest stratum of the nobility to be granted _kabane_ during that reign.

CHAPTER X
Kabane Patterns

This brief discussion here of kabane patterns is primarily a summary in graphic form of much that has been written thus far. Chart A, below, illustrates the pattern of relationships between traditional kabane and the new ones of the eight-rank system for the 177 uji that were granted kabane during Tenmu's and Jitō's reigns. The listing sequence of the traditional kabane is a reflection of the relative ranking of the new kabane; that is to say, the relative ranking of the former are extrapolated from the relative ranking of the latter. However, it will be seen that only in the case of mahito, the top ranking kabane of the new system, is there an absolute equation in rank with a single, traditional kabane, in that case, with kimi (kō). For the balance of the three ranks of asomi, sukune and imiki we must be satisfied with more general equations: asomi is primarily equivalent in rank to the traditional kabane of omi and kimi (kun); sukune is primarily equivalent in rank to the traditional muraji; and imiki is primarily equivalent in rank to the traditional atahi.

The new muraji rank is more complex, because sixty-six uji were granted that kabane during Tenmu's reign, but fifteen of them were later granted either sukune (4 uji) or imiki (11 uji). For the remaining fifty-one uji the rank of their muraji within the new system is primarily equivalent to the rank of the traditional miyatsuko, but included with miyatsuko are a number of kabane that are undifferentiated in terms of relative ranking. They include obito, kishi, fuhito, agata-nushi, suguri, kurahito, etc. The new kabane of muraji apparently acted in many instances as a transitional kabane between a traditional ranking and a new ranking within the top four kabane of the new system.

Kabane *Patterns*

Chart B, below, graphically illustrates on a percentage basis the traditional-kabane constituents of the five separate groups of uji granted the new kabane of either mahito, asomi, sukune, imiki or muraji during Tenmu's reign. In each case the dominant traditional-kabane constituent is placed within the circle.

Based on data found in Appendix I, Part B, useful information is obtained regarding the overall relative prominence of lineage groups based on NSK frequency. If we lump together all NSK references for the period A.D. 507-686 on the basis of the highest grade of kabane granted to all lineage groups during Tenmu's reign, and if we then lump together all such references to lineage groups and/ or individuals that were not granted kabane or whose identification is in question, the following relative NSK reference frequency figures obtain:

New Kabane	No. of NSK References
mahito	61
asomi	508
sukune	277
imiki	136
muraji	120
nonrecipients	446
Totals	1548

The following graphically illustrates the distribution of these figures in terms of percentages:

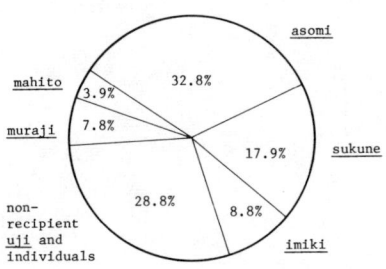

These figures are subject to many uses, one of the most striking of which is to illustrate in numerical or in graphic form the dimension of what we might call the new nobility that was elevated to higher social status by Tenmu through his grants of new kabane. Of course, this dimension can only be illustrated in terms relative to the dimension of the old nobility who were not granted kabane during Tenmu's reign. With this restriction in mind, it will be seen that 71.2% of the NSK kabane-related references refer to uji that were granted one of the new kabane, and 28.8% refer to uji and individuals that did not receive any of the new kabane titles.

In dealing with such figures as these it must be kept in mind that they reflect the trends or patterns of the NSK for the sixth and seventh centuries, and they therefore may be less than fully accurate reflections of the historical realities of those centuries. Nevertheless, it would appear that despite such uncertainty the kabane patterns herein described do give a basis of judgment. For example, they provide a sort of standard by which one may measure variations of kabane patterns found in other source materials of later periods, particularly of those of the SNG covering the Nara period.

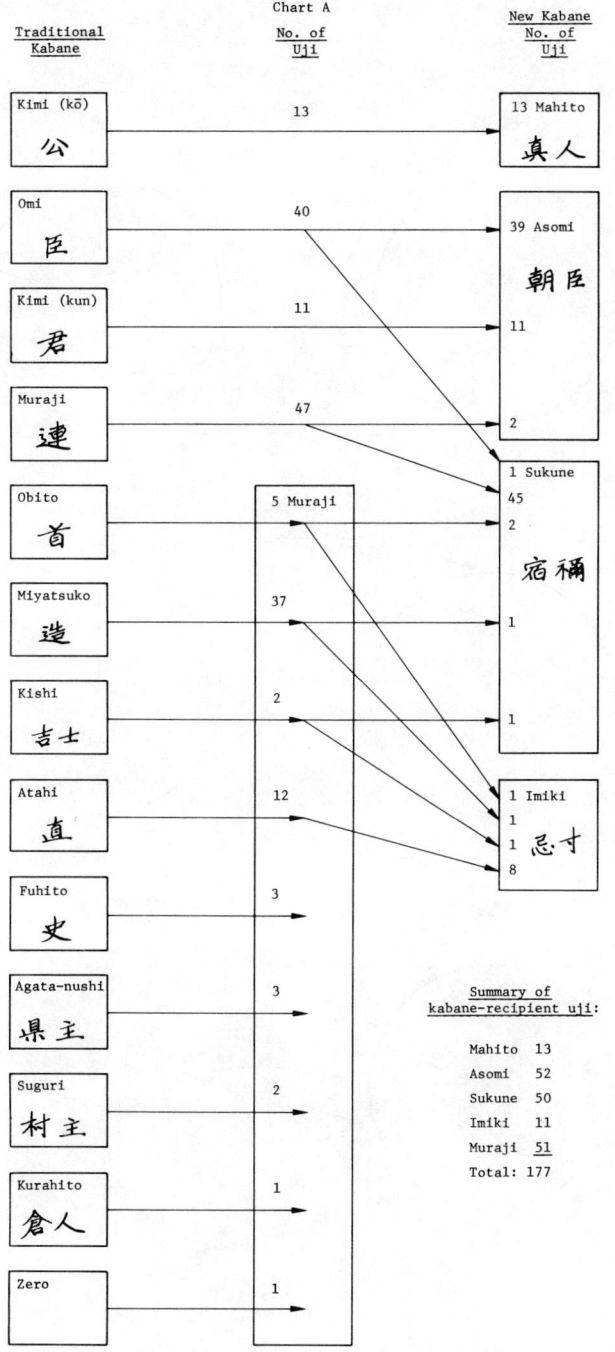

Chart B

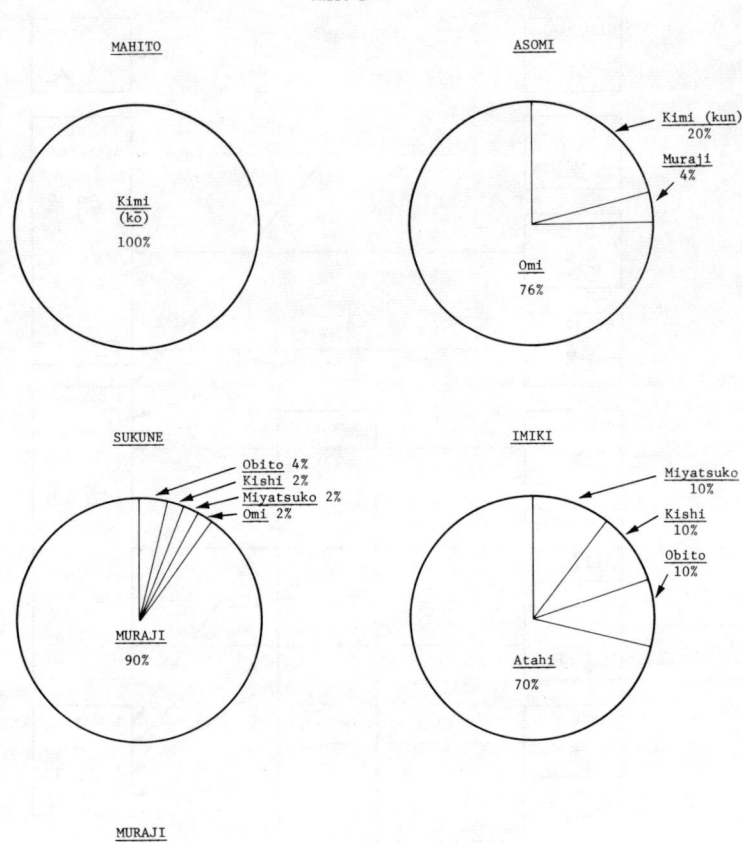

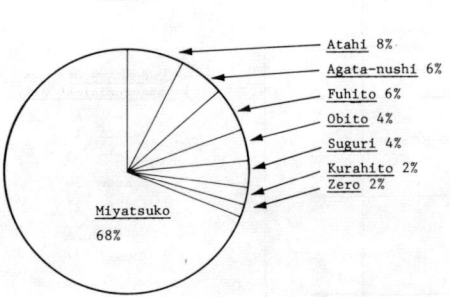

CHAPTER XI
Sample Analyses

It has been suggested in this monograph that it is valuable to employ certain analytic and comparative approaches to selected data relating to lineage groups, in order to estimate their social status and ranking relative to other lineage groups. It was mentioned in Chapter I, above, that this approach involves analyses of specific components comprising what may be termed the "profile" of the group or groups being studied. These components include the nature and implications of the kabane and prior kabane borne by the members of the groups being studied, their respective types of lineage and ancestry, the number of NSK references made to each of the groups, their listing sequences (if available) in the NSK, SSJR, etc.

While the word "analytic" is here employed in reference to such an approach, it is recognized that the scientific method cannot be applied wholly to the more variable and less isolable data with which the social scientist often must deal. The restrictions on such an approach become even more apparent when dealing with problems relating to social institutions in the centuries prior to the Nara period, because of the inadequacies of the sources. Nevertheless, it is my conviction that an analytic approach, limited though it may be by the available social-science data, yields at least some elucidation and some new insights to many problems of interest and importance.

The first problem discussed below in Section A deals with the relative ranking of the Nakatomi no Asomi and the Imibe no Sukune clans, a subject that was first documented in the early ninth century by Imibe no Hironari. The second problem discussed below in Section B deals with a rather enigmatic list of eighteen clans that appears in the NSK in the fifth year of Jitō's reign (691). Both of these problems are analyzed in terms of the profile components explained earlier. These analyses are merely examples of what may be expected from the application of the approaches suggested in this monograph. An additional matter is then presented below in Section C to illustrate briefly that slightly more refined methods of quantification may be of value in the determination of relative ranking factors based on types or categories of activities with which personalities and clans are identified in the NSK.

A. LAMENTATIONS ACCORDING TO IMIBE NO HIRONARI

Imibe no Hironari compiled a history of his uji on imperial request and presented it to the emperor in either A.D. 807 or 808. The results of his labors are entitled Kogoshūi, which has been translated into English by Genchi Katō and Hikoshirō Hoshino (1926) and published as Gleanings from Ancient Stories. Hironari's fundamental contention was that his and the Nakatomi uji were, as far as priestly duties and Shintō affairs were concerned, the two most important lineage groups, and that their mutual importance dated from Japan's very earliest times, from as far back as to the mythological events centering around the Sun Goddess and the earliest imperial descendants of the Sun Line. It was also Hironari's contention that his and the Nakatomi lineage groups were equals but that his lineage group had been unjustly lowered in status in the preceding two centuries.

The KJK and the NSK contain traditions concerning both of these uji. Very often it would appear that these two earliest texts of Japanese myth and history imply that the Nakatomi and Imibe uji were of equal status; for example in a number of accounts contained therein the names of these two uji appear jointly. In some of the accounts of mythical events occurring during the "Age of the Gods" one finds closely associated in a single event the names of the kami ancestors of these two uji, that of Ame no Koyane no Mikoto, the reputed ancestor of the Nakatomi, and that of Ame no Futo Tama no Mikoto, the reputed ancestor of the Imibe. The following excerpt taken from Philippi's translation of the KJK will serve to illustrate this point.

> They [the eight-hundred myriad deities] summoned AME-NO-KO-YANE-NO-MIKOTO and PUTO-TAMA-NO-MIKOTO to remove the whole shoulder-bone of a male deer of the mountain AME-NO-KAGU-YAMA, and take heavenly PAPAKA wood from the mountain AME-NO-KAGU-YAMA, and [with these] perform a divination.
>
> They uprooted by the very roots the flourishing MA-SAKAKI trees of the mountain AME-NO-KAGU-YAMA; to the upper branches they affixed long strings of myriad MAGA-TAMA beads; in the middle branches they hung a large-dimensioned mirror; in the lower branches they suspended white NIKITE cloth and blue NIKITE cloth.
>
> These various objects were held in his hands by PUTO-TAMA-NO-MIKOTO as solemn offerings and AME-NO-KO-YANE-NO-MIKOTO intoned a solemn liturgy.[1]

The apparent equal status that the Imibe and Nakatomi enjoyed during the "Age of the Gods" and as portrayed in the KJK and NSK may reflect one of the two following possibilities: First, in protohistoric and early historic times the two uji may very well have functioned jointly and equally in certain Shintō matters and ceremonies, and the traditions of such were preserved by both lineage groups through oral or written transmissions. Second, the portrayal of equal status may have resulted from the fact that a Nakatomi and an Imibe were part of a committee of twelve members who were ordered by Tenmu in 681 (Tenmu 10/3/3) "to commit to writing a chronicle of the Emperors, and also of matters of high antiquity."[2] It is generally accepted that a direct relationship exists between the materials compiled as the result of that order and the two ear-

---

[1] KJK I, pp. 82-83. Philippi's diacritics omitted. For similar descriptions of mythological events in which the Imibe and Nakatomi together participated, see NSK I, pp. 42-43, 45, 47-48.
[2] NSK I, v. 2, p. 350; NSK V, v. 2, p. 446.

liest extant accounts of Japan's pre-Nara history, the KJK and NSK.[3] Although twelve members comprised that compilation committee, the Imibe and Nakatomi representatives, Imibe no Muraji Kobito and Nakatomi no Muraji Ohoshima, apparently played a more active role than the other committee members, for the NSK notation ends with the statement, "Ohoshima and Kobito took the pen in hand themselves, and made notes." It is entirely possible that these two members of the committee were particularly careful to assure that the achievements and genealogical accounts of their respective uji were balanced in the work the committee prepared.

Even though the data found in the KJK and NSK accounts for the period of the "Age of the Gods" support the proposition that the Imibe and Nakatomi were of equal status, the question arises as to whether they really were of equal status in later times during the sixth and seventh centuries, the essential period of this present study. Hironari's Kogoshūi claims that,

> When the Empress (Suiko) reigned at the Oharida Palace, the descendants of Futotama fell into insignificance, but, thanks to the Imperial grace, they were still permitted to retain the office of a Court Shintō Priest, although greatly reduced or impoverished and far inferior in rank to that of their ancestors.[4]

Neither of the accounts of Suiko's reign in the KJK or NSK refers to the members of the Imibe uji, but the NSK does confirm the fact that the Imibe and Nakatomi did on some occasions later on in the second half of the seventh century so jointly function. For example, the NSK contains references to events or situations of religious significance in which members of both the Imibe and Nakatomi either participated or are mentioned: For example, in 673 (Tenmu 2/12/5) an Imibe and a Nakatomi (the first names lacking in the NSK), along with other officials, were given presents for having participated in the Festival of the First Fruits.[5] In 681 (Tenmu

---

[3] NSK I, v. 2, Supplementary Note 29-17, pp. 593-594.
[4] Katō and Hoshino, Kogoshūi, pp. 42-43.
[5] For details on this festival see Kanname-sai and Niiname-sai in F. Bock, Engi-Shiki.

10/3/16), as already mentioned above, Imibe no Muraji Kobito and Nakatomi no Muraji Ohoshima, along with ten other persons, were commanded to compile a chronicle of the emperors and of other ancient matters. In 690 (Jitō 4/1/1) Nakatomi no Ohoshima no Asomi and Imibe no Sukune Shikobuchi participated in Empress Jitō's enthronement ceremonies, Ohoshima conveying the blessings of the heavenly deities (Ama-tsu-kami) and Shikobuchi conveying the three imperial regalia to the empress. While these three notations refer to times rather later than the reign of Suiko, they do tend to confirm or support that part of Hironari's statement that the Imibe were "still permitted to retain the office of Court Shintō Priest."

Hironari laments that during the Tempyō period (729-749) the Nakatomi, because they were by that time the most influential at court in Shintō matters, took advantage of that situation to enhance their own prestige at the expense of the Imibe and other uji that also traditionally had responsibilities related to Shintō matters. Hironari describes that situation as follows:

> It was in the Taihō Era that Japan first possessed official records of the Shintō Gods. Even then, however, a complete list of the names of Shintō Gods and Shrines was lacking and the national Shintō rites were not well established. When the Government Authorities began to compile a book on the Shintō Shrines officially registered during the Tempyō Era, the Nakatomi family, being then most influential at court in religious affairs, took arbitrary measures, strictly superintended the compilation, and consequently, the shrines, no matter how insignificant, were all recorded in the registry, if they had any connection with the Nakatomi, whilst, on the contrary, even the greater, more renowned shrines, if not related to that house, were omitted from all mention therein. Thus, the Nakatomi family, being then all-powerful, made an unwarranted use of its authority in Shintō matters to the detriment of the other families.[6]

[6] Katō and Hoshino, Kogoshūi, pp. 44-45.

Hironari was correct in claiming that the Nakatomi uji had become most influential at court in Shintō matters. Actually the NSK records that as early as 644 (Kōgyoku 3/1/1) Nakatomi no Kamako no Muraji was appointed Director of the Council of Kami Affairs (Kamu Tsukasa no Kami). This text has been questioned and some believe that no such post existed at that time and that the reference was inserted later by the NSK compilers. However, there is no question but that the head of the Nakatomi uji, particularly since he was the famous and influential Kamako, exercised unusual influence in the last half of the seventh century.[7]

In the course of his argumentation Hironari refers to Tenmu's eight-rank kabane system. He points to the disparity in kabane rank created between the Nakatomi and Imibe, because the Nakatomi had been granted the second rank of asomi, while the Imibe merely had been granted the third rank of sukune, a situation he describes as follows:

> During the reign of the Emperor (Tenmu) who ruled at the Kiyomihara Palace, the hereditary titles [kabane] of all the families were revised and re-arranged in eight classes. To my great regret, however, the titles were bestowed in recognition of the services then performed to the Government, without taking into account any of the past duties rendered to the Heavenly Grandson by the forefathers of the respective families when he descended to earth from Heaven. The second class title "Asomi" together with a larger sword was conferred on the Nakatomi family; and the third class title "Sukune" together with a smaller sword was bestowed on the Imibe family. The fourth class title "Imiki" was awarded to the three families, Hata, Aya, and Fumi of Kudara.[8]

Hironari's argument was based on the assumption that relative ranking of aristocratic lineage groups in the seventh and eighth cen-

---

[7] See NSK V, v. 2, p. 253, n. 22.
[8] Katō and Hoshino, Kogoshūi, pp. 43-44.

turies should have been founded primarily on precedent and on the nature of the services rendered by members of those groups when they participated in events centering around the Sun Goddess, the Heavenly Grandson or Emperor Jinmu. From the point of view of <u>kabane</u> alone, Hironari's pique is understandable when judged exclusively in terms of traditional relative ranking of social as opposed to power groups. Nakatomi's original <u>kabane</u> was <u>muraji</u>, and of the many <u>uji</u> that were awarded <u>kabane</u> during Tenmu's reign, the vast majority of those that were awarded the third rank of <u>sukune</u> had originally borne <u>muraji</u>. In fact, of the fifty <u>uji</u> that were awarded <u>sukune</u>, forty-five had originally borne <u>muraji</u>. Nevertheless, the Nakatomi no Muraji <u>uji</u> (GR97) was granted Tenmu's second rank of <u>asomi</u> in 684, and of the fifty-two <u>uji</u> that were awarded <u>asomi</u> at that time only two had originally borne <u>muraji</u>, the other one being the Mononobe no Muraji <u>uji</u> (GR94). Of the fifty-two <u>asomi</u> recipients, thirty-nine had previously borne <u>omi</u> and eleven had previously borne <u>kimi</u> (kun).

By contrast with the Nakatomi, the Imibe's original <u>kabane</u> was <u>obito</u>, which in the pre-Tenmu, traditional <u>kabane</u> system was of lower rank than <u>muraji</u>.[9] In fact, it is well known that <u>omi</u> and <u>muraji</u> were the two most numerous <u>kabane</u> and were borne by the most powerful and influential lineage groups in the pre-Tenmu period in the sixth and seventh centuries. Of the 201 <u>kabane</u> grants made during Tenmu's reign, only five were made to individuals or <u>uji</u> that had originally borne the traditional <u>kabane</u> of <u>obito</u>. For purposes of judging the respective status of the Nakatomi and Imibe lineage groups, it is instructive to compare the profile of those five <u>uji</u> whose original <u>kabane</u> was <u>obito</u> with that of the Nakatomi <u>uji</u>. With so few samples it is not possible to construct a very satisfactory profile, but the data that are available seem to demonstrate that the five <u>obito</u> <u>uji</u> were far less important and in a very different class than the Nakatomi.

[9] See "Obito" in <u>NRD</u>, v. 2, p. 427.

Uji and Original Kabane	Kabane granted by Tenmu and number of the grant				NSK Reference Frequency
	Muraji	Asomi	Sukune	Imiki	
1. Imibe no Obito	GR1	0	GR142	0	6
2. Kurukuma no Obito	GR21	0	0	0	2
3. Mononobe no Obito[10]	GR29	0	GR188	0	4
4. Fumi no Obito	GR54	0	0	GR199	7
5. Yoshino no Obito	GR65	0	0	0	1
6. Nakatomi no Muraji	0	GR97	0	0	60

This table demonstrates that the five obito-bearing uji were of a lower rank than the Nakatomi no Muraji uji. First, none of the five obito uji was granted asomi during Tenmu's reign. Second, all five uji were first granted muraji and subsequently two of these were granted sukune and one was granted imiki. Third, the NSK reference frequencies of the five obito uji show how far less prominent they were, either individually or as a group, than the Nakatomi.

Elsewhere in the Kogoshūi, Hironari claims that other uji which traditionally had participated in Shintō-related ceremonies should be better represented by having some of their members in the Council of Kami Affairs (Jingikan). Hironari lists seven such uji that had been "reduced to poor and miserable circumstances."[11] There is no way to measure how poor and miserable these uji were when Hironari wrote in the ninth century, but the record indicates that they did not play an important role in the sixth and seventh centuries, or perhaps one would be more accurate in saying that the roles they may have played were not of the type to attract notation in the NSK when it was compiled in the early eighth century. The following table demonstrates that the seven uji mentioned by Hironari ranked relatively low by the end of the seventh century.

---

[10] Not to be confused with the famous and influential Mononobe no Muraji uji (GR94). The Mononobe no Obito uji became known later as the Furu no Muraji uji (GR188).

[11] Katō and Hoshino, Kogoshūi, p. 50

Sample Analyses

Uji	Kabane Granted by Tenmu	Grant No.	NSK Reference Frequency
1. Sarume	0	0	0
2. Kagami Tsukuri	muraji	GR71	1
3. Tama Tsukuri	0	0	0
4. Tatenui	0	0	0
5. Kamuhatori	sukune	GR162	1
6. Shitsuori	sukune	GR169	1
7. Omi	0	0	0

First, it will be seen that only three of these seven were granted kabane by Tenmu, one having been awarded muraji and two, sukune, the latter being of the same rank as that which was awarded to the Imibe themselves. Second, none was awarded asomi, the rank of kabane granted to the Nakatomi by Tenmu. Third, all seven of these uji are of virtually zero prominence when judged in terms of NSK reference frequencies pertaining to events of the sixth and seventh centuries. During that period there is only one reference in the NSK to each of three of the uji, and those three references merely record the grants of kabane during Tenmu's reign and are not otherwise informative.

The conclusion that must be drawn is that Hironari was probably right when he wrote to his great regret that "the titles [kabane] were bestowed in recognition of the services then performed to the government, without taking into account any of the past duties rendered to the Heavenly Grandson by the forefathers of the respective families...." If the data provided in the table immediately above comes anywhere near being an accurate reflection of the relative ranking enjoyed by this group of seven uji in the seventh century, it must be concluded that Hironari's claims of equality with the Nakatomi were weak. Hironari's identification of the plight of his own Imibe uji with that of these seven uji shows how removed his argument was from the power-political considerations of the time. His was the voice of conservatism of the early ninth century, which called for a return to the social, political, and religious state of affairs as he believed they had existed in much earlier times.

The SSJR, which was compiled within a decade of Hironari's Kogoshūi, also reflects quite clearly the relatively low rank of the Imibe lineage group, as compared with the Nakatomi, in the early ninth century. Even though the SSJR primarily delineates the varying status differentiations of aristocratic blood-related groups on the basis of ancestral types, it also reflects indirectly and through other means general degrees of varying status. For example, in the case of the shinbetsu category, or uji of "deity" ancestry, it is noticeable that the kami ancestors of important uji are more frequently mentioned than those of less important uji. It must be assumed that such a situation resulted, at least in part, from numerous uji attempting to enhance their prestige and position by claiming as their ancestor one which was also claimed by a more powerful and influential uji.[12] There is an interesting parallel to such a tendency in the cases of the respective "deity" or kami ancestors of the Nakatomi and Imibe. The kami ancestor of the former was Ame no Koyane no Mikoto and of the latter, Ame no Futo Tama no Mikoto, and, whereas, the SSJR contains eighteen references to the ancestor of the Nakatomi, it contains only one to that of the Imibe. For purposes of comparison, it is germane to mention here that Ohokuni Nushi, the ancestor of the Ohomiwa no Asomi uji (GR87) rates eight references; Nigi Haya Hi no Mikoto, the ancestor of the Mononobe no Asomi uji (GR94) rates twenty-four references; and Ame no Oshi Hi no Mikoto, the ancestor of the Ohotomo no Sukune uji (GR139) rates seven references.

If it can be assumed that the compilers of the SSJR prepared their genealogy in the belief that "birds of a feather [should] flock together," then the Imibe no Sukune uji did not fly in very distinguished company. As just mentioned, there is only one genea-

---

[12] For a related discussion, see ch. VII, sec. C, above, particularly the table entitled "Groupings of Asomi and Sukune-Recipient Uji Grouped on the Basis of Common Kami Ancestry."

logical reference to the Imibe no Sukune uji in the SSJR, and that is found in the "Ukyō Shinbetsu, Jō" chapter, or what might be rendered into English as "Right-side Sector of the Capital, [Uji of] Deity Classification, First [of Two Parts]."[13] The ancestries of thirty-six uji are listed in that chapter, of which eight bear the kabane of sukune. Six of these eight, including the Imibe no Sukune, were awarded sukune on the same day in 684 (Tenmu 13/12/2). The following is a list of these six uji together with their NSK reference frequencies:

Uji	Grant No.	NSK Reference Frequency
Imibe no Sukune	GR142	6
Kamunakibe no Sukune	GR151	1
Nukatabe no Sukune	GR163	7
Tamanoya no Sukune	GR167	1
Yatsume no Sukune	GR173	1
Tame no Sukune	GR178	2

As far as NSK references for the sixth and seventh centuries are concerned, this is not a prominent group. Virtually nothing is known about the activities of four of these uji. In the case of Nukatabe no Sukune (GR163), the available references indicate that members of that uji held protocol positions of a diplomatic nature during the reigns of Kinmei and Suiko (four references). While these five uji, other than the Imibe, may have been important in Shintō affairs in earlier times, they were seldom even mentioned during the period of this study.

In summary, from whatever angle one considers the relative-ranking problem of the Imibe and Nakatomi lineage groups, one must agree that Hironari's lamentations in the Kogoshūi were based on fact: the Imibe and Nakatomi uji were of unequal status. While the two may have been of equal status when it came to sacerdotal traditions and responsibilities, the evidence is clear that by the

---

[13]SSJR I, p. 755; SSJR II, p. 230. See also Appendix II, sec. A.

seventh century the Nakatomi enjoyed much higher political status than the Imibe. The Nakatomi, from as early as the Taika coup in 645, rapidly constructed a power base that virtually overwhelmed the state during the Heian period; by contrast, the Imibe remained solely a lineage group that was proud of its priestly position in a society that had largely turned its interests in other directions. Hironari's frustrations, certainly, must have evolved out of his belief in, and appeal to, tradition as adequate support for his contention that the Imibe should enjoy equal status with the Nakatomi. However, the Nakatomi had been of far greater service to the crown in more recent centuries and for that reason acquired a higher status than the Imibe.

B. GRAVES AND ANCESTORS

Among the events described by the NSK in the year A.D. 691 (Jitō 5/8/13) there is found an interesting but troublesome notation that reads, "Eighteen uji were commanded to present [to the throne] the records of their ancestral graves."[14] Some NSK manuscripts have a variant reading, which would then convert the above translation into "the records of their ancestors."[15] An interlinear gloss provides us with a list of these eighteen uji in the following order: Ohomiwa, Sazakibe, Isonokami, Fujihara, Ishikaha, Kose, Kashihade, Kasuga, Kamitsukeno, Ohotomo, Ki, Heguri, Hata, Ahe, Saheki, Uneme, Hozumi and Azumi. The most recent critical edition of the NSK states that the criteria for the listing of this group of uji are unknown.[16] While it may not be possible ever to determine the actual criteria for the listing of these particular uji, an analysis of this list of uji in terms of our present knowledge of the relative ranking systems of the late seventh century, as provided by the NSK, and of the early ninth century, as provided by the SSJR, does furnish grounds for what may be a more accurate conjecture.

[14] 墓記
[15] 纂記
[16] NSK, v. 2, p. 510, n. 18.

It is immediately apparent that all of the uji in this list were recipients of kabane during Tenmu's reign. Fifteen of them were granted asomi on Tenmu 13/11/1, and three were granted sukune on Tenmu 13/12/2. The three uji of sukune rank were the Ohotomo (GR139), Saheki (GR140) and Azumi (GR141), which appear in the first three places on the list of the fifty uji that were granted sukune at that time.[17] It is significant to note that this list does not include any recipients of either mahito or imiki, which means that those uji that were collaterally most closely related to the imperial house, as well as immigrant uji, are absent from the list.

From these few observations alone it is clear that this list of eighteen uji is composed of some of the most important representatives of the several social and political strata that ranked just below those lineage groups that had been granted mahito by Emperor Tenmu. First, the list contains ten uji which are classified by the SSJR as being of kōbetsu, that is, of "imperial" descent. They were granted asomi by Tenmu, as were many other collateral relatives of the imperial house, since they were more distant relatives than the mahito recipients. Second, the list also contains five uji which are classified by the SSJR as being of shinbetsu, that is, of "deity" descent. These were granted asomi by Tenmu, and three of them were among Japan's most powerful and prominent lineage groups; namely, the Ohomiwa (GR87), the Mononobe/Isonokami (GR94) and the Nakatomi/Fujihara (GR97). Third, the list finally contains three uji that are classified by the SSJR as also being of "deity" descent, and these were granted by Tenmu the next lower kabane rank of sukune. These three are also counted among Japan's most powerful and prominent lineage groups; they were the Ohotomo (GR139), the Saheki (GR140), and the Azumi (GR141).

The important status of eleven of these eighteen uji is further attested by their very high NSK reference frequency. In the list

---

[17]See ch. VI, sec. D, above, for comments on the correlation between NSK reference frequency and list sequence.

of the ten asomi-recipient uji with the highest NSK reference frequencies presented in Chapter VI, Section D, above, eight of these eighteen uji will be found, and in a similar list of the six sukune-recipient uji with the highest NSK reference frequencies presented in Chapter VII, Section D, above, three of these eighteen uji will be found. Thus, eleven of these eighteen uji, in terms of NSK reference frequency, are among the most prominent of the 102 lineage groups granted asomi or sukune by Tenmu.

There is one additional element reflecting the fact that this list of eighteen uji included some of the lineage groups that were among Japan's most important and powerful at the end of the seventh century. In Chapter VII, Section C, above, dealing with the sukune awards there are discussed and listed six broad groupings of uji, which, according to the SSJR, each had a common kami ancestor. Five of the six groupings are headed by particularly influential lineage groups, namely, the Ohomiwa (GR87), the Mononobe/Isonokami (GR94), the Nakatomi/Fujihara (GR97), the Ohotomo (GR86) and the Azumi (GR141). It is informative to note that all five of these important uji are in the list of eighteen uji under discussion.

In summary, a number of conclusions can be drawn on the basis of this analysis. First, this list of eighteen uji includes eleven uji that were among Japan's most powerful lineage groups in the sixth and seventh centuries. Second, in terms of the social stratification prevailing during the last quarter of the seventh century these eleven uji represent the third broad echelon from the top of the hierarchy, the first being the emperor and the imperial house and the second being composed of the lineage groups that were awarded the kabane of mahito based upon the relatively close degree of their collateral relationship with the imperial line. Third, there is included in this list the five leading uji of the six major groupings of uji that may be classified as being "related" through common kami ancestry. Fourth, the list of eighteen uji does not include any lineage groups of immigrant origin. Fifth, it is conjectured that one reason for the relatively uniform high NSK reference frequencies of these eighteen uji may be a result of these uji having turned their records over to the government, and it is possible that those family records supplied a significant quantity of data that was included later in the NSK when it was compiled and presented to the court almost three decades later.

The Eighteen Uji that were ordered on Jitō 5/8/13
to Submit Records to the Government,
Listed in the Order of their Appearance in the NSK:

Uji	Grant No.	Original Kabane	Granted Asomi	Granted Sukune	SSJR Classification Kōbetsu	Shinbetsu	NSK Reference Frequency
1. Ohomiwa	GR87	kimi (kun)	X			X	32
2. Sazakibe	GR96	omi	X		X		1
3. Isonokami	GR94	muraji	X			X	53
4. Fujihara	GR97	muraji	X			X	60
5. Ishikaha	GR100	omi	X		X		3
6. Kose	GR90	omi	X		X		44
7. Kashihade	GR91	omi	X		X		16
8. Kasuga	GR88	omi	X		X		5
9. Kamitsukeno	GR119	kimi (kun)	X		X		7
10. Ohotomo	GR139	muraji		X		X	83
11. Ki	GR92	omi	X		X		28
12. Heguri	GR95	omi	X		X		5
13. Hata	GR93	omi	X		X		4
14. Ahe	GR89	omi	X		X		56
15. Saheki	GR140	muraji		X		X	20
16. Uneme	GR102	omi	X			X	8
17. Hozumi	GR105	omi	X			X	22
18. Azumi	GR141	muraji		X		X	15

C. QUANTIFICATION OF NIHON SHOKI ACTIVITIES CATEGORIES

This monograph has illustrated that the determination of some relative-ranking factors through quantitative analysis is of value when applied to controlled data extracted from the NSK. Thus far, the emphasis has been on the relative ranking of the various clan groups that were granted one of Tenmu's new kabane. The relative ranking of these groups has been indicated by analyses of such factors as original kabane, SSJR categories, NSK reference frequency and list sequence. It is suggested here, however, that it is possible to go a further step and determine for any two clan groups their quantitative relative ranking in terms of the categories or types of activities in which the groups' kabane-bearing personalities were involved. Basically, the NSK is a collection of miscellaneous accounts that are arranged chronologically and are overwhelmingly concerned with the aristocratic strata of society. By comparison with the Chinese standard histories (cheng-shih), the NSK is deficient in form and organization, and the accounts it contains are fragmentary at best. Quantitative analysis helps to overcome some of these deficiencies by providing the investigator with abstractions of broader patterns that may be present in that text.

As was described in Chapter I, above, almost 1550 references relating to kabane-bearing individuals and uji were extracted from the NSK covering the approximate 200-year period from the beginning of Keitai's reign in 507 to the end of Jitō's in 697. In the preparation of this present aspect of quantification, each reference was then assigned to one of twenty-three possible "activities categories," and these categories were arranged in sequence, starting with the category with the largest number of references and ending with the one with the smallest. The following table reflects in quantitative terms the relative ranking of these twenty-three categories.

Activities Categories	Number of NSK References
1. Diplomatic affairs (within Japan and abroad)	305
2. Grants of a kabane	204
3. Unclassified references	100–150
4. Pro-Tenmu in the Jinshin War	
5. Military affairs (foreign and domestic)	
6. Appointment or reconfirmation to an office or post	

Sample Analyses 129

7. Buddhist affairs
8. Fiscal matters (<u>miyake</u>, occupational groups (<u>be</u>), etc.)
9. Participation in selection process of an emperor

} 50-100

10. Anti-imperial activities
11. Pro-imperial or subordinate to imperial house
12. Pro-Kōbun in the Jinshin War
13. Participation in imperial obsequies
14. Grants of cap ranks
15. Gifts from or to an emperor
16. Technological matters
17. Genealogical references
18. Activities indicative of being pro-Soga
19. Clan members selected as imperial consorts
20. Good omens and natural anomalies

} 25-50

21. Giving advice to the emperor
22. Shintō affairs
23. Participation in enthronement ceremonies

} 5-25

A review of these twenty-three activities categories reveals that four of them deal with matters concerned exclusively with the seventh century, namely, categories 2 (grants of <u>kabane</u>), 4 (pro-Tenmu in the Jinshin War), 12 (pro-Kōbun in the Jinshin War) and 14 (grants of cap ranks). In order to adjust the other nineteen activities categories more within their seventh-century context, the <u>NSK</u> references were separated chronologically into two groups: the first referring to personalities before the reign of Suiko (i.e., before 592), and the second referring to personalities between that date and the end of the <u>NSK</u>, that is, to the last year of Jitō's reign in 697. This procedure yielded 397 references for the earlier period and 1151 for the later. This ratio demonstrates the sharp increase in the number of <u>NSK</u> references to personalities in its seventh-century accounts.

The next step taken was to determine the quantitative relative ranking of separate groups of clans in relation to these twenty-three NSK activities categories. By the end of Tenmu's reign it can be said that six groups or types of clans existed as follows: the five clan groups that had been granted one of Tenmu's five new kabane and all other clans. Of the clans that had not been granted one of the new kabane, the most important was the Soga that had risen to a position of great power during the sixth century and maintained that position until the Taika coup of 645. For present purposes, the Soga clan was treated as the sixth clan grouping, and data concerning all other personalities and clans that had not been granted one of the new kabane were set aside. This procedure made it possible to determine the Soga's quantitative ranking by NSK activities categories relative to each of the five clan groups that had been awarded Mahito, Asomi, Sukune, Imiki and Muraji. This procedure also reduced the number of NSK references to 969, divided among the six clan groups as follows:

Clan Groups	Number of NSK References
1. Mahito	55
2. Asomi	397
3. Sukune	211
4. Imiki	110
5. Muraji	99
6. Soga Clan	97

The next step taken was to determine the number of references (i.e., the subtotals) within each of the twenty-three activities categories for each of these six clan groups. Then, in order to arrive at the quantitative relative ranking for each clan grouping within each of the twenty-three activities categories, abstract values of from six to zero were assigned to the subtotals in each category. For example, if the subtotals within a given activities category for the Mahito, Asomi, Sukune, Imiki and Muraji clan groups and the Soga clan were 4, 54, 42, 28, 14 and 2, respectively, the relative ranking of these subtotals would be expressed by the abstract values of 2, 6, 5, 4, 3, and 1, respectively. The next step was to construct graphs on which to plot the quantitative relative ranking of any two of the six clan groups within any one or more of the twenty-three activities categories. Eight samples of these graphs will be found below, which are intended merely as demonstrations of this methodology.[18]

Graphs I through V demonstrate the quantitative relative ranking of the Asomi clans and each of the other five clan groups within the twenty-three activities categories. Each small circle represents the relative ranking of a single activities category for the two clan groups concerned. Clusters of these circles represent the activities categories in which the two concerned clan groups may be found upon further investigation to have been in either highly competitive or cooperative positions. This possibility would be particularly indicated when the clusters are located in the upper right quadrant (i.e., the highest ranking quadrant) of any one of the graphs, and more particularly so to the degree that the clusters fall on or astride the diagonal balance line. Graphs I through V demonstrate that the Asomi clan group ranks relatively higher than any one of the other five clan groups, since a large majority of the activities categories in all five graphs fall high on the Asomi side of the diagonal balance line. Only in the case of Graph V, which relates the Asomi clans and the Soga, does a cluster of nine of the twenty-three activities categories fall quite evenly on either side of the balance line in the graph's highest ranking quadrant.

Correlation of the categories that fall within the highest ranking quadrant on each of Graphs I through V indicates that it is within the following categories where one may anticipate the greatest degree of cooperation and/or competition between the Asomi clan groups and any one of the other five groups:

---

[18]I am indebted to Mr. Shuzō Koyama, my colleague at the University of California, Davis, for suggesting this particular method, which he has used successfully in comparing archaeological data.

Actvities Categories	Asomi-Mahito	Asomi-Sukane	Asomi-Imiki	Asomi-Muraji	Asomi-Soga
8. Fiscal matters	0	X	X	X	X
11. Pro-imperial or subordinate to imperial house	X	X	0	0	X
12. Pro-Kōbun in the Jinshin War	0	X	X	0	X
14. Award of cap ranks	X	X	X	0	0
16. Technological matters	0	X	X	X	0
18. Pro-Soga	0	X	X	X	0

Graphs VI through VIII illustrate the quantitative relative ranking of the Soga clan and the Asomi, Sukune and Muraji clan groups, respectively, within selected activities categories. These categories involve matters that might well be reflective of the economic and political power bases of the clan groups concerned. Here again the superior ranking of the Asomi group can be seen, followed by the Sukune and Muraji groups. Only activities categories 6 (appointment or reconfirmation to an office or post) and 8 (fiscal matters) fall within the highest quadrant of Graph VI, but only category 8 falls within that quadrant in all three graphs. This configuration indicates that the investigation of fiscal matters would likely yield more informative data on inter-clan relationships than the investigation of activities categories 1 (diplomatic affairs) or 16 (technological matters).

These few examples of quantification have been presented here as an indication that the analytic approach to the NSK holds some promise for the investigator. While it is true that the products of such analysis are abstractions of broad patterns that exist in the NSK, they do provide a framework of sorts within which the unique events or facts of history may better be understood and focused. And given the nature of the text of the NSK itself, and the paucity of other literary sources for Japan's history of the sixth and seventh centuries, the quantification of data that are available is not unreasonable. It is hoped that the approach briefly suggested here will be pursued more extensively by other Western investigators.

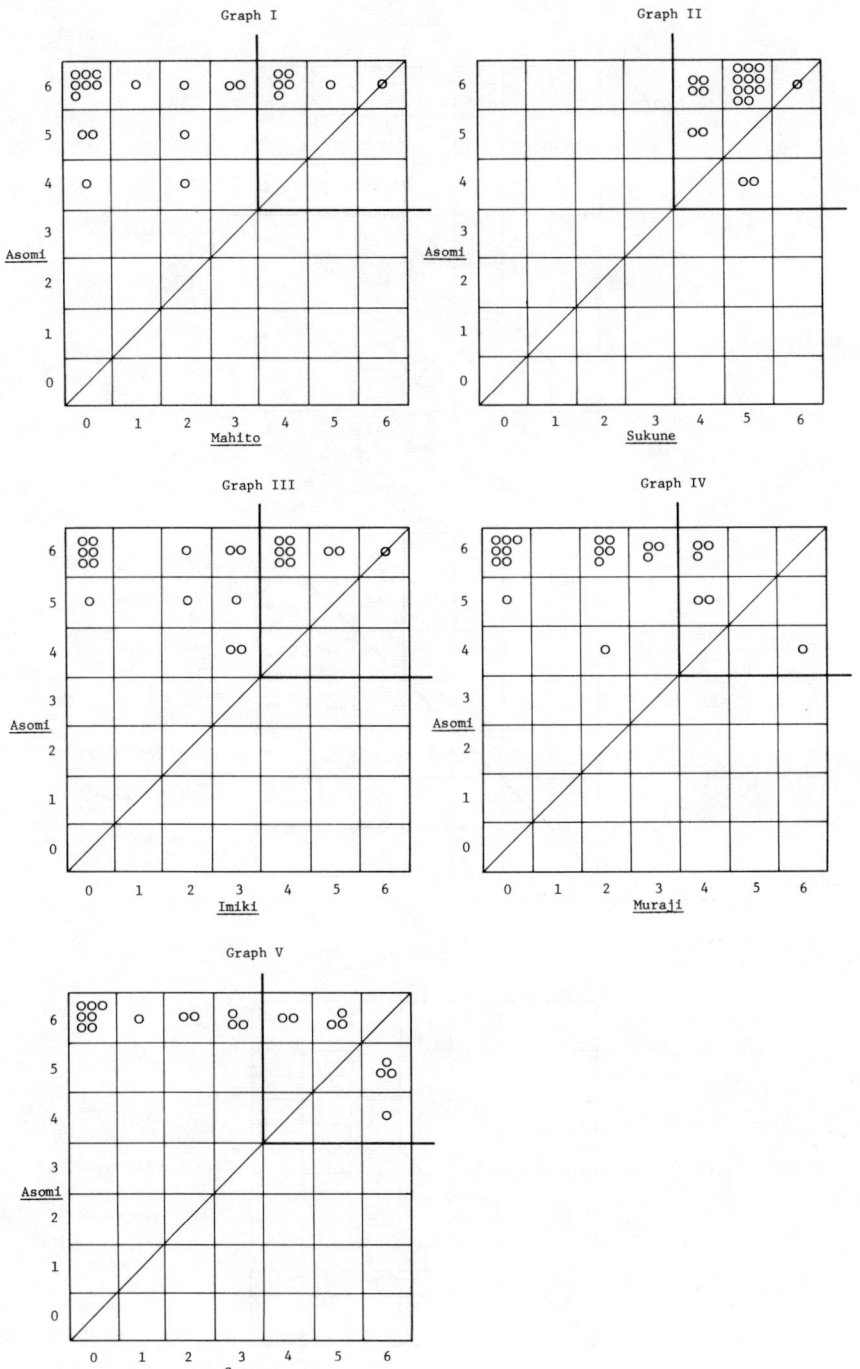

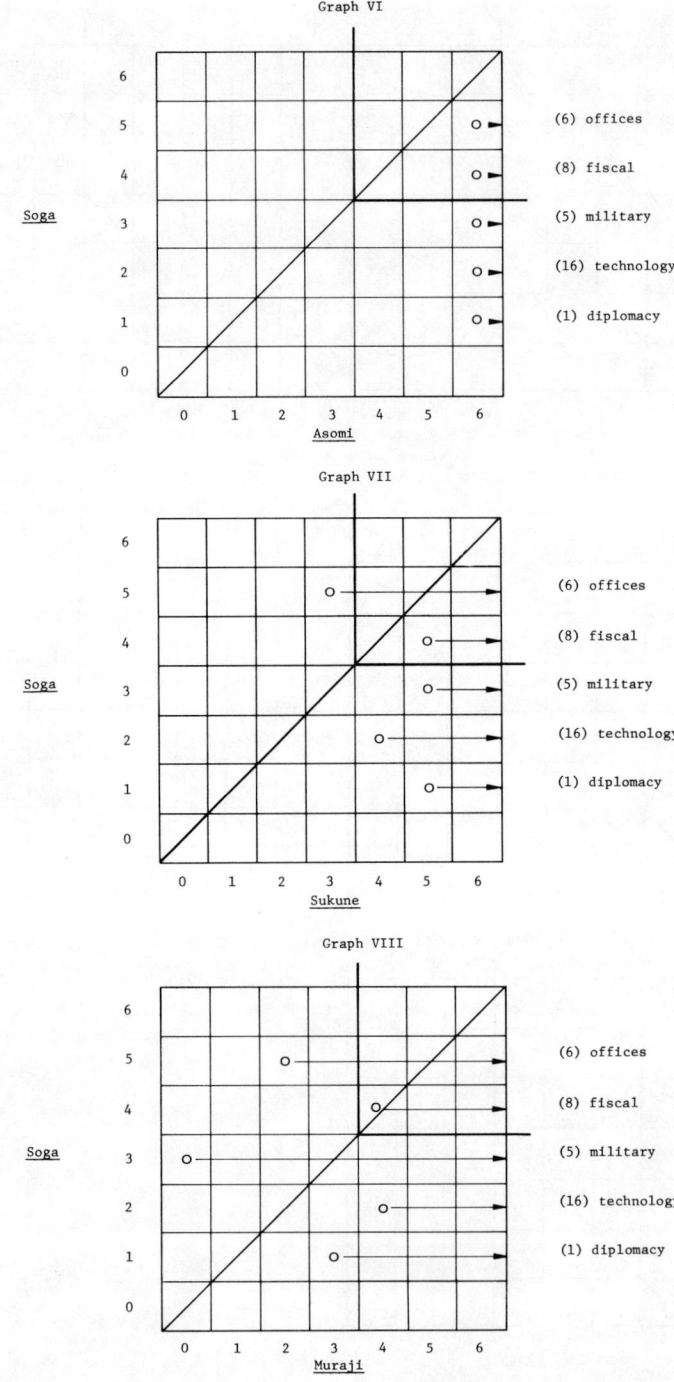

CHAPTER XII
Conclusions

Japan's seventh century was a period of rapid change politically, socially and economically; some of the change was dramatic, some of it subtle. Change was dramatic to the degree that it was new and innovative, and subtle to the degree it represented modification of traditional institutions. For example, the Chinese-style government structure that was adopted from continental models and adapted to Japanese needs during the last half of that century represented a dramatic organizational transformation, when compared with the form of the clanlike governmental structure of the pre-Taika period; but the modification of the kabane system under Tenmu was subtle by contrast. Construction of the Chinese-style governmental structure was highly innovative and was carried out under the impact of foreign influence, while the modification of the kabane system represented merely a change in the traditional social-ranking system within a familiar frame of reference.

Whether constituting fundamental transformations or mere modifications, in some respects those changes of the second half of the seventh century amounted to a "rectification" program aimed at bringing into closer harmony the linguistic designations of office and rank with the new political and social realities that had evolved by the second half of the seventh century. That rectification program was necessitated by earlier alterations that had occurred in the philosophy of government, in Japan's aristocratic social structure, and in the values attached to position, rank and status. The philosophy of government and the values attached to position, rank and status were, in fact, inseparable and constituted the generative drive that brought about the dramatic transformations and subtle modifications that were thought to be necessary.

In dealing with Japan's history of the sixth and seventh centuries it must be remembered that those who wrought the changes, and those who profited from them, comprised a very small segment of the whole of Japanese society. The extremely restricted sources for the study of the period refer but seldom to commoners; the compilers of the sources were aristocrats, and their interests were aristocratic in orientation and scope. Thus, when we speak of values, we speak not so much of the values of the Japanese people but of the values of the aristocratic apex of society in a given age. The kabane ranking system was limited to Japan's nobility below the level of the imperial house, and above the infinitely more numerous masses. Therefore, the detectable values attached to kabane in the sixth and seventh centuries were highly specialized and restricted in their usage and application.

Faith and value are often identical, and such was certainly the case in ancient Japan, for it was then that mythology and genealogy were intertwined to produce a fundamental value on the basis of which aristocratic social differentiation ideally and in theory rested. Realities and mythologies existed side by side, as in so many other societies, then and now, but apparently it was the mythologies that were the more valued or thought to be the more ideal of the two in differentiating the stratifications of aristocratic society. Certainly such is an accurate description of the situation that existed by the last quarter of the seventh century during the reign of Tenmu, and there is no doubt but that it had evolutionary antecedents stretching back for a considerable but unknown time. However, since the KJK and NSK were completed in the early eighth century and the SSJR in the early ninth, we are on solid ground only to state that the values of Japan's aristocratic components of the late seventh and the early eighth and ninth centuries are delineated in those sources, rather than to claim that those sources, reflect the values of earlier centuries.

Despite the certainty that power considerations, which were based on varying combinations of political, economic and military strength, exerted fundamental influences on the earlier courses of Japanese history, and while such power considerations most emphatically were often decisive in determining the differentiations of social distinction and rank, the available sources imply that mythological genealogies were the more fundamental. Even though we may question that the available sources accurately reflect the values of earlier centuries, it is certain that the values inherent in Tenmu's eight-rank kabane system of A.D. 684 was in certain regards, the culmination of a considerable evolution of the ideas that the emperor and the Sun Line occupied, by right of descent from the Sun Goddess, the pinnacle of the sociopolitical hierarchy, that the variations in social status of noble lineages below the rank of that pinnacle were determined by the relative rank of their respective ancestors or progenitors, and that the relative rank of those ancestors or progenitors was decided in large degree on the basis of their relationships with the Sun Line in mythological times. But the reality of the situation was more probably quite the reverse: the relative ranking of those various progenitors was largely determined in much later times by the relative ranks of their descendants.

Determining the details and evolution of the social values that culminated in Tenmu's new kabane system is an elusive business at best, but what is relatively clear are the configurations in ranking, and the values they represented, for those selected lineage groups that were honored by grants of kabane. To the degree that lineage and descent types were the principal criteria for the higher ranks of the new system, the determination of the values involved is simplified; but to the degree that other considerations progressively comprised the criteria for the lower grants, the determination is complicated and less certain.

The importance placed on mythological genealogy is demonstrated by the fact that kami or deity ancestry was possessed by an overwhelming majority of the lineage groups granted kabane during Tenmu's reign. The SSJR uses the triple lineage categories of kōbetsu (imperial lineages), shinbetsu (deity lineages) and shoban (non-Japanese or immigrant lineages), but the ultimate progenitors in the cases of both the kōbetsu and shinbetsu lineage categories were kami or deities. The kōbetsu lineage groups traced their descent from specific imperial ancestors, but their ultimate progenitrix in all cases was the Sun Goddess, and the shinbetsu groups traced theirs from other specific kami. One may say, therefore, that ultimate kami ancestry was a fundamental criterion for the ranking of the following four social categories: the emperor, other members of the imperial family, uji claiming descent from imperial progenitors, and uji claiming descent from kami other than the progenitrix of the Sun Line.

By the end of the seventh century, differentiations in social rank within the broad general category of lineage groups claiming ultimate kami ancestry coincided with the four social categories listed above. Then, within each of these categories, but below the level of the emperor and the other members of the imperial family, more specific criteria, such as the progenitor of a given lineage group, constituted additional refinements affecting the group's relative social ranking. For example, lineage groups claiming descent from imperial ancestors, and thus ultimately from the Sun Goddess, comprised the most elite lineage groups below the level of the Sun Line. This lineage category was further stratified by the end of the seventh century in terms of the degree of collateral relationship with the then reigning monarch, namely Tenmu. By that time, lineage groups claiming descent from emperors who reigned primarily in the sixth century comprised the most elite of all lineage groups of ultimate kami descent. It was only to this specific category of uji that the kabane of mahito, the top rank in Tenmu's new system, was granted.

The next lower stratum of uji claiming ultimate kami ancestry, was comprised of uji claiming descent from imperial ancestors who reigned before the sixth century, some harking all the way back to the first mythological emperor, Jinmu. To selected uji falling into this category Tenmu granted the _kabane_ of _asomi_, the second lower rank in the new eight-rank system. Of the fifty-two _uji_ recipients of this _kabane_, forty-four fall into the _kōbetsu_ or imperial category of lineages, but it was at this point that a significant, new element appeared: there were also included among the _asomi_ recipients seven _uji_ of the _shinbetsu_ or deity category of lineage groups. Included among the seven were two of Japan's most famous and powerful lineage groups, the Mononobe and the Nakatomi, not to mention the Ohomiwa, all of which are found to possess prominent reference frequency in the _NSK_. The inclusion of these groups demonstrates that power or service considerations, and not lineage alone, were included in the criteria or determinants for the receipt of the rank of _asomi_.

A greater diversity of lineage types is next found among the fifty lineage groups that were granted _sukune_, the third ranking _kabane_ of Tenmu's new system. The recipient _uji_ were predominantly the _shinbetsu_ or _kami_ category of lineage groups (thirty-seven out fifty) but seven were of the _kōbetsu_ or imperial category. Thus, in respect of lineage-type patterns, the _sukune_ recipients were just the reverse of the _asomi_. It was at this point that another significant element appeared with the inclusion among the _sukune_ recipients of one lineage group of the _shoban_ or immigrant category. The inclusion of this lineage group amongst these grantees indicates that to a degree considerations other than lineage influenced or acted as determinants of the relative ranking of at least one of the _sukune_ recipients. While _kami_ ancestry was certainly the prime criterion for the majority of the _sukune_ recipients, lineage groups of both imperial and immigrant descent were included.

The _kabane_ of _imiki_, the fourth rank in the new system, was next granted to a small group of _uji_ that was almost evenly divided between lineages of the _shinbetsu_ and _shoban_ categories. While the data concerning these _imiki_ recipients is limited in scope, since only eleven _uji_ are involved, certain significant factors are ap-

parent. First, on the basis of the types of kabane originally borne
by these uji prior to the reign of Tenmu, it is highly probable
that they were selected as recipients of one of Tenmu's new kabane
because of services they had performed for the imperial line, services which were largely of a managerial nature. Second, the inclusion of possibly five uji of the shoban or immigrant category
demonstrates that a significant degree of integration of selected
foreign elements of continental origin into Japan's sociopolitical
hierarchy had occurred by the late seventh century.

Tenmu granted muraji to eighteen named individuals and fifty-
five uji between 680 and 684, before the institution of his new
eight-rank system, and also to two named individuals in 686, the
last year of his reign, but uncertainty exists as to whether the
rank of those muraji grants represented the seventh rank of his
new system. It can be said, however, that the general profile of
the muraji recipient groups, which is based primarily on types of
lineage categories and the diversity of the traditional kabane they
had borne before being granted muraji, indicates that the ranking
of the kabane of muraji granted by Tenmu was below that of imiki.

In summary, it can be seen that although the term "lineage
group" has been used most frequently in this monograph to render
the term uji, lineage categories were a far more important criterion for determining the relative ranking of the recipients of the
top three grades of the new system, namely, mahito, asomi and sukune, than for determining that of the recipients of either the
fourth grade of imiki or the uncertain grade of muraji. An increasing degree of diversity of background, in both lineage types and
traditional kabane originally borne by the recipients, characterized the grants of kabane for each descending rank within the new
system.

When one speaks of Tenmu's eight-rank kabane system as being
new, an important qualification is required: Tenmu's system was
indeed new but it did not replace entirely the traditional kabane
system that had evolved during previous centuries. Tenmu's system

was superimposed on an older one, and the recipients of *kabane* during Tenmu's reign constituted the nucleus of a "new" nobility. Many of the traditional, pre-Tenmu *kabane* continued to be used after Tenmu's reign, and they appear in significant numbers in the sources of the Nara period. And while a description of the patterns of *kabane* usage during the Nara period does not fall within the scope of this present monograph, many of the bearers of traditional pre-Tenmu *kabane* continued during the eighth century to be granted grades of the new *kabane* that had originated with Tenmu's new system.

While the *NSK* fails to afford the reader with any precise statement of the original objectives for the implementation of Tenmu's new *kabane* system, analyses of available data, and inferences drawn therefrom, indicate that superimposing the new system on the old performed a number of useful functions for crown and state. First, it provided a means of enhancing the relative status of a number of the traditionally most powerful or prestigious *uji*, at the same time that it enabled recognition by the crown of the higher degree of status attained by *uji* of more recent origin. In this respect Tenmu's *kabane* system served to constitute a new nobility comprised of a graded coalition of older and newer elements.

Second, it obviated serious social strife that might have occurred had the traditional *kabane* system been abolished. For example, anti-imperial forces were not granted one of the new *kabane*, but they continued to bear their traditional ones. The superimposition of the new system on the old was an indirect means of lowering the relative social ranking of such forces below the level of that of the recipients of the top four grades of the new system, without directly denying them the right to bear *kabane*.

Third, the very use of *kabane* by Tenmu, even though his new ones were superimposed on the old, provided in principle a traditional and well-understood technique for differentiating social status at a time when many noble lineage groups must have feared possible negative social consequences due to the rapid sinification of the political structure that was occurring in the second half of the seventh century.

Fourth, and most important from the point of view of the Sun Line, the new system clearly designated the reigning sovereign's closest collaterally related lineage groups as constituting the top social ranks of the new nobility below the level of the sovereign and the other members of the imperial house. As such, the new system, even though traditionally oriented, served to further bolster the claims of imperial supremacy that lay at the base of so many other reforms carried out in the second half of the seventh century following the Taika coup of 645.

The various grants of kabane to numerous uji during Tenmu's reign represented a restructuring of Japan's aristocratic hierarchy. One result was to tie more closely to the sovereign a significant number of lineage groups that had for centuries made their contributions to the growth of the imperial institution. The new kabane system represented recognition on the part of the sovereign of the new patterns of loyalty, respect, and service to the imperial institution that had evolved by the last quarter of the seventh century. Although only 177 uji were granted one of the new kabane during Tenmu's reign, one should not draw the conclusion that all of the numerous uji not granted new kabane at that time represented opposing or anti-imperial forces. As mentioned above, the new kabane continued to be granted to uji throughout the Nara period, but further research will be required before clarification can be made of the social and political implications of the numerous uji that were not granted new kabane during Tenmu's reign nor subsequently during the Nara period.

It is clear, however, that the new social hierarchy created by Tenmu also reflected the continuation of a process begun from before the time of the Taika coup, namely, to restrict the number of uji allowed to participate actively in affairs of state. And we know this process of restriction, at least in the political area, continued and accelerated during the Nara and Heian periods to the point where the majority of the individuals enjoying the highest social status and occupying the most important political positions derived from the Sun Line and Fujihara lineage groups.

Another restriction must be noted concerning the new nobility created by Tenmu's kabane system: the geographic distribution of the recipient uji was overwhelmingly limited to areas close to the court and coincided largely with the areas encompassed by the Home Provinces. It must be admitted that this conclusion derives primarily, but not exclusively, from the SSJR's early ninth-century classification of uji by lineage categories and their geographic distribution, although the KJK and NSK do supply some significant but less comprehensive supporting data. The nearly twelve-hundred lineage groups listed in the SSJR are classified by geographic location in the capital area and in the provinces (kuni) of Yamashiro, Yamato, Settsu, Kafuchi and Izumi. While it is entirely possible that the geographic distribution pattern of the SSJR reflects to an uncertain degree changes that occurred during the Nara period, one is on relatively firm ground to assert that the SSJR distribution patterns reflect to like degree the late seventh-century geographic distribution of the uji that were granted kabane by Tenmu. At the very least, the available evidence indicates that uji located geographically near the sovereign and court in the Home Provinces were given preferential status over those residing in other, more distant, locales.

One is tempted to theorize that in seventh-century Japan a relative-ranking pattern was applied to geographic areas that was a direct reflection of the pattern of sociopolitical relative ranking enjoyed by the noble residents of those areas. This would not be unlike the relative ranking pattern that was applied to kami ancestors based upon the pattern of actual relative ranking enjoyed by their respective descent groups. In other words, the question logically may be asked as to whether, and to what extent, the grants of Tenmu's new kabane depended on the degree of proximity of the land holdings of the recipients to the geographic power center controlled by the Sun Line.

By the end of the seventh century the ideal existed that mythological genealogy should be the prime determinant of status, but the fact remains that other determinants existed, as has been demonstrated in this monograph by recourse to analyses of what I term "NSK reference frequency" and "list sequence." In the two long lists in the NSK enumerating the 102 uji that were granted either asomi or sukune during Tenmu's reign, a definite correlation for selected uji exists between a high rate of reference frequency in the NSK and the general sequence in which those uji are noted in those lists. The implication must be drawn that it was not the supposed rank of their mythological progenitors that alone placed these uji in preferred positions in society, but other factors came into play as well.

It is true that the use of NSK reference frequency is more informative when applied to the asomi and sukune recipients than to either the mahito at the highest rank, or to the imiki and muraji at the lowest ranks; in the case of the mahito recipients, their prestige derived primarily from their lineage type, and, additionally, their NSK reference frequencies are too low to be analyzed relative to those of the asomi and sukune recipients. And in the cases of the imiki and muraji recipients, lineage considerations were of relatively little importance and their occupational or service contributions were primary. But in the cases of asomi and sukune the respective numbers of recipient uji are evenly balanced with fifty-two in the former and fifty in the latter.

For the asomi and sukune groups it would appear that lineage considerations, service to the imperial line, as well as real strength and power constituted an amalgam of criteria for their respective relative ranking. The kabane-related data for these two groups of uji, when analyzed in conjunction with their respective NSK reference frequencies, reveal that the majority of the uji granted these two kabane appear but very infrequently in the pages of the NSK for the period covering the sixth and seventh centuries.

This fact may well indicate that the uji comprising this majority may well have enjoyed high social status in the noble social hierarchy of the late seventh century but enjoyed relatively low political status. By contrast, one can be fairly certain that any detailed study of the ten uji with the highest NSK reference frequencies in each of the two groups of uji granted either asomi or sukune would reveal far more of the workings of the top level of the "establishment" than a similar study devoted to the uji in the asomi and sukune categories with the lowest NSK reference frequencies.

In concluding this monograph a few remarks seem in order concerning another important, though broader, implication of this technical study of kabane. No scholar today believes that the apical social and political position occupied by the emperor and the other scions of the Sun Line derived in ancient Japan from the exalted position and prestige of their ancestress, Amaterasu Ohomikami, and yet this idea or feeling still lurks in the emotional recesses of some people who believe or feel that the remarkable survival and continuity of the imperial line and the imperial institution may be so attributed. By the Heian period, and certainly during the entire feudal period, the emperor, though most often politically impotent, was viewed as the fountain from which flowed the right for others to exercise sovereignty in his name. Before 1945 modern scholarship relating to the imperial institution was also significantly influenced by the exalted position attributed to the emperor by political theorists during the Meiji period and until the end of World War II. Despite such later developments, this present monograph on kabane demonstrates that the mythology of ancestry was also much in vogue at the end of the seventh century, and it was doubtless due in large part to this fact that there was generated some of the mystique and otherworldly aura which engulfed the imperial person through subsequent centuries.

However, the mythology of ancestry in those times performed a most practical social role in supporting the emperor and the other

Sun Line descendants in their claims to position of social paramountcy within the state, as well as in providing a means of ranking the various aristocratic social strata relative to that supreme position. It is in this regard that one may safely seek at least one explanation for the survival of Shintō practice and belief during the seventh and eighth centuries when Shintō might otherwise have been lost in the tidal wave of Buddhism that swept over Japan. Ancestral typology was one thing and played a certain inextricable role in the society of those times, and Buddhism and its beliefs and practices were quite another thing; how else can one attempt a rational explanation of what appears to have been the religious duality practiced in Japan in those early centuries after the arrival of Buddhism? There appears to have been little if any intellectual conflict aroused by a Japanese sovereign playing his role as the chieftain and high priest of the imperial house, on the one hand, and his espousal of Buddhist belief and practice, on the other.

Buddhism served the spiritual and esthetic appetites of the time, but traditional mythological and ancestral beliefs served as the pivot of the social structure and as a means of calibrating the graduated distinctions of status within that structure. Shintō survived because it performed the service of preserving and symbolizing the mythological ancestral typologies that were socially essential to the highly stratified aristocratic structure of ancient Japan. It is in this respect that kabane, more especially the three top grades of Tenmu's eight-rank system of mahito, asomi and sukune, cannot be wholly separated from the beliefs and practices of the native cult.

Appendix I
INVENTORY OF KABANE-BEARING UJI AND INDIVIDUALS
NOTED IN THE NIHON SHOKI FROM
THE BEGINNING OF THE REIGN OF KEITAI THROUGH THAT OF JITŌ

Note:

This inventory contains all NSK references to kabane that are accompanied by the name of an uji, or by the given name of an individual (na), or by both, from the first year of the reign of Keitai through the last year of the reign of Jitō. The Nihon Koten Bungaku Taikei edition of the NSK, annotated by Sakamoto Tarō, Ienaga Saburō, Inoue Mitsusada and Ōno Susumu, and published in 1965, was used as the authoritative text for compiling the inventory. The spellings of all names and kabane are transliterations in the Hepburn system of the kana readings found in that edition. The inventory is presented in two parts. Part A is an alphabetically arranged list of kabane-bearing uji and individuals that did not receive kabane grants during Tenmu's reign. It also contains references to both uji and individuals whose identity is in question. Part B is a list of the uji and individuals representing 177 uji that were granted kabane during Tenmu's reign. The uji in this list are arranged chronologically in the sequence in which the grants were made. To each grantee, whether an individual or an uji, is given a grant number (GR) ranging from 1 to 202. All kabane references to individuals belonging to a single uji are grouped together under the GR number representing the last and highest rank of kabane which was granted to that particular uji during Tenmu's reign. For example, the Osakabe no Miyatsuko uji is listed as a kabane recipient under GR25, but the reader is referred to GR152, which represents the subsequent kabane grant made to that uji. All NSK references to this uji and its members will be found under GR152.

Following each notation in the inventory will be found four columns indicating the date of the reference, the page numbers for it in each of the NSK I and NSK V, and the number of references in that particular form of notation to be found on the indicated page or pages of the NSK V edition. The dates indicate the exact location of the notation in the NSK, and are therefore useful for locating them in any edition of the NSK one may have available. The dates thus represent locations in the NSK rather than reconstructions of the date on which any particular event occurred. Years are indicated by either the year of an emperor's reign or by year periods (nengō). For example, "Kinmei 23/6/0" indicates that the reference in question will be found in the NSK under the sixth month of the twenty-third year of the reign of Kinmei, and "Taika 1/9/3" indicates that the reference will be found under the third day of the ninth month of the first year of the Taika year period. The abbreviation of "IC" stands for an intercalary month as, for example, in "Jitō 3/IC8/27." The abbreviation "BA" stands for "Before Accession," that is, it stands for the introductory notations to a given emperor found in the NSK prior to the dated first year of his reign. In other words, "BA" is equivalent to those portions of the NSK that are classified as "sokui-zen ki" or "the NSK account [of a given emperor] prior to [his] accession." An example would be "Tenchi BA/8/0" which stands for the eighth month prior to accession of Emperor Tenchi.

Following the column of dates will be found the page references in Aston's translation and in the Nihon Koten Bungaku Taikei edition of the NSK. No effort has been made to indicate variations in the readings of the former from those of the latter. The page references to NSK I notations are included in the hope that they will be helpful in gaining a better understanding for those who use the English translation. The fourth column lists the number of times a particular notation is referred to on the indicated page or pages of the NSK V. These figures are for the convenience of the reader in clarifying the basis for the simple statistical analyses in this monograph that are referred to as "NSK reference frequency".

There are a few exceptions to the statement found above to the effect that all NSK references to kabane, if accompanied by the name of an uji or an individual or both, are included in this inventory. The first exception involves sukune which was used as an honorific title (keishō) in the centuries before sukune was made the third rank of Tenmu's new eight-rank kabane system in 684. Individuals of uji that bore the traditional pre-Tenmu kabane of omi are occasionally listed in the NSK as bearing sukune as an honorific title rather than as a kabane. In these cases, such notations are included in the inventory and are counted as references to the traditional pre-Tenmu kabane of omi. Examples of these exceptions are the references to Soga no Iname no Sukune, which are listed in Part A of the inventory, and to Ki no Womaro no Sukune, which is listed in Part B under GR92. The other exceptions of this nature involve the titles of ohoomi and ohomuraji, which, technically speaking, are not kabane, because they were not borne by all members of a given uji. Nevertheless, omi was the traditional pre-Tenmu kabane of all uji in which a single member bore the title of ohoomi, and muraji was the traditional pre-Tenmu kabane of all uji in which a single member bore the title of ohomuraji. Conse-

Appendix I

quently, all references to ohoomi and ohomuraji, which appear in the NSK for the period of this study in company with an uji name or the personal name of an individual or both, are included in this inventory and are counted as bearing respectively the traditional pre-Tenmu kabane of omi and muraji.

In a number of places in the inventory brackets are employed for the purpose of clarification of abbreviated NSK notations. For example, under the Ahe no Omi uji (GR89), Ahe no Tori no Omi is referred to on Suiko 16/8/12, and four years later on Suiko 20/2/20 he is referred to as Tori no Omi. The last notation is listed in the inventory as [Ahe no] Tori no Omi. Brackets are also employed for purposes of clarification when the members of a given uji are referred to in the NSK bearing what appear to be the names of their sub-uji, usually derived from place names. Again, the following examples drawn from the Ahe no Omi uji (GR89) will suffice to illustrate this point:

Ahe no Hiketa no Hirabu no Omi
[Ahe no] Hiketa no Asomi Hirome
Ahe no Asomi Minushi
[Ahe no] Fuse no Minushi no Asomi

Lastly, brackets are employed when there are indications that the name of an uji had been changed as in the cases of the Mononobe no Muraji uji (GR94) and the Nakatomi no Muraji uji (GR97). An example of the former is [Mononobe]/Isonokami no Asomi Maro, and of the latter, [Nakatomi]/Fujihara no Asomi Ohoshima.

PART A:

INVENTORY OF KABANE-BEARING UJI AND INDIVIDUALS
NOT GRANTED KABANE DURING TENMU'S OR JITŌ'S REIGNS

	Date		NSK I v.2	NSK V v.2	No. of Ref.
Afu no Omi Sanuki	Kinmei	23/6/0	lacking	120	1
Afu no Omi Shima	Tenmu	1/6/24	304	386	1
Afumi no Omi Mitsu	Sushun	2/7/1	118	168	1
Afumi no Anamu no Omi Ihifuta	Suiko	31/0/0	151	207	1
Afumi no Kena no Omi	Keitai	21/6/3	15	34	1
		23/3/0	18	38	1
		23/4/0	19	40	1
[Afumi no] Kena no Omi	Keitai	21/6/3			3
		23/4/7	15-24	34-46	6
		24/9/0			7

Agata-nushi Ihibo:
    Cf. Mishima no Agata-nushi

Akasome no Miyatsuko Tokotari	Tenmu	1/6/25	306	388	1
[Anato no] Kuni no Miyatsuko Obito	Hakuchi	1/2/9	236	312	1
Aratawo no Atahi Akamaro	Tenmu	1/7/3	313	398	1
Aratawo no Muraji Maro	Tenmu	14/10/10	372	472	1
Asakura no Kimi	Taika	2/3/19	214-6	288-90	4
Ashikita no Kimi	Bidatsu	12/0/0	100	147	1
Asono Kimi	Senka	1/5/1	34	58	1
Asuka no Kinunuhi no Miyatsuko	Sushun	1/0/0	118	168	1
Enowi no Muraji: Cf. Mononobe no Enowi					
Enu no Omi Moshiro	Kinmei	31/4/2	87	128	1
Funato no Atahi	Hakuchi	4/6/0	244	320	1
Harima no Atahi	Kinmei	17/1/0	78	116	1
Hayashi no Omi: Cf. Soga no Iruka					
Hi no Ashikita no Kuni no Miyatsuko Arishito	Bidatsu	12/7/1	97	142	1
Hi no Ashikita no Kuni no Miyatsuko Wosakabe no Yukehi Arishito	Bidatsu	12/0/0	98	144	1
Himuka no Omi: Cf. Soga no Himuka					
Hita no Atahi: Cf. Ikehe no Hita					
Iga no Kuni no Miyatsuko	Jitō	6/3/17	406	514	1
Ihaki no Suguri Oho	Tenchi	3/12/0	283	362	1
Ihohara no Kimi Omi	Tenchi	2/8/13	279	358	1
Ihowi no Miyatsuko Kujira	Tenmu	1/7/4	317	403	1
		1/7/23	318	405	1
Ijimi no Kuni no Miyatsuko	Ankan	1/4/1	27	49	1
[Ijimi no] Kuni no Miyatsuko Wakugo no Atahi	Ankan	1/4/1	27	49	1
[Ijimi no Kuni no Miyatsuko] Wakugo no Atahi	Ankan	1/4/1	27	50	1
Ikago no Omi Ahe	Tenmu	1/6/25	306	388	1
		1/7/2	312	396	1
Ikehe no Atahi	Kinmei	14/5/1	68	104	2
Ikehe no Atahi Hita	Bidatsu	13/0/0	101	148	1
[Ikehe no] Hita no Atahi	Bidatsu	13/0/0	101	148	1

Appendix I 151

Ikuha no Omi	Kinmei	5/3/0	52-54	83-86	6
		14/8/7	69	106	1
Ikuha no Omi Makuhi	Sushun	BA/6/7	112	161	1
Imaki no Ayahito Kōsai	Suiko	16/9/11	139	192	1
Imaki no Ayahito Nichimon	Suiko	16/9/11	139	192	1
Imaki no Ayahito Ohokuni	Suiko	16/9/11	139	192	1
Imaki no Ayahito Saimon	Suiko	20/0/0	144	198	1
Iname no Sukune: Cf. Soga no Iname					
Inukahi no Muraji Ikimi	Tenmu	1/7/23	315	400	1
			317	403	1
Iruka no Omi: Cf. Soga no Iruka					
Ise no Kuni no Miyatsuko	Jitō	6/3/17	406	514	1
Ise no Ohoka no Obito Woguma	Bidatsu	4/1/0	94	138	1
Iyobe no Muraji Umakahi	Jitō	3/6/2	392	498	1
Izumo no Kuni no Miyatsuko	Saimei	5/0/0	263	340	1
Izumo no Omi Koma	Tenmu	1/7/2	312	398	1
		1/7/22	315	400	1
Kafuka no Omi	Bidatsu	13/9/0	101	148	1
Kahara no Muraji Kane	Tenmu	13/10/3	365	464	1
Karashima no Suguri Saba	Tenchi	10/11/10	298	378	1
Kasahara no Atahi Omi, Musashi no Kuni no Miyatsuko	Ankan	1/12/0	31	54	1
Kashima no Omi Kusu	Jitō	6/7/2	409	517	1
Kazuraki no Wonara no Omi	Sushun	4/11/4	119	170	1
Kazuraki no Omi Wonara	Sushun	BA/7/0	113	162	1
Kena no Omi: Cf. Afumi no Kena					
Ki no Omi Nasochi Mimasa	Kinmei	5/2/0	49	78	1
Ki no Kuni no Miyatsuko Oshikatsu	Bidatsu	12/7/1	97	142	1
		12/10/0	97	142	1
Kibi no Ama no Atahi Hashima	Bidatsu	12/7/1	97	142	1
		12/0/0	97	142	1
Kibi no Ama no Atahi Naniha	Bidatsu	2/5/3	92	136	1
Kibi no Omi	Kinmei	2/4/0	42	68	1
		5/3/0	53	84	1
		5/11/0	56-58	88-91	4
Kibi no Otokimi no Omi	Kinmei	5/3/0	53	84	1
Kibi no Kasa no Omi Shidaru	Taika	1/9/3	204	277	1
		1/9/12	204	278	2
Kifumi no Eshi	Suiko	12/9/0	133	186	1

Kishi no Akahato	Kinmei	31/7/0	88	129	1
Kishi no Harima	Tenchi	4/0/0	284	364	1
Kishi no Kimi	Tenchi	4/0/0	284	364	1
Kishi no Koma	Hakuchi	4/5/12	242	318	1
		5/7/0	247	322	1
Kishi no Kuraji	Suiko	31/0/0	151	206	2
[Kishi no] Kuromaro	Jomei	5/1/26	166	230	1
Kishi no Nagani	Hakuchi	4/5/12	242	318	1
		5/7/24	246	322	1
		5/7/0	247	322	1
Kishi no Okina	Keitai	23/3/0	17	38	1
Kishi no Woguro: Cf. Woguro no Kishi					
Kishi no Womaro	Jomei	5/1/26	166	230	1
Kishi no Wosahiko	Bidatsu	4/4/6	94	138	1
Kishi no Woshibi	Tenchi	7/11/5	290	370	1
Koma no Wekaki Komaro	Saimei	5/0/0	263	341	1
Wekaki Koma no Tatebe no Komaro	Hakuchi	4/6/0	244	320	1
Komada no Suguri Oshihito	Tenmu	1/6/26	307	390	1
Komotsumebe no Obito Tomi	Kinmei	23/7/0	83	122	1
Kosohe no Omi Ohokuchi	Tenmu	1/7/13	314	400	1
Kuhita no Fubito Nakura	Tenmu	6/4/11	336	427	1
Kuni no Miyatsuko Obito: Cf. Anato no Kuni no Miyatsuko					
Kuni no Miyatsuko Wakugo: Cf. Ijimi no Kuni no Miyatsuko					
Kura no Omi Wokuso	Hakuchi	1/2/15	238	314	1
Kura no Yamada no Omi: Cf. Soga no Kura no Yamada					
Kuraji no Kimi	Kinmei	15/12/0	75	113	1
Kuratsukuri no Omi: Cf. Soga no Iruka					
Kuratsukuri no Suguri Shimedachito	Bidatsu	13/0/0	101	148	1
Kusu no Omi Ihate	Tenmu	1/6/26	308	390	1
Mano no Obito Deshi	Suiko	20/0/0	144	198	1
Marise no Omi: Cf. Sakahibe no Marise					
Maro no Omi Cf. Soga no Kura no Yamada					
Maroko no Muraji	Taika	2/3/19	216	290	1

Appendix I 153

Mibube no Muraji Tora	Jitō	3/7/20	393	498	1
Masuta no Atahi Komushō	Tenmu	14/10/8	371-2	472	1
Michi no Kimi	Kinmei	31/5/0	88	128	1
Michi no Kimi Iratsume	Tenchi	7/2/23	288	368	1
Michi no Omi	Keitai	21/8/1	16	36	1
		24/2/1	21	42	1
Mikaha no Ohotomo no Atahi	Taika	2/3/19	216	290	1
Minabuchi no Ayahito Shōan	Suiko	16/9/11	139	192	1
[Mishima no] Agata-nushi Ihibo	Ankan	1/12/4	29-30	52	3
Miwo no Kimi Katahi	Keitai	1/3/14	6	24	1
Miwo no Tsunowori no Kimi	Keitai	1/3/14	5	24	1
[Mononobe no] Enowi no Muraji	Taika	2/3/19	214	288	1
[Mononobe no] Enowi no Muraji Komaro	Tenmu	9/7/17	347	442	1
Mononobe no Enowi no Muraji Shibi	Saimei	4/11/5	256	334	1
Mononobe no Enowi no Muraji Shihinomi	Taika	1/9/3	204	277	1
[Mononobe no] Enowi no Muraji Wokimi	Tenmu	1/5/0	303	384	1
		1/6/24	305	387	1
Mononobe no [Enowi no] Wokimi no Muraji	Tenmu	5/6/0	332	423	1
Mononobe no Futsuta no Miyatsuko Shiho	Taika	5/3/26	234	309	1
Mononobe no Magamu no Muraji	Kinmei	15/12/0	73	110	1
Mononobe no Muraji Nasochi Yōgata	Kinmei	5/2/0	49	78	1
Mononobe no Yosami no Muraji Idaki	Suiko	16/8/12	137	190	1
Mononobe no Yosami no Muraji Oto	Suiko	31/0/0	151	206	1
[Mononobe no] Yosami no Muraji Wakugo	Saimei	3/0/0	252	330	1
Mori no Kimi Karita	Jitō	1/1/19	385	488	1
		7/6/4	412	521	1
Mori no Kimi Ohoiha	Saimei	4/11/9	256	334	1
		4/11/11	256-7	335	2
	Tenchi	BA/8/0	275	352	1
		4/0/0	284	364	1
Mozu no Haji no Muraji Tsuchitoko	Hakuchi	5/10/10	247	323	1
Mugetsu Kimi Hiro	Tenmu	1/6/22	304	386	1
Murakuni no Muraji Woyori	Tenmu	1/6/22	304	386	1
		1/7/2	312	396	1
		5/7/0	333	424	1

Murohara no Obito Mita	Hakuchi	4/5/12	244	319	1
Musa no Kimi Katsushi	Jomei	BA/9/0	162	224	1
Musa no Omi	Kōgyoku	3/1/0	185	255	1
Nagawo no Atahi Masumi	Tenmu	1/7/23	315	401	1
Nakatomi no Hashihito no Muraji Oyu	Hakuchi	5/2/0	246	322	1
Nara no Wosa no Emyō	Suiko	16/9/11	139	192	1
Ne no Muraji Kanemi	Tenmu	1/6/26	307	390	1
Nihinomi no Muraji	Senka	1/5/1	34	58	1
Nonaka no Kahara no Fubito Mitsu	Taika	5/3/0	235	310	1
Noto no Omi Mamutatsu	Saimei	6/3/0	264	342	1
Nunoshi no Obito Iha	Tenchi	10/11/10	298	378	1
Ohochi no Miyatsuko Wosaka	Yōmei	2/4/0	110	159	1
Ohochi no Muraji	Taika	2/3/19	215	288	1
Ohochi no Obito	Suiko	20/0/0	Lacking	198	1
Ohokida no Kimi Wakami	Tenmu	1/6/26	307	390	1
		1/7/22	314	400	1
		8/3/6	341	434	1
Ohokida no Kimi Wesaka	Tenmu	1/6/24	304	386	1
		1/6/26	307	390	1
		4/6/23	329	419	1
Ohoshima no Obito Ihahi	Bidatsu	2/7/1	92	136	1
		3/7/20	93	136	1
Ohotomo no Kimi Inatsumi	Saimei	4/7/4	254	332	1
Ohotomo no Suguri Kōsō	Suiko	10/10/0	126	178	1
Okisome no Muraji Ohoku	Hakuchi	5/2/0	246	322	1
Okisome no Muraji Usagi	Tenmu	1/7/2	312	396	1
		1/7/9	314	399	1
		1/7/23	317	404	1
Oshisaka no Muraji	Taika	2/3/19	214	288	1
Oshisakabe no Fubito Kekuso	Yōmei	2/4/2	110	158	1
Saheki no Miyatsuko Mimuro	Bidatsu	14/3/30	103	150	1
Sakahibe no Omi	Suiko	8/2/0	124	176	1
		31/11/0	152	208	1
	Jomei	BA/9/0	162-64	224-26	3
Sakahibe no Omi Marise	Suiko	20/2/20	143	197	1
Sakahibe no Marise no Omi	Jomei	BA/9/0	158	218	1
[Sakahibe no] Marise no Omi	Jomei	BA/9/0	162	224	1
		BA/9/0	163	226	3
Sakahibe no Omi Womaro	Suiko	31/0/0	151	206	1

Appendix I 155

Sakamoto no Kishi Nagae	Kōgyoku	1/2/22	173	238	1
Sakita no Obito	Suiko	20/0/0	Lacking	198	1
Sawoka no Obito Mase	Bidatsu	2/7/1	92	136	1
Shiga no Ayahito Weon	Suiko	16/9/11	139	192	1
Shihida no Kimi	Senka	1/3/8	34	58	1
Shihoya no Muraji Konoshiro	Saimei	4/11/9-11	256-7	334-5	4
Shima no Kuni no Miyatsuko	Jitō	6/3/17	406	514	1
Shima no Ohoomi: Cf. Soga no Umako					
Shimo no Wosa no Morota	Jitō	9/3/23	418	528	1
Shinoda no Fubito Mu	Tenchi	3/12/0	283	362	1
Shirawi no Fubito	Kinmei	30/4/0	87	127	1
Shirawi no Fubito Hone	Tenmu	13/12/6	367	467	1
Shirawi no Fubito Itsu	Bidatsu	3/10/9	94	137	1
Shirawi no Obito	Kinmei	30/4/0	87	127	1
[Soga no] Woane no Kimi	Sushun	BA/0/0	112	160	1
Soga no Ohoomi	Bidatsu	14/2/24	102	149	1
	Sushun	BA/7/0	115	164	2
	Suiko	11/2/4	126	178	1
	Kōgyoku	1/4/10	173	238	1
		1/7/23	174	240	1
		1/7/25	175	240	1
		1/7/27	175	240	1
		1/10/15	176	242	1
	Taika	1/9/12	204	276	1
Soga no Omi	Kinmei	16/2/0	76	114	1
	Bidatsu	14/3/1	103	150	1
	Kōgyoku	1/0/0	178	244	1
		3/6/6	187	257	1
Soga no Omi Akae	Saimei	4/11/11	257	335	1
	Tenmu	1/8/25	319	406	1
Soga no Akae no Omi	Saimei	4/11/3	255	334	1
	Tenchi	8/1/9	290	370	1
		8/10/19	292	372	1
		10/1/2	294	374	1
		10/1/5	294	375	1
		10/11/23	298	380	2
	Tenmu	BA/10/19	302	383	1
Soga no Akae no Ohoomi	Tenmu	2/2/27	321	410	1
Soga no Ohoomi Emishi	Kōgyoku	1/0/0	178	244	1
		2/10/6	181	248	1
		2/11/0	183	252	1
		3/11/0	189	259	1
[Soga no] Ohoomi Emishi	Kōgyoku	4/6/12	192	264	1
Soga no Omi Emishi	Kōgyoku	1/1/15	171	236	1
		4/6/13	193	264	2

Soga no Emishi no Omi	Jomei	BA/9/0	157	216	1
Soga no Toyura no Emishi no Omi	Suiko	18/10/9	141	194	1
[Soga no Emishi] Toyura no Ohoomi	Jomei	8/7/1	167	230	1
	Kōgyoku	3/3/0	186	256	1
		3/6/6	187	257	1
Soga no Omi Hatayasu	Tenmu	1/7/2	312	397	3
		1/8/25	319	406	1
Soga no Hatayasu no Omi	Tenchi	10/1/5	294	375	1
		10/11/23	298	380	1
	Tenmu	BA/10/19	302	383	1
Soga no Omi Himuka	Taika	5/3/24	232	306	1
		5/3/26	234	309	1
Soga no Himuka no Omi	Taika	5/3/25	234	308	1
[Soga no] Himuka no Omi	Taika	5/3/0	235	310	1
Soga no Iname no Sukune	Senka	1/2/1	33	56	1
	Taika	1/8/8	202	276	1
[Soga no] Iname no Sukune	Kinmei	13/10/0	67	102	1
	Sushun	BA/0/0	112	160	1
	Suiko	34/5/20	154	212	1
	Taika	1/8/8	203	276	1
Soga no Iname no Sukune no Ohoomi	Kinmei	BA/12/5	38	64	1
		23/8/0	86	126	1
Soga no Ohoomi Iname no Sukune	Senka	1/5/1	34	58	1
	Kinmei	2/3/0	40	66	1
		13/10/0	66	102	1
		14/7/4	68-9	104	1
		16/7/4	77	116	1
		17/7/6	78	117	1
		17/10/0	77	116	1
		31/3/1	87	128	1
	Yōmei	1/1/1	107	155	1
Soga no Omi Iruka	Kōgyoku	1/7/23	174	240	1
		2/10/12	181	249-50	2
		2/11/1	181-2	250-1	2
		3/1/1	184	254	1
		4/6/12	Lacking	263	1
Soga no Iruka no Omi	Kōgyoku	4/6/12	191	262	1
[Soga no] Iruka no Omi	Kōgyoku	1/0/0	178	244	1
		3/11/0	189	259	1
		4/6/12	191-92	262-63	2
		4/6/13	194	265	1
[Soga no Iruka] Hayashi no Omi	Kōgyoku	2/11/0	183	252	2
[Soga no] Kuratsukuri no Omi [Iruka]	Kōgyoku	4/6/12	191-92	262-64	3
Soga no Kura no Yamada no Ishikaha no Maro no Omi	Kōtoku	BA/6/14-15	196-7	270	2
[Soga no] Kura no Yamada no Omi [Maro]	Kōgyoku	3/1/1	185	255	1

Appendix I

[Soga no Kura no Yamada no] Maro no Omi	Kōgyoku	4/6/8	191	262	1
[Soga no] Kura no Yamada no Maro no Omi	Kōgyoku	4/6/8 4/6/12	191 191	261 262	1 2
Soga no Kura no Yamada no Maro no Ohoomi	Taika	5/3/24	232	307	1
Soga no [Kura no] Yamada no Ohoomi	Taika	5/3/30	234	310	1
[Soga no Kura no] Yamada no Ohoomi	Taika	5/3/0	234	310	1
Soga no Yamada no Ishikaha no Maro no Ohoomi	Kōtoku Taika Tenchi	BA/6/15 1/7/2 7/2/23	197 198 287	270 271 367	1 1 1
Soga no [Yamada no] Ishikaha no Maro no Ohoomi	Taika	1/7/12-14	199	272	3
Soga no Umako no Sukune	Bidatsu Yōmei Sushun Taika	1/4/0 13/0/0 BA/9/5 1/5/0 BA/6/7 BA/8/2 1/0/0 5/10/10 5/11/3 5/11/0 1/8/8	90 101 106 108-9 112 117 118 119 119 120 203	132 148 119 157 161 167 168 170 170 171 276	1 1 1 1 1 1 1 1 1 1 1
[Soga no] Umako no Sukune	Bidatsu Yōmei Sushun Taika	13/0/0 14/3/30 14/6/0 1/5/0 5/11/3 5/11/0 1/8/8	102 103 104 109 119-20 120 203	148 150 151-2 157-8 170 171 276	4 3 5 3 2 1 2
Soga no Umako no Ohoomi	Bidatsu Sushun	3/10/9 BA/7/0	93 114	137 164	1 1
[Soga no] Umako no Sukune no Ohoomi	Bidatsu	4/2/1 14/8/15	94 104-5	138 152	1 2
[Soga no] Umako no Ohoomi	Yōmei	2/4/2	110-1	159-60	2
Soga no Ohoomi Umako no Sukune	Bidatsu	14/2/15	102	148	1
[Soga no] Ohoomi Umako no Sukune	Suiko	BA/11/0	121	172	1
Soga no Umako no Sukune no Ohoomi	Yōmei Sushun	2/4/2 BA/7/0	110 113	158 162	1 2
Soga no Shima no Ohoomi [Umako]	Jomei	2/1/12	165	228	1
[Soga no] Shima no Ohoomi [Umako]	Suiko Jomei Kōgyoku	28/0/0 34/5/20 BA/9/0 4/6/13	148 154 162 193	203 212 224 264	1 1 1 1

Soga no Taguchi no Omi Kahahori	Taika	1/9/3 1/9/12	204 204	277 278	1 1
[Soga no] Taguchi no Omi	Taika	2/3/19	215	289	1
[Soga no] Taguchi no Omi Tsukushi	Taika	5/3/26 5/3/30	234 234	309 310	1 1
Soga no Kuramaro no Omi Womasa	Jomei	BA/9/0	158	218	1
Soga no Omi Yasumaro	Tenmu	BA/10/17	301	382	1
[Soga no] Zentoko no Omi	Suiko	4/11/0	124	174	1
Sone no Muraji Karainu	Tenmu	4/4/10 10/12/29	328 353	418 450	1 1
Susukiwo no Atahi	Taika	2/3/19	216	290	1
Tabe no Muraji	Jomei	1/4/1 2/9/0	164 165	227 228	1 1
Tabe no Muraji Kunioshi	Tenmu	10/12/29	353	450	1
Taguchi no Omi: Cf. Soga no Taguchi					
Tajihi no Wozaha no Muraji Kuniso	Saimei	4/11/11	256	334	1
Takamuku no Ayahito Genri	Suiko Jomei	16/9/11 12/10/11	139 170	192 234	1 1
Takamuku no Fubito Genri	Kōtoku Hakuchi	BA/6/14 5/2/0	197 245	270 321	1 1
Takata no Obito Ihanari	Jitō	3/11/8	395	500	1
Takata no Obito Nemaro	Hakuchi	4/5/12	244	319	1
Takata no Obito Nihinomi	Tenmu	1/6/25 14/10/10	306 372	388 472	1 1
Tanahe no Fubito Tori	Hakuchi	5/2/0	246	322	1
Taniha no Omi	Taika	2/3/19	215	289	1
Tomi no Obito Ichihi	Sushun	BA/7/0	114-5	164	2
Toyura no Ohoomi: Cf. Soga no Emishi					
Tsu no Omi Kutsuma	Saimei	3/0/0	252	330	1
Tsuki no Kishi	Keitai	24/9/0 24/10/0	23 23	44 45	2 1
Tsuki no Kishi Ikina	Kinmei	23/7/0	84	124	1
Tsuki no Obito Afumi	Tenmu	1/6/24	305	387	1
Tsukushi no Fubito Masaru	Jitō	5/1/14	401	508	1
Tsukushi no Kimi Kuzuko	Keitai	22/12/0	17	36	1
Tsukushi no Hi no Kimi	Kinmei	17/1/0	78	116	1
Tsukushi no Kimi	Kinmei	17/1/0	78	116	1
Tsukushi no Kimi Sachiyama	Tenchi Jitō	10/11/10 4/10/22	298 400	378 506	1 1

Appendix I

Tsukushi no Kuni no Miyatsuko	Kinmei	15/12/0	75	112	1
Tsukushi no Kuni no Miyatsuko Ihawi	Keitai	21/6/3	15	34	1
Tsukushi no Miyake no Muraji Tokuko	Tenmu	13/12/6	367	467	1
Uchi no Omi	Kinmei	14/6/0	68	104	1
		14/8/7	69	104	1
		15/1/9	71	108	3
		15/5/3	72	110	1
Uchi no Omi	Kinmei	15/12/0	72-4	110	4
Ugoha no Omi	Kinmei	5/3/0	52	83	1
Uhe no Atahi Yumi	Tenmu	13/3/8	362	461	1
Uhe no Suguri Kōbu	Tenmu	8/11/23	344	438	1
Uhe no Suguri Kudara	Jitō	5/4/1	402	509	1
		7/3/5	411	520	1
Umako no Sukune no Ohoomi: Cf. Soga no Umako					
Utena no Atahi Sumi	Taika	2/3/19	214	288	1
Utena no Imiki Yashima	Jitō	8/3/2	414	524	1
Wakugo no Atahi: Cf. Ijimi no Kuni no Miyatsuko					
Wani no Omi no Kafuchi	Keitai	1/3/14	6	24	1
Wanibe no Omi Kimite	Tenmu	1/6/22	304	386	1
		1/7/2	312	396	1
Watoko no Fubito	Taika	2/3/19	214	288	1
Wika [no] Kimi	Kinmei	5/2/0	50	80	1
Wikaka no Kimi	Kinmei	5/2/0	50	80	1
Winouhe no Kimi	Taika	2/3/19	214	288	1
Woane no Kimi: Cf. Soga no Woane					
Woguro no Kishi	Bidatsu	6/5/5	95	140	1
Woka no Kimi Yoroshi	Hakuchi	5/2/0	245	322	1
Womidori no Omi	Taika	2/3/19	215	289	1
Yago no Fubito	Suiko	10/10/0	126	178	1
Yakuchi no Asomi Otokashi	Jitō	BA/10/2	383	486	1
Yamada no Fubito Mikata	Jitō	6/10/11	410	518	1
Yamanohe no Kimi Yasumaro	Tenmu	1/6/26	307	390	1
Yamashiro no Weshi	Suiko	12/9/0	133	186	1
Yamato no Weshi Otokashi	Tenmu	6/5/3	336	428	1
Yosami no Muraji: Cf. Mononobe no Yosami					

Yuge no Muraji Ganhō   Jitō   4/10/22   400   506   1

Zentoko no Omi:
   Cf. Soga no Zentoko

PART B:

INVENTORY OF KABANE GRANTEES
DURING TENMU'S AND JITŌ'S REIGNS GROUPED BY UJI

			Date	NSK I v.2	NSK V v.2	No. of Ref.
GR1	Imibe no Obito Kobito: Cf. GR142					
GR2	Kusakabe no Kishi Ohokata: Cf. GR59, GR193					
GR3	Nishikori no Miyatsuko Wokida: Cf. GR34					
GR4	Tawi no Atahi Yoshimaro	Tenmu	10/4/12	351	446	1
GR5	Sukita no Kurahito Mukutari	Tenmu	10/4/12	351	446	1
GR6	[Sukita no Kurahito] Ishikatsu	Tenmu	10/4/12	351	446	1
GR7	Kafuchi no Atahi	Kinmei	2/7/0	44	72	2
			4/11/8	48	76	2*
			4/12/0	49	78	1
			5/2/0	50	80	2
			5/3/0	53	84	2
			5/10/0	56	88	1
			5/11/0	58	90	1
	Kafuchi no Atahi Agata	Tenmu	10/4/12	351	446	1
	Kafuchi no Atahi Kujira	Tenchi	8/0/0	292	373	1
GR8	Oshinumi no Miyatsuko Kagami: Cf. GR52					
GR9	Oshinumi no Miyatsuko Arata: Cf. GR52					
GR10	Oshinumi no Miyatsuko Yoshimaro: Cf. GR52					
GR11	Ohokoma no Miyatsuko Momoe: Cf. GR39					
GR12	Ohokoma no Miyatsuko Ashitsuki: Cf. GR39					
GR13	Yamato no Atahi Tatsumaro: Cf. GR20, GR189					
GR14	Kadobe no Atahi Ohoshima: Cf. GR33					

*One reference lacking in NSK I, p. 48.

GR15	Shishihito no Miyatsuko Okina	Tenmu	10/4/12	351	446	1
GR16	Yamashiro no Koma no Ikamaro	Tenmu	10/4/12	351	446	1
GR17	Toneri no Miyatsuko Nukamushi	Tenmu	10/12/29 11/1/9 11/2/0	354 354 354	450 450 450	1 1 1
GR18	Fumi no Atahi Chitoko: Cf. GR19, GR195					
GR19	Yamato no Aya no Atahi: Cf. GR18, GR195					
GR20	Yamato no Atahi: Cf. GR13, GR189					
GR21	Kurukuma no Obito	Tenmu	12/9/23	361	458	1
	Kurukuma no Obito Tokomaro	Tenchi	7/2/23	288	368	1
GR22	Mohitori no Miyatsuko	Tenmu	12/9/23	361	458	1
GR23	Yatabe no Miyatsuko	Suiko	22/6/13 23/9/0	145 146	200 200	1 1
		Tenmu	12/9/23	361	458	1
GR24	Fujiharabe no Miyatsuko	Tenmu	12/9/23	361	458	1
GR25	Osakabe no Miyatsuko: Cf. GR152					
GR26	Sakikusabe no Miyatsuko	Tenmu	12/9/23	361	458	1
GR27	Ohoshi Kafuchi no Atahi: Cf. GR191					
GR28	Kafuchi no Aya no Atahi: Cf. GR196					
GR29	Mononobe no Obito: Cf. GR188					
GR30	Yamashiro no Atahi: Cf. GR192					
GR31	Kazuraki no Atahi: Cf. GR190					
GR32	Tonohatori no Miyatsuko	Tenmu	12/9/23	361	458	1
GR33	Kadobe no Atahi	Tenmu	12/9/23	361	458	1
	Kadobe no Atahi Ohoshima	Tenmu	10/4/12	351	446	1
GR34	Nishikori no Miyatsuko	Tenmu	12/9/23	361	458	1
	Nishikori no Miyatsuko Wokida	Tenmu	10/4/12	351	446	1
	Nishikori no Obito Akawi	Jomei	BA/9/0	162	224	1
	Nishikori no Obito Kuso	Suiko	18/10/17	141	195	1
	Nishikori no Obito Ohoishi	Kinmei	31/7/0	88	129	1
GR35	Kazura no Miyatsuko	Tenmu	12/9/23	361	458	1
	Kazura no Miyatsuko Oshikatsu	Tenmu	8/8/22	343	436	1

GR36	Totori no Miyatsuko	Tenmu	12/9/23	361	458	1
GR37	Kume no Toneri no Miyatsuko	Tenmu	12/9/23	361	458	1
GR38	Hinokuma no Toneri no Miyatsuko	Tenmu	12/9/23	361	458	1
GR39	Ohokoma no Miyatsuko	Tenmu	12/9/23	361	458	1
	[Ohokoma no Miyatsuko] Ashitsuki	Tenmu	10/4/12	351	446	1
	Ohokoma no Miyatsuko Momoe	Tenmu	10/4/12	351	446	1
	Ohokoma no Muraji Momoe	Jitō	10/5/13	420	530	1
GR40	Hada no Miyatsuko: Cf. GR197					
GR41	Kahase no Toneri no Miyatsuko	Tenmu	12/9/23	361	458	1
GR42	Yamato no Umakahi no Miyatsuko	Tenmu	12/9/23	361	458	1
	Yamato no Umakahibe no Miyatsuko	Shuchō	1/9/29	381	482	1
	Yamato no Umakahibe no Miyatsuko Muraji	Tenmu	8/11/23	344	438	1
	Yamato no Umakahi no Obito	Kōgyoku	2/11/1	181	250	1
GR43	Kafuchi no Umakahi no Miyatsuko	Tenmu	12/9/23	361	458-9	1
	[Kafuchi no] Umakahi no Miyatsuko	Taika	1/7/10	199	272	1
	Kafuchi no Umakahibe no Miyatsuko	Shuchō	1/9/29	381	482	1
	[Kafuchi no] Umakahi no Obito	Keitai	1/1/6	3	20	1
	Kafuchi no Umakahi no Obito Arako	Keitai	1/1/6	3	20	1
	Kafuchi no Umakahi no Obito Mikari	Keitai	23/4/0	20	41	1
	Kafuchi no Omonoki no Umakahi no Obito Mikari	Keitai	24/9/0	22	44	1
	Kafuchi no Umakahi no Obito Oshikatsu	Kinmei	22/0/0	80	118	1
	[Kafuchi no] Umakahi no Obito Utayori	Kinmei	23/6/0	82	120-1	2
GR44	Kifumi no Miyatsuko	Tenmu	12/9/23	361	459	1
	Kifumi no Miyatsuko Honjichi	Tenchi	10/3/3	296	376	1
	Kifumi no Muraji Honjichi	Jitō	8/3/2	414	524	1
	Kifumi no Miyatsuko Ohotomo	Tenmu	1/6/24	304-5	386-7	2
	Kifumi no Muraji Ohotomo	Jitō	1/8/28	386	490	1

Appendix I 163

GR45	Komotsume no Miyatsuko	Tenmu	12/9/23	361	459	1
GR46	Magari no Hakozukuri no Miyatsuko	Tenmu	12/9/23	361	459	1
GR47	Isonokamibe no Miyatsuko	Tenmu	12/9/23	361	459	1
GR48	Takara no Himatsuri no Miyatsuko	Tenmu	12/9/23	361	459	1
GR49	Hazukashibe no Miyatsuko	Tenmu	12/9/23	361	459	1
GR50	Anahobe no Miyatsuko	Tenmu	12/9/23	361	459	1
GR51	Shirakabe no Miyatsuko	Tenmu	12/9/23	361	459	1
	Shirakabe no Muraji Abumi	Hakuchi	1/0/0	240	316	1
GR52	Oshinumi no Miyatsuko	Tenmu	12/9/23	361	459	1
	Oshinumi no Miyatsuko Arata	Tenmu	10/4/12	351	446	1
	Oshinumi no Miyatsuko Kagami	Tenmu	10/4/12	351	446	1
	Oshinumi no Miyatsuko Ohokuni	Tenmu	3/3/7	325	415	1
	Oshinumi no Miyatsuko Wotatsu	Tenchi	7/2/23	288	368	1
	Oshinumi no Miyatsuko Yoshimaro	Tenmu	7/9/0 10/4/12	338 351	431 446	1 1
GR53	Hatsukashi no Miyatsuko	Tenmu	12/9/23	361	459	1
GR54	Fumi no Obito: Cf. GR199					
GR55	Wohatsuse no Miyatsuko	Tenmu	12/9/23	361	459	1
GR56	Kudara no Miyatsuko	Tenmu	12/9/23	361	459	1
GR57	Katari no Miyatsuko	Tenmu	12/9/23	361	459	1
GR58	Miyake no Kishi: Cf. GR154					
GR59	Kusakabe no Kishi: Cf. GR2, GR193					
GR60	Hahaki no Miyatsuko	Tenmu	12/10/5	361	459	1
GR61	Fune no Fubito	Kinmei Bidatsu Tenmu	14/7/4 1/5/15 12/10/5	69 91 361	104 133 459	1 1 1
	Fune no Fubito Ōhei	Suiko	16/6/15	137	190	1
	Fune no Fubito Ōjin	Bidatsu	3/10/11	94	137-8	1
	Fune no Fubito Tatsu	Suiko	17/4/4	140	193	1
	Fune no Fubito Wesaka	Kōgyoku	4/6/13	193	264	1
	Fune no Muraji	Kinmei	14/7/4	69	104	1
GR62	Iki no Fubito	Tenmu	12/10/5	361	459	1
	Iki no Muraji Hakatoko	Saimei	5/7/3 6/7/16 7/5/23	260-2 266 271	338-40 344 349	2 1 1

		Tenchi	6/11/13	286	366	1
		Jitō	BA/10/2	383	486	1
			9/7/26	419	528	1
	Iki no Fubito Karakuni	Tenmu	1/7/23	315	402	1
			1/7/23	316	402	1
			1/7/23	318	404	1
	Iki no Fubito Maro	Taika	2/3/19	214	288	1
	Iki no Fubito Oto	Jomei	4/10/4	166	230	1
GR63	Sarara no Umakahi no Miyatsuko	Tenmu	12/10/5	361	459	1
GR64	Uno no Umakahi no Miyatsuko	Tenmu	12/10/5	361	459	1
GR65	Yoshino no Obito	Tenmu	12/10/5	361	459	1
GR66	Ki no Sakahito: Cf. GR194					
GR67	Uneme no Miyatsuko	Tenmu	12/10/5	361	459	1
GR68	Atoki no Fubito	Tenmu	12/10/5	361	459	1
GR69	Takechi no Agatanushi	Tenmu	12/10/5	361	459	1
	Takechi no Agatanushi Kome	Tenmu	1/7/0	317	404	1
GR70	Shiki no Agatanushi	Tenmu	12/10/5	361	460	1
GR71	Kagami Tsukuri no Miyatsuko	Tenmu	12/10/5	361	460	1
GR72	Mino no Agatanushi	Tenmu	13/1/17	362	460	1
GR73	Kura no Kinunuhi no Miyatsuko	Tenmu	13/1/17	362	460	1
	Ohokura no Kinunuhi no Miyatsuko Maro	Saimei	2/9/0	250	328	1
GR74	Moriyama no Kimi	Tenmu	13/10/1	365	464	1
GR75	Michi no Kimi	Tenmu	13/10/1	365	464	1
	Michi no Mahito Tomi	Tenmu	14/9/15	370	470	1
		Jitō	1/12/10	387	490	1
			11/2/28	422	532	1
GR76	Takahashi no Kimi	Tenmu	13/10/1	365	464	1
GR77	Mikuni no Kimi	Keitai	1/3/14	6	24	1
		Tenmu	13/10/1	365	464	1
	Mikuni no Kimi Maro	Hakuchi	1/2/15	238	314	2
	Mikuni no Maro no Kimi	Taika	5/3/24	232-3	307	2
	Mikuni no Mahito Tomotari	Tenmu	14/9/18	371	471	1
GR78	Tagima no Kimi	Yōmei	1/1/1	107	156	1
		Tenmu	13/10/1	365	464	1
	Tagima no Kimi Hiromaro	Tenmu	4/4/8	328	418	1
	Tagima no Kimi Hiroshima	Tenmu	1/6/26	308	391	1
	Tagima no Kimi Tate	Tenmu	10/7/4	351	447	1
	Tagima no Kimi Toyohama	Tenmu	10/2/30	350	445	1

Appendix I 165

	Name	Reign	Date	P1	P2	N
	Tagima no Mahito Chitoku	Jitō	2/11/11	389	493	1
			6/3/3	406	513	1
	Tagima no Mahito Hiromaro	Tenmu	14/5/19	369	469	1
	Tagima no Mahito Kunimi	Shuchō	1/9/27	380	481	1
		Jitō	11/2/28	421	532	1
	Tagima no Mahito Sakurawi	Jitō	3/2/26	390	494	1
GR79	Umaraki no Kimi	Tenmu	13/10/1	365	464	1
GR80	Tajihi no Kimi	Senka	1/3/8	34	57	1
		Tenmu	13/10/1	365	464	1
	Tajihi no Kimi Maro	Tenmu	6/10/14	337	429-30	1
	Tajihi no Mahito Ikemori	Jitō	7/6/4	412	521	1
	Tajihi no Mahito	Jitō	10/10/17	421	531	1
			10/10/22	421	531	1
	Tajihi no Mahito Maro	Jitō	1/3/20	385	488	1
	Tajihi no Mahito Shima	Tenmu	11/4/21	355	452	1
			12/1/2	359	456	1
		Jitō	3/IC8/27	394	499-500	1
	Tajihi no Shima no Mahito	Jitō	4/1/2	396	500	1
			4/7/5	398	503	1
			5/1/13	401	507	1
GR81	Wina no Kimi	Senka	1/3/8	34	57	1
	Wina no Kimi	Tenmu	13/10/1	365	464	1
	Wina no Kimi Ihasuki	Tenmu	1/6/26	308	390	1
			1/6/27	309	394	1
	Wina no Kimi Takami	Hakuchi	1/2/15	238	314	1
	Wina no Kimi Takami	Tenmu	1/12/0	320	408	1
GR82	Sakata no Kimi	Keitai	1/3/14	6	25	1
		Tenmu	13/10/1	365	464	1
	Sakata no Kimi Ikazuchi	Tenmu	5/9/0	334	426	1
GR83	Hata no Kimi	Tenmu	13/10/1	365	464	1
	Hata no Kimi Yakuni	Tenmu	1/7/2	312	397	1
			1/7/22	315	400	1
			12/12/13	361	460	1
	Hata no Mahito Yakuni	Shuchō	1/3/6	375	476	1
			1/3/25	375	476	1
GR84	Okinaga no Kimi	Tenmu	13/10/1	365	464	1
	Okinaga no Yamada no Kimi	Kōgyoku	1/12/14	177	244	1
	Okinaga no Mahito Oyu	Jitō	6/11/8	410	518	1
			7/3/16	411	520	1
GR85	Sakahito no Kimi	Keitai	1/3/14	6	25	1
		Tenmu	13/10/1	365	464	1
GR86	Yamaji no Kimi	Tenmu	13/10/1	365	464	1
GR87	Ohomiwa no Kimi	Tenmu	13/11/1	366	465	1
	Miwa no Fumiya no Kimi	Kōgyoku	2/11/1	182	250	1

			2/11/1	182	250	1
			2/11/1	183	252	1
	Miwa no Kimi Kobito	Tenmu	1/6/25	306	388	1
			1/7/2	312	396	1
	Ohomiwa no Makamuda no Kobito no Kimi	Tenmu	5/8/0	334	424	1
	Ohomiwa no Makamuda no Mukahe no Kimi	Tenmu	5/8/0	334	425	1
	Miwa no Kimi Mikaho	Hakuchi	1/2/15	238	314	1
	Miwa no Kimi Nemaro	Tenchi	2/3/0	279	357	1
	Miwa no Kimi Ohokuchi	Taika	2/3/19	214	288	1
	Miwa no Kimi Sakafu	Bidatsu	14/8/15	105	152	1
		Yōmei	1/5/0	107-9	156,158	3
	[Miwa no] Sakafu no Kimi	Yōmei	1/5/0	108	156-7	4
	Ohomiwa no Sakafu no Kimi	Bidatsu	14/8/15	104	152	1
	Miwa no Kimi Shikobu	Taika	5/5/1	236	311	1
	Miwa no Shikobu no Kimi	Taika	1/8/8	203	277	1
	Miwa no Kimi Takechimaro	Tenmu	1/6/29	311	396	1
			1/7/0	317	404	1
	Miwa no Asomi Takechimaro	Jitō	6/2/19	406	513	1
	Ohomiwa no Asomi Takechimaro	Shuchō	1/9/28	380	482	1
		Jitō	6/3/3	406	513	1
	Miwa no Kimi Wosazaki	Jomei	8/3/0	167	230	1
	Ohomiwa no Asomi Yasumaro	Jitō	3/2/26	391	494	1
	Miwa no Hiketa no Kimi Nanihamaro	Tenmu	13/5/28	364	463	1
	Miwa no Kurukuma no Kimi Azumahito	Taika	1/7/10	199	272	1
	Miwa no Kimi Azumahito	Taika	1/7/10	199	272	1
GR88	Kasuga no Omi	Sushun	BA/7/0	113	162	1
	Ohokasuga no Omi	Tenmu	13/11/1	366	465	1
	Kasuga no Hitsume no Omi	Kinmei	2/3/0	41	68	1
	Kasuga no Omi Nakatsukimi	Bidatsu	4/1/0	94	138	1
	Kasuga no Ahata no Omi Kudara	Kōtoku	4/5/12	243	318	1
GR89	Ahe no Omi	Senka	1/5/1	34	58	1
		Kinmei	17/1/0	78	116	1
		Sushun	2/7/1	118	168	1
		Suiko	16/8/12	138	192	1
		Jomei	BA/9/0	157-9	216-8	3
		Jomei	BA/9/0	162	223-4	2
		Saimei	4/4/0	252	330	1
			5/3/0	260	337	2
			6/3/0	263-4	342	5
		Tenmu	13/11/1	366	465	1
	Ahe no Ohoomi	Taika	1/9/12	204	278	1
			4/2/8	230	306	1
			5/3/17	232	306	1

Appendix I 167

	Ahe no Omi Hito	Sushun	BA/7/0	113	162	1
	Ahe no Kosohe no Omi	Taika	1/9/12	204	278	1
	Ahe no Kurahashi Maro no Ohoomi	Kōtoku Taika	BA/6/15 1/7/2 1/7/12-13	197 198 199	270 271 272	1 1 2
	Ahe no Omi Maro	Suiko	32/10/1	154	210	1
	Ahe no Maro no Omi	Jomei	BA/9/0	157	216	1
	Ahe no Me no Omi	Bidatsu	12/0/0	98	144	1
	Ahe no Ohomaro no Omi	Senka	1/2/1	33	56	1
	Ahe no Tori no Omi	Suiko	16/8/12	137	190	1
	[Ahe no] Tori no Omi	Suiko	20/2/20	143	197	1
	Ahe no Uchi no Omi Tori	Suiko	20/2/20	143	196	1
	Ahe no Toriko no Omi	Suiko	18/10/9	141	194	1
	Ahe no Uchimaro no Omi	Kōtoku	BA/6/14	196	270	1
	[Ahe no] Fuse no Omi	Taika	2/3/19	213	287	1
	[Ahe no] Fuse no Omi Mimimaro	Tenchi	7/9/29	289	370	1
	Ahe no Hiketa no Omi	Saimei	6/5/0	265	343	1
	Ahe no Hiketa no Omi Hirabu	Saimei Tenchi	4/0/0 5/3/0 2/3/0	257 260 279	336 338 357	1 1 1
	Ahe no Hiketa no Hirabu no Omi	Tenchi	BA/8/0	275	352	1
	[Ahe no] Kuno no Omi Maro	Tenmu	4/4/8 4/4/14	328 328	418 418	1 1
	[Ahe no] Hiketa no Asomi Hirome	Jitō	7/6/4	412	521	1
	Ahe no Asomi Minushi	Jitō	10/10/22	421	531	1
	[Ahe no] Fuse no Minushi no Asomi	Jitō	4/1/2 5/1/13	396 401	500 508	1 1
	[Ahe no] Fuse no Asomi Minushi	Shuchō Jitō	1/9/28 1/1/1 2/11/11 8/1/2	380 384 389 414	482 488 493 523	1 1 1 1
	[Ahe no] Fuse no Asomi Shikofuchi	Jitō	6/7/2	409	516	1
	[Ahe no] Hiketa no Asomi Sukunamaro	Jitō	7/11/23	414	523	1
	Ahe no Kuno no Asomi Maro	Shuchō	1/9/29	381	482	1
GR90	Kose no Omi	Kinmei Jomei	5/3/0 16/2/0 BA/9/0	54 76 159	86 114 218	1 1 1
	Kose no Omi	Kinmei	5/3/0	54	86	1
	Kose no Omi	Tenmu	13/11/1	366	465	1

	Kose no Omi Hirabu	Sushun	BA/7/0	113	162	1
	Kose no Omi Hito	Tenmu	1/7/2	312	397	2
			1/8/25	319	406	1
	Kose no Hito no Omi	Tenchi	10/1/2	294	374	1
			10/1/5	294	375	1
			10/11/23	298	380	1
	Kose no Omi Inamochi	Kinmei	1/9/5	39	65	1
	Kose no Omi Kusuri	Hakuchi	4/5/12	243-4	318	1
	Kose no Omi Ohomaro	Jomei	BA/9/0	158	218	1
	Kose no Omi Saru	Kinmei	31/7/0	88	129	1
	Kose no Saru no Omi	Sushun	4/11/4	119	170	1
	Kose no Omi Shitano	Taika	2/3/19	213	287	1
	Kose no Omi Tokoda	Kōgyoku	1/12/13	177	244	1
	Kose no Tokoda no Omi	Kōgyoku	2/11/1	181-2	250	3
			4/6/12	192	264	1
		Taika	1/7/10	198	271	1
		Saimei	4/1/13	252	330	1
	Kose no Tokoda Ko no Omi	Taika	5/4/20	235	311	1
	Kose no Tokone no Omi	Taika	2/3/19	213	288	1
			2/3/19	215	290	1
	[Kose no] Toyotari no Omi	Hakuchi	5/4/12	244	318	1
	Kose no Ohoomi Wohito	Keitai	21/6/3	15	35	1
	Kose no Wohito no Ohoomi	Keitai	1/1/4	2	20	1
			1/2/4	4	22	1
			23/9/0	21	42	1
		Ankan	1/3/6	27	48	1
	Kose no Kamusaki no Omi Wosa	Tenchi	2/3/0	279	357	1
	Kose no Asomi Ahamochi	Tenmu	14/9/15	370	470	1
		Jitō	11/2/28	422	532	1
	Kose no Asomi Maro	Jitō	7/6/4	412	521	1
	Kose no Asomi Shitano	Tenmu	14/3/16	369	468	1
	Kose no Asomi Tayasu	Jitō	BA/10/2	383	486	1
			3/2/26	391	494	1
			3/6/2	392	498	1
			7/6/4	412	521	1
	Kose no Asomi Umakahi	Tenmu	14/10/12	372	472	1
GR91	Kashihade no Omi	Kinmei	31/5/0	88	128	3
		Tenmu	13/11/1	366	465	1
	Kashihade no Omi Hasuhi	Kinmei	6/3/0	59	92	1
			6/11/0	60	93	1
	Kashihade no Omi Hatsumi	Saimei	2/9/0	250	328	1
	Kashihade no Omi Katabu	Sushun	BA/7/0	113	162	1
	Kashihade no Omi Katabuko	Kinmei	31/5/0	88	128	1
	Kashihade no Omi Maro	Tenmu	11/7/9	356	452	1
			11/7/18	356	452	1

Appendix I   169

	[Kashihade no] Maro no Omi	Tenmu	11/7/21	356	453	1
	Kashihade no Omi Momoyori	Taika	2/3/19	214-5	288	1
	Kashihade no Omi Ohomaro	Ankan	1/4/1	27	49	2
	Kashihade no Omi Ohotomo	Suiko	18/10/8	141	194	1
GR92	Ki no Omi	Jomei	BA/9/0	159	218	1
			BA/9/0	161	222	1
		Taika	2/3/19	214	288	1
		Tenmu	13/11/1	366	465	1
	Ki no Omi Ahemaro	Tenmu	1/7/2	312	396	1
			1/7/9	314	399	1
			2/8/9	323	412	1
			3/2/28	325	414	1
	Ki no Omi Kasamaro	Tenmu	5/4/22	331	422	1
	Ki no Omi Katamaro	Tenmu	2/12/17	325	414	1
			8/2/3	340	434	1
	Ki no Marikita no Omi	Taika	2/3/19	214	288	1
			2/3/19	215	290	1
	Ki no Omi Maro	Taika	5/3/26	234	309	1
	Ki no Omi Ohoto	Tenmu	1/7/0	316	402	1
	Ki no Omi Shihote	Jomei	BA/9/0	158	218	1
	Ki no Ushi no Omi	Tenchi	10/1/5	294	375	1
			10/11/23	298	380	1
	Ki no Womaro no Sukune	Kinmei	23/7/0	83	122	2
		Sushun	BA/7/0	113	162	1
			4/11/4	119	170	1
	Ki no Omi Womaro Kida	Hakuchi	1/2/15	238	314	1
	Ki no Asomi Mahito	Shuchō	1/9/27	380	481	1
		Jitō	1/1/1	384	488	1
	Ki no Asomi Maro	Jitō	7/6/4	412	521	1
	Ki no Asomi Yumihari	Shuchō	1/9/28	381	482	1
		Jitō	6/3/3	406	513	1
GR93	Hata no Omi	Taika	2/3/19	215	289	1
	Hata no Omi	Tenmu	13/11/1	366	465	1
	Hata no Omi Hironiwa	Suiko	31/0/0	151	207	1
	Hata no Asomi Mugohe	Jitō	3/6/2	392	498	1
GR94	Mononobe no Muraji	Keitai	9/2/4 to 10/9/0	13-14	32-33	6
		Tenmu	13/11/1	366	465	1
	Mononobe no Chichi no Muraji	Keitai	9/2/4	13	32	1
	Mononobe no Ise no Muraji Chichine	Keitai	23/3/0	17	38	1
	Mononobe no Muraji Kuma	Tenchi	BA/8/0	275	352	1
	Mononobe no Muraji Maro	Tenmu	1/7/23	315	400	1
			5/10/10	335	426	1

			6/2/1	335	427	1
			10/12/29	353	450	1
	Mononobe no Niheko no Muraji	Bidatsu	12/0/0	98	144	1
	Mononobe no Yuge no Moriya no Muraji	Yōmei	BA/9/5	106	154	1
	Mononobe no Ohomuraji	Keitai	6/12/0	8	26	1
		Sushun	2/5/0	112	160	1
	Mononobe no Ohomuraji Arakahi	Keitai	6/12/0	8	26	1
			21/6/3	15	35	1
			22/11/11	16	36	1
		Senka	1/5/1	34	58	1
	Mononobe no Arakahi no Ohomuraji	Keitai	1/1/4	2	20	1
			1/2/4	4	22	1
			21/8/1	16	36	1
		Ankan	BA/2/0	26	48	1
		Senka	1/2/1	33	56	1
			1/7/0	35	58	1
	Mononobe no Moriya no Ohomuraji	Yōmei	1/5/0	108	156	1
			2/4/2	109-110	158	2
		Sushun	BA/7/0	113	162	1
			BA/7/0	115	164	2
	[Mononobe no] Moriya no Ohomuraji	Yōmei	1/5/0	108	156	1
	[Mononobe no] Niheko no Ohomuraji	Bidatsu	12/0/0	100	146	1
	Mononobe no Ohomuraji Wokoshi	Ankan	1/IC12/0	30-31	53	2
		Kinmei	1/9/5	39	65-66	2
			13/10/0	66-67	102	2
	Mononobe no Wokoshi no Ohomuraji	Kinmei	BA/12/5	38	64	1
	Mononobe no Yuge no Ohomuraji	Kōgyoku	2/10/6	181	249	1
	Mononobe no Yuge no Moriya no Ohomuraji	Bidatsu	1/4/0	90	132	1
			14/3/1	102	150	1
			14/3/30	103	150	1
			14/8/15	105	152	1
	[Mononobe no] Yuge no Moriya no Ohomuraji	Bidatsu	14/8/15	105	152	1
	[Mononobe]/Isonokami no Asomi Maro	Shuchō	1/9/28	380	482	1
		Jitō	3/9/10	394	500	1
			10/10/22	421	532	1
	Mononobe no Maro no Asomi	Jitō	4/1/1	395	500	1
GR95	Heguri no Omi	Taika	2/3/19	215	289	1
		Tenmu	13/11/1	366	465	1
	Heguri no Omi Kamute	Sushun	BA/7/0	113	162	1
	Heguri no Omi Kobito	Tenmu	10/3/17	350	446	1
	Heguri no Omi Ushi	Suiko	31/0/0	151	207	1

GR96	Sazakibe no Omi	Tenmu	13/11/1	366	465	1
GR97	Nakatomi no Muraji	Jomei	BA/9/0	159	218	1
			BA/9/0	161-2	222-24	3
		Tenmu	13/11/1	366	465	1
	Nakatomi no Ihare no Muraji	Bidatsu	14/6/0	104	152	1
	Nakatomi no Muraji Kamako	Kinmei	13/10/0	67	102	2
	Nakatomi no Kamako no Muraji	Kōgyoku	3/1/1	184-6	253-6	8
			4/6/12	191	262	3
			4/6/13	193	264	1
		Kōtoku	BA/6/14	195-7	268-70	4
	Nakatomi no Kamatari no Muraji	Hakuchi	5/1/5	245	321	1
	Nakatomi no Muraji Kane	Tenmu	1/8/25	319	406	2
	Nakatomi no Kane no Muraji	Tenchi	9/3/9	293	374	1
			10/1/5	294	374-5	2
			10/11/23	298	380	1
		Tenmu	BA/10/19	302	383	1
	Nakatomi no Katsumi no Muraji	Yōmei	2/4/2	109-10	158-9	2
	[Nakatomi no] Katsumi no Muraji	Yōmei	2/4/0	110	159	1
	Nakatomi no Kome no Muraji	Hakuchi	4/5/12	242-3	318	1
	Nakatomi no Muraji Kuni	Suiko	31/0/0	150-1	206	2
	Nakatomi no Muraji Mike	Jomei	BA/9/0	158	218	1
			BA/9/0	160	220	1
	Nakatomi no Muraji Mutsuki	Taika	2/3/19	215	289	1
	Nakatomi no Muraji Oshikuma	Taika	3/0/0	230	305	1
	Nakatomi no Muraji Ohoshima	Tenmu	10/3/17	350	446	1
			10/12/29	353	450	1
			12/12/13	361	460	1
	Nakatomi no Miyadokoro no Muraji Womaro	Suiko	16/6/15	136-7	190	1
			20/2/20	143	196	1
	Nakatomi no Asomi Ohoshima	Jitō	5/11/24	404	512	1
	[Nakatomi]/Fujihara no Asomi Ohoshima	Tenmu	14/9/18	371	472	1
		Shuchō	1/1/0	375	475	1
			1/9/28	381	482	1
		Jitō	1/8/28	386	490	1
			2/3/21	388	492	1
			7/3/11	411	520	1
	Nakatomi no Ohoshima no Asomi	Jitō	4/1/1	395	500	1
	Nakatomi no Asomi Omimaro	Jitō	BA/10/2	383	486	1
			3/2/26	391	494	1
	[Nakatomi]/Fujihara no Asomi Omimaro	Jitō	7/6/4	412	521	1

	[Nakatomi]/Fujihara no Asomi Fubito	Jitō	3/2/26	390	494	1
	[Nakatomi]/Fujihara no Asomi Fubito	Jitō	10/10/22	421	532	1
GR98	Ohoyake no Omi	Tenmu	13/11/1	366	465	1
	Ohoyake no Omi Ikusa	Suiko	31/0/0	151	207	1
	Ohoyake no Omi Kamatsuka	Tenchi	2/3/0	279	357	1
	Ohoyake no Asomi Maro	Jitō	3/2/26	390	494	1
			8/3/2	414	524	1
GR99	Ahata no Omi	Tenmu	13/11/1	366	465	1
	Ahata no Omi Hosome	Kōgyoku	1/12/13	177	244	1
	Ahata no Hosome no Omi	Suiko	19/5/5	142	196	1
	Ahata no Omi Ihimushi	Hakuchi	1/2/15	238	314	1
	Ahata no Omi Mahito	Tenmu	10/12/29	353	450	1
	Ahata no Asomi Mahito	Tenmu	14/5/19	369	469	1
	Ahata no Mahito no Asomi	Jitō	3/1/9	390	494	1
			3/6/20	393	498	1
GR100	Ishikaha no Omi	Tenmu	13/11/1	366	465	1
	Ishikaha no Asomi Mushina	Tenmu	14/9/15	370	470	1
		Jitō	3/9/10	394	500	1
GR101	Sakurawi no Omi	Jomei	BA/9/0	159–62	219–23	6
		Tenmu	13/11/1	366	465	1
	Sakurawi no Omi Wajiko	Jomei	BA/9/0	158	218	1
GR102	Uneme no Omi	Jomei	BA/9/0	159	218	1
		Tenmu	13/11/1	366	465	1
	Uneme no Omi Mareshi	Jomei	BA/9/0	158	218	1
	Uneme no Omi Omimaro	Taika	5/3/25	234	308	1
	Uneme no Asomi Tsukura	Tenmu	14/9/18	371	472	1
		Shuchō	1/9/27	380	481	1
	Uneme no Omi Tsukura	Tenmu	10/7/4	351	447	1
			13/2/28	362	461	1
GR103	Tanaka no Omi	Suiko	31/0/0	150	206	2
		Tenmu	13/11/1	366	465	1
	Tanaka no Omi Kanuchi	Tenmu	10/12/29	353	450	1
	Tanaka no Omi Tarimaro	Tenmu	1/6/25	306	388	1
			1/7/2	312	396	1
	Tanaka no Asomi Norimaro	Jitō	1/1/19	385	488	1
			3/1/8	390	494	1
			3/5/22	391	496	1
			3/8/21	394	498	1
			5/7/3	403	510	1
GR104	Woharida no Omi	Jomei	BA/9/0	162	223	1
		Tenmu	13/11/1	366	465	1
	Woharida no Omi Maro	Tenmu	10/7/4	351	447	1
			11/5/16	355	452	1

Appendix I   173

GR105	Hozumi no Omi	Suiko	8/0/0	124	176	1
		Tenmu	13/11/1	366	465	1
	Hozumi no Ihayumi no Omi	Kinmei	16/7/4	77	116	1
	Hozumi no Omi Ihoe	Tenmu	1/6/29	311	396	1
	Hozumi no Omi Kuhi	Taika	2/3/19	213	287	1
	Hozumi no Omi Kuhi	Taika	5/3/26	234	309	2
	Hozumi no Kuhi no Omi	Taika	2/3/19	215	290	1
	Hozumi no Kuhi no Omi	Taika	5/3/24	232-3	307	2
	Hozumi no Omi Momotari	Tenmu	1/6/26	308	390	1
			1/6/29	311	395	2
	Hozumi no Omi Oshiyama	Keitai	6/4/6	7	26	1
			6/12/0	7,9	26,28	2
			7/6/0	9	28	1
	Hozumi no Oshiyama no Omi	Keitai	23/3/0	17	37	1
	[Hozumi no] Oshiyama no Omi	Keitai	23/3/0	17	37	1
	Hozumi no Asomi Mushimaro	Shuchō	1/1/0	375	475	1
			1/9/29	381	482	1
	Hozumi no Asomi Yamamori	Jitō	3/2/26	390	494	1
GR106	Yamashiro no Omi	Tenmu	13/11/1	366	465	1
	Yamashiro no Omi Hitate	Suiko	10/10/0	126	178	1
GR107	Kamo no Kimi	Tenmu	13/11/1	366	465	1
	Kamo no Kimi Emishi	Tenmu	1/6/29	311-2	396	1
			1/7/23	315	401	1
	Kamo no Asomi Emishi	Jitō	9/4/17	418	528	1
GR108	Wono no Omi	Tenmu	13/11/1	366	465	1
	Wono no Omi Imoko	Suiko	15/7/3	136	189	1
			16/4/0	136	189	1
			17/9/0	140	194	1
	Wono no Imoko no Omi	Suiko	16/9/11	139	192	1
	[Wono no] Imoko no Omi	Suiko	16/4/0	136	189-90	2
			16/6/15	137	190	1
	Wono no Asomi Keno	Jitō	9/7/26	419	528	1
			9/9/6	419	528	1
GR109	Kahahe no Omi	Kinmei	23/7/0	84	123-4	4
		Suiko	26/0/0	147	202	4
		Jomei	BA/9/0	159	218	1
			BA/9/0	161-2	222-3	2
		Tenmu	13/11/1	366	465	1
	Kahahe no Omi Ihatsutsu	Taika	2/3/19	214	288	1
	Kahahe no Omi Kobito	Tenmu	10/12/10	353	450	1
	Kahahe no Omi Maro	Hakuchi	5/2/0	245	321	1
		Saimei	1/8/1	249	327	1
	Kahahe no Omi Momoe	Tenmu	6/10/14	337	429	1

	Kahahe no Momoe no Omi	Tenchi	BA/8/0	275	352	1
	Kahahe no Omi Momoyori	Taika	2/3/19	214-5	288	1
	Kahahe no Omi Nezu	Suiko	31/0/0	151	206	1
	Kahahe no Omi Nihe	Kinmei	23/7/0	83-4	122-4	4
	Kahahe no Omi Shihatsu	Taika	2/3/19	214	288	1
	Kahahe no Omi Yumaro	Taika	2/3/19	215	288	1
GR110	Ichiwi no Omi	Tenmu	13/11/1	366	465	1
GR111	Kakinomoto no Omi	Tenmu	13/11/1	366	465	1
	Kakinomoto no Omi Saru	Tenmu	10/12/29	353	450	1
GR112	Karube no Omi	Tenmu	13/11/1	366	465	1
	Karube no Asomi Taruse	Tenmu	14/10/10	372	472	1
GR113	Wakasakurabe no Omi	Tenmu	13/11/1	366	465	1
	Wakasakurabe no Omi Ihose	Tenmu	1/6/24	305	387	1
			1/6/26	307	390	1
	Wakasakurabe no Asomi Ihose	Tenmu	10/9/15	421	531	1
GR114	Kishita no Omi	Taika	2/3/19	215	289	1
		Tenmu	13/11/1	366	465	1
	Kishita no Omi Maro	Tenchi	BA/0/0	276	354	1
GR115	Takamuku no Omi	Jomei	BA/9/0	159	218	1
		Tenmu	13/11/1	366	465	1
	Takamuku no Omi Kunioshi	Kōgyoku	2/11/0	182	251	1
			4/6/12	193	264	1
	Takamuku no Omi Maro	Tenmu	10/12/29	353	450	1
			13/4/20	363	462	1
	Takamuku no Omi Uma	Jomei	BA/9/0	158	218	1
	Takamuku no Asomi Maro	Tenmu	14/5/26	369	469	1
GR116	Shishihito no Omi	Tenmu	13/11/1	366	465	1
	Shishihito no Omi Kari	Sushun	2/7/1	118	168	1
	Shishihito no Omi Ohomaro	Tenmu	2/2/27	322	410	1
GR117	Kume no Omi	Taika	1/8/8	203	277	1
		Tenmu	13/11/1	366	465	1
	Kume no Omi Shihoko	Tenmu	1/7/23	316	402	1
GR118	Inukami no Kimi	Suiko	22/9/0	146	200	1
		Tenchi	2/5/1	279	358	1
		Tenmu	13/11/1	366	465	1
	Inukami no Kimi Mitasuki	Suiko	22/6/13	145	200	1
			23/9/0	145	200	1
		Jomei	2/8/5	165	228	1
	Inukami no Kimi Shiromaro	Saimei	2/9/0	250	328	1
	Inukami no Takebe no Kimi	Kōtoku	BA/6/14	196	270	1
GR119	Kamitsukeno no Kimi	Tenmu	13/11/1	366	465	1

Appendix I

	Kamitsukeno no Kimi Katana	Jomei	9/0/0	168	232	1
	Kamitsukeno no Kimi Michiji	Tenmu	10/3/17	350	446	1
			10/8/11	352	448	1
	Kamitsukeno no Kimi Wakako	Tenchi	2/3/0	278	357	1
			2/6/0	279	358	1
	Kamitsukeno no Kimi Wokuma	Ankan	1/IC12/0	31	54	1
GR120	Tsuno no Omi	Tenmu	13/11/1	366	465	1
	Tsuno no Omi Ushikahi	Tenmu	13/4/20	363	462	1
	Tsuno no Asomi Ushikahi	Tenmu	14/5/26	369	469	1
			14/9/15	370	470	1
GR121	Hoshikaha no Omi	Tenmu	13/11/1	366	465	1
	Hoshikaha no Omi Maro	Tenmu	9/5/27	346	441	1
GR122	Oho no Omi	Tenmu	13/11/1	366	465	1
	Oho no Omi Homuji	Tenmu	1/6/22	304	386	1
			1/7/2	312	396	2
			1/7/6	313	398	1
			12/12/13	361	460	1
		Jitō	10/8/25	421	530	1
	Oho no Omi Komoshiki	Tenchi	BA/9/0	275	353	1
	Oho no Asomi Homuji	Tenmu	14/9/18	371	472	1
GR123	Munakata no Kimi	Tenmu	13/11/1	366	465	1
	Munakata no Kimi Tokuzen	Tenmu	2/2/27	322	410	1
GR124	Kurumamochi no Kimi	Tenmu	13/11/1	366	465	1
GR125	Aya no Kimi	Tenmu	13/11/1	366	465	1
GR126	Shimotsumichi no Omi	Tenmu	13/11/1	366	465	1
GR127	Iga no Omi	Senka	1/5/1	34	58	1
		Kinmei	5/2/0	51	82	2
		Tenmu	13/11/1	366	465	1
GR128	Ahe no Omi	Tenmu	13/11/1	366	465	1
	Ahe no Omi Ohoko	Suiko	18/10/9	141	194	1
GR129	Hayashi no Omi	Tenmu	13/11/1	366	465	1
GR130	Hami no Omi	Tenmu	13/11/1	366	465	1
GR131	Shimotsukeno no Kimi	Tenmu	13/11/1	366	465	1
	Shimotsukeno no Asomi Komaro	Jitō	3/10/22	395	500	1
GR132	Sami no Kimi	Tenmu	13/11/1	366	466	1
	Sami no Kimi Sukunamaro	Tenmu	1/6/29	311	396	1
			1/7/23	315	401	1
	Sami no Asomi Sukunamaro	Tenmu	14/9/15	370	470	1
		Jitō	3/6/2	392	498	1
GR133	Chimori no Omi	Tenmu	13/11/1	366	466	1
	Chimori no Omi Maro	Tenchi	7/11/5	290	370	1

GR134	Ohono no Kimi	Tenmu	13/11/1	366	466	1
	Ohono no Kimi Hatayasu	Tenmu	1/7/4	313	398	1
GR135	Sakamoto no Omi	Kinmei	23/7/0	84	124	1
		Tenmu	13/11/1	366	466	1
	Sakamoto no Omi Arate	Sushun	BA/7/0	113	162	1
		Suiko	9/3/5	125	177	1
			10/6/3	126	178	1
	Sakamoto no Arate no Omi	Suiko	18/10/9	141	194	1
	Sakamoto no Omi Takara	Tenmu	1/7/23	315	401	2
	Sakamoto no Takara no Omi	Tenmu	2/5/29	323	412	1
GR136	Ikeda no Kimi	Tenmu	13/11/1	366	466	1
GR137	Tamate no Omi	Tenmu	13/11/1	366	466	1
GR138	Kasa no Omi	Tenmu	13/11/1	366	466	1
	Kasa no Omi Moroiha	Tenchi	6/11/13	286	366	1
GR139	Ohotomo no Muraji	Suiko	31/0/0	151	207	1
		Jomei	BA/9/0	158-9	218	2
			BA/9/0	161-2	222-3	2
		Taika	5/3/25	234	308	1
		Tenmu	13/12/2	367	466	1
	Ohotomo no Arate no Muraji	Sushun	1/3/0	117	167	1
	Ohotomo no Arateko no Muraji	Bidatsu	12/0/0	98,100	144,146	3
	[Ohotomo no] Arateko no Muraji	Bidatsu	12/0/0	100	146	1
	Ohotomo no Muraji Fukehi	Tenmu	1/6/29	310-11	394-5	2
			1/7/9	314	399	1
	Ohotomo no Hirabu no Muraji	Yōmei	2/4/2	111	160	1
	[Ohotomo no] Hirabu no Muraji	Yōmei	2/4/2	111	160	1
	Ohotomo no Koma no Muraji	Taika	5/3/24	232	307	1
			5/3/25	234	308	1
	Ohotomo no Muraji Kuhi	Sushun	BA/7/0	113	162	1
		Suiko	9/3/5	125	177	1
	Ohotomo no Kuhi no Muraji	Suiko	18/10/9	141	194	1
	Ohotomo no Kuhi no Muraji	Sushun	4/11/4	119	170	1
		Suiko	16/8/12	138	192	1
	Ohotomo no Kujira no Muraji	Jomei	BA/9/0	158	217	1
	Ohotomo no Muraji Kunimaro	Tenmu	4/7/7	329	420	1
			5/2/0	331	422	1
	Ohotomo no Muraji Maguta	Tenmu	1/6/24	305	387	1
			1/6/26	309	392	1
			12/6/3	360	458	1
	Ohotomo no Muraji Miyuki	Tenmu	4/3/16	327	418	1

Appendix I

Ohotomo no Moriya no Muraji	Tenmu	8/6/26	342	436	1
Ohotomo no Enomoto no Muraji Ohokuni	Tenmu	1/6/24	305	388	1
Ohotomo no Muraji Sadehiko	Kinmei	23/8/0	86	126	1
Ohotomo no Sadehiko no Muraji	Kinmei	23/8/0	86	126	1
	Sushun	3/0/0	118	168	1
Ohotomo no Muraji Tomokuni	Tenmu	1/6/24	305	387	1
Ohotomo no Nagatoko (Umakahi) no Muraji	Kōtoku	1/6/14	196	270	1
Ohotomo no Nagatoko no Muraji (Umakahi)	Taika	5/4/20	235	311	1
Ohotomo no Muraji Umakahi	Jomei	4/10/4	166	229	1
	Kōgyoku	1/12/13	177	244	1
Ohotomo no Umakahi no Muraji	Kōgyoku	3/6/1	186	256	1
Ohotomo no Muraji Wofukehi	Tenmu	12/8/5	360	458	1
Ohotomo no Muraji Yasumaro	Tenmu	1/6/29	311	396	1
		13/2/28	362	460	1
Ohotomo no Ohomuraji	Keitai	1/2/4	3	21	2
		1/2/10	4	22	1
		6/12/0	9	28	1
		21/6/3	15	35	1
		23/4/7	19	40	1
	Ankan	BA/2/0	26	48	1
		1/IC12/4	29-30	52-3	3
Ohotomo no Ohomuraji Kanamura	Keitai	6/12/0	8	26	1
		21/6/3	15	35	1
		23/4/7	19	39	1
	Ankan	1/10/15	28-9	50-2	3
		1/IC12/4	29	52	1
	Kinmei	1/9/5	39	65-6	2
Ohotomo no Kanamura no Ohomuraji	Keitai	BA/12/21	2	18	1
		1/1/4	2	20	1
		1/2/4	3-4	22	1
	Senka	1/2/1	33	56	1
		2/10/1	35	59	1
	Kinmei	BA/12/5	38	64	1
	Bidatsu	12/0/0	98	144	1
Ohotomo no Ohomuraji Muroya	Keitai	1/2/10	4	22	1
Ohotomo no Sukune Kokimi	Jitō	7/3/16	411	520	1
Ohotomo no Sukune Miyuki	Tenmu	14/9/18	371	471	1
	Jitō	2/11/11	389	493	1
		8/1/2	414	523	1
		10/10/22	421	531	1
Ohotomo no Miyuki no Sukune	Jitō	5/1/13	401	508	1

	Ohotomo no Sukune Teuchi	Jitō	3/6/2	392	498	1
	Ohotomo no Sukune Tomokuni	Jitō	6/4/2	407	514	1
	Ohotomo no Sukune Yasumaro	Shuchō	1/1/0	375	475	1
			1/9/28	380	482	1
		Jitō	2/8/10	388	492	1
GR140	Saheki no Muraji	Kinmei	15/1/9	71	108	1
			17/1/0	78	116	1
		Bidatsu	13/9/0	101	148	1
		Tenmu	13/12/2	367	466	1
	Saheki no Muraji Azumahito	Jomei	BA/9/0	158	218	1
	Saheki no Muraji Hirotari	Tenmu	4/4/10	328	418	1
			10/7/4	351	447	1
			11/5/16	355	452	1
	Saheki no Muraji Komaro	Kōgyoku	3/1/0	186	256	1
			4/6/12	191-2	262-3	2
			4/6/13	194	265	1
	Saheki no Komaro no Muraji	Tenchi	5/3/0	284	364	1
	Saheki no Muraji Nifute	Sushun	BA/6/7	112	161	2
	Saheki no Muraji Ohome	Tenmu	1/6/24	305	387	1
	Saheki no Muraji Takunaha	Saimei	2/0/0	251	329	1
	Saheki no Muraji Wotoko	Tenmu	1/6/26	308	390	1
	Saheki no Sukune Hirotari	Tenmu	14/9/15	371	470	1
	Saheki no Sukune Ohome	Jitō	5/9/23	404	510	1
GR141	Azumi no Muraji	Suiko	31/11/0	152	208	1
			32/4/17	153	210	1
			32/10/1	154	210	1
		Taika	2/3/19	214	288	1
		Tenmu	13/12/2	367	466	1
	Azumi no Yamashiro no Muraji Hirabu	Kōgyoku	1/2/2	172	237	1
	Azumi no Yamashiro no Muraji [Hirabu]	Kōgyoku	1/2/24	173	238	1
	Azumi no [Yamashiro] Muraji Hirabu	Kōgyoku	1/1/29	171	236	1
	Azumi no Hirabu no Muraji	Tenchi	BA/8/0	275	352	1
			1/5/0	277	355	1
	Azumi no Muraji Inashiki	Tenmu	1/3/18	302	384	1
			10/3/17	350	446	1
	Azumi no Muraji Tsuratari	Saimei	3/0/0	252	330	1
			4/0/0	259	336	1
		Tenchi	9/9/1	294	374	1
GR142	Imibe no Muraji	Tenmu	13/12/2	367	466	1
	Imibe no Obito Kobito	Tenmu	1/7/3	313	398	1
			9/1/8	345	439	1
	Imibe no Obito Komaro	Taika	1/7/14	200	272	1

	Imibe no Muraji Obito	Tenmu	10/3/17	350	446	1
	Imibe no Sukune Shikobuchi	Jitō	4/1/1	395	500	1
GR143	Wohari no Muraji	Senka	1/5/1	34	58	1
		Tenmu	13/12/2	367	466	1
	Wohari no Muraji Kusaka	Keitai	1/3/14	5	24	1
	Wohari no Sukune Ohosumi	Jitō	10/5/8	420	530	1
GR144	Kura no Muraji	Tenmu	13/12/2	367	466	1
GR145	Nakatomi no Sakahito no Muraji	Tenmu	13/12/2	367	466	1
GR146	Haji no Muraji	Tenmu	13/12/2	367	466	1
	Haji no Muraji Chishima	Tenmu	1/7/13	314	400	1
	Haji no Muraji Hodo	Jitō	4/10/22	400	506	1
	Haji no Muraji Ihamura	Sushun	BA/6/7	112	161	1
	Haji no Muraji Mashiki	Tenmu	11/3/0	355	452	1
	Haji no Muraji Mu	Taika	5/3/24	234	308	1
	Haji no Sukune Nemaro	Jitō	3/2/26	390	494	1
			3/5/22	391	496	1
	Haji no Muraji Umate	Tenmu	1/6/24	305	388	1
			1/6/26	307	390	1
	Haji no Muraji Usagi	Suiko	18/10/9	141	194	1
	Haji no Saba no Muraji	Kōgyoku	2/11/1	181-2	250	2
	[Haji no] Saba no Muraji	Suiko	11/2/4	127	179	1
	Haji no Saba no Muraji Wite	Kōgyoku	2/9/17	180	248	1
	Haji no Muraji Wite	Suiko	11/2/4	126	179	1
	[Haji no] Wite no Muraji	Suiko	11/2/4	127	179	1
	Haji no Sukune Wohi	Tenmu	13/12/6	367	467	1
		Jitō	4/10/15	399	505	1
	Haji no Yashima no Muraji	Yōmei	2/4/0	111	160	1
	Haji no Muraji Yatsute	Hakuchi	4/5/12	244	319	1
GR147	Kanimori no Muraji	Tenmu	13/12/2	367	466	1
	Kanimori no Muraji Tsunomaro	Taika	5/5/1	236	311	1
	Kanimori no Muraji Womaro	Hakuchi	4/5/12	244	319	1
GR148	Sakahibe no Muraji	Tenmu	13/12/2	367	466	1
	Sakahibe no Muraji Ihasuki	Saimei	2/9/0	250	328	1
	Sakahibe no Muraji Ihashiki	Saimei	5/7/3	260	338	1
	Sakahibe no Ihashiki no Muraji	Saimei	5/7/3	260	338	1
	[Sakahibe no] Ihashiki no Muraji	Saimei	5/7/3	261	338	1

	Sakahibe no Muraji Ihatsumi	Hakuchi Tenchi	4/5/12 4/0/0 6/11/9	244 284 286	319 364 366	1 1 1
		Tenmu	10/1/11 11/3/13	349 354	444 450	1 1
	Sakahibe no Muraji Inatsumi	Saimei	5/7/3	261	338	1
	Sakahibe no Muraji Kusuri	Saimei	4/11/9 4/11/11	256 256	334 335	1 1
		Tenmu	1/7/7	314	399	1
	Sakahibe no Sukune Ihatsumi	Tenmu	14/9/18	371	471	1
	Sakahibe no Sukune Konoshiro	Shuchō	1/1/0	375	475	1
GR149	Sakurawi no Tabe no Muraji	Ankan Tenmu	2/9/3 13/12/2	32 367	55 466	1 1
	Sakurawi no Tabe no Muraji Inu	Sushun	BA/7/0	117	166	1
GR150	Ihokibe no Muraji	Tenmu	13/12/2	367	466	1
	Ihokibe no Muraji Kikoyu	Ankan	1/IC12/0	30	53	1
GR151	Kamunakibe no Muraji	Tenmu	13/12/2	367	466	1
GR152	Osakabe no Miyatsuko	Tenmu	12/9/23	361	548	1
	Osakabe no Miyatsuko Karakuni	Jitō	8/6/8	417	526	1
	Osakabe no Muraji	Tenmu	13/12/2	367	466	1
GR153	Kusakabe no Muraji	Tenmu	13/12/2	367	466	1
	Kusakabe no Muraji Shikobu	Hakuchi	1/2/9 1/2/15	236 239-40	312 316	1 1
GR154	Miyake no Kishi	Tenmu	12/10/5	361	459	1
	Miyake no Kishi Irishi	Tenmu	4/7/7	329	420	1
	Miyake no Muraji	Tenmu	13/12/2	367	466	1
	Miyake no Muraji Ihatoko	Tenmu	1/6/25 9/7/23	306 347	388 442	1 1
GR155	Kobe no Muraji	Tenmu	13/12/2	367	466	1
GR156	Tasuki no Tajihi no Muraji	Tenmu	13/12/2	367	466	1
GR157	Yuki no Tajihi no Muraji	Tenmu	13/12/2	367	466	1
GR158	Nuribe no Miyatsuko Ani	Yōmei	2/4/0	110-11	159	1
	Nuribe no Muraji	Tenmu	13/12/2	367	466	1
GR159	Ohoyuwe no Muraji	Tenmu	13/12/2	367	466	1
GR160	Wakayuwe no Muraji	Tenmu	13/12/2	367	466	1
GR161	Yuge no Muraji	Tenmu	13/12/2	367	466	1
GR162	Kamuhatori no Muraji	Tenmu	13/12/2	367	466	1
GR163	Nukatabe no Muraji	Kinmei Tenmu	22/0/0 13/12/2	79 367	118 466	1 1

Appendix I   181

	Nukatabe no Muraji Hirabu	Suiko	16/8/3	137	190	1
			18/10/8	141	194	1
	Nukatabe no Hirabu no Muraji	Suiko	19/5/5	142	196	1
	Nukatabe no Muraji Ohi	Taika	1/8/8	203	277	1
	Nukatabe no Yuwe no Muraji	Taika	5/3/30	234	310	1
GR164	Tsumori no Muraji	Kinmei	4/11/8	48	76	1
			5/2/0	49-51	79-82	5
			5/3/0	53	84	2
			5/11/0	56	88	1
		Tenmu	13/12/2	367	466	1
	Tsumori no Muraji Kisa	Saimei	5/7/3	260	338	1
	Tsumori no Kisa no Muraji	Saimei	5/7/3	260	338	1
	[Tsumori no] Kisa no Muraji	Saimei	5/7/3	261	338	1
	Tsumori no Muraji Ohoama	Kōgyoku	1/2/22	173	238	1
GR165	Agata no Inukahi no Muraji	Ankan	2/9/3	32	55	1
		Tenmu	13/12/2	367	466	1
	Agata no Inukahi no Muraji Ohotomo	Tenmu	1/6/24	305	386-7	2
	[Agata no] Inukahi no Muraji Ohotomo	Tenmu	9/7/5	347	442	1
	Agata no Inukahi no Muraji Tasuki	Tenmu	13/10/3	365	464	1
	Agata no Inukahi no Sukune Ohotomo	Tenmu	14/9/18	371	471	1
		Shuchō	1/9/27	380	481	1
GR166	Wakainukahi no Muraji	Tenmu	13/12/2	367	466	1
	Wakainukahi no Muraji Amita	Kōgyoku	4/6/12	192	263	1
			4/6/13	194	265	1
	Kazuraki no Wakainukahi no Muraji Amita	Kōgyoku	3/1/0	186	256	1
			4/6/12	191	262	1
GR167	Tamanoya no Muraji	Tenmu	13/12/2	367	466	1
GR168	Nihitabe no Muraji	Tenmu	13/12/2	367	466	1
	Nihitabe no Muraji Komemaro	Saimei	4/11/11	256	334	2
GR169	Shitsuori no Muraji	Tenmu	13/12/2	367	466	1
GR170	Hi no Muraji	Tenmu	13/12/2	367	466	1
	Hi no Muraji Okina	Hakuchi	4/5/12	244	318	1
			5/2/0	246	322	1
	Hi no Muraji Oyu	Jitō	4/10/22	400	506	1
GR171	Ohoshiama no Muraji	Tenmu	13/12/2	367	466	1
	Ohoshiama no Sukune Arakama	Shuchō	1/9/27	380	481	1
GR172	Yamabe no Muraji	Tenmu	13/12/2	367	466	1
GR173	Yatsume no Muraji	Tenmu	13/12/2	367	466	1

GR174	Sawi no Muraji	Tenchi	1/12/1	277	356	1
		Tenmu	13/12/2	367	466	1
	Sawi no Muraji Ajimasa	Tenchi	BA/8-9/0	275	352-3	2
GR175	Hatakumi no Muraji	Tenmu	13/12/2	367	466	1
GR176	Ato no Muraji	Tenmu	13/12/2	367	466	1
	Ato no Muraji Akafu	Tenmu	1/6/26	307	390	1
	Ato no Muraji Chitoko	Tenmu	1/6/24	305	387	1
	Ato no Muraji Kusuri	Shuchō	1/1/14	374	474	1
GR177	Mamuta no Muraji	Tenmu	13/12/2	367	466	1
	Mamuta no Muraji Womochi	Keitai	1/3/14	6	24	1
GR178	Tame no Muraji	Kōgyoku	2/11/1	182	250	1
		Tenmu	13/12/2	367	466	1
GR179	Chihisakobe no Muraji	Tenmu	13/12/2	367	466	1
	Chihisakobe no Muraji Sahichi	Tenmu	1/6/27	309	393	1
			1/8/25	319	406	1
GR180	Uji no Muraji	Tenmu	13/12/2	367	466	1
GR181	Woharida no Muraji	Tenmu	13/12/2	Lacking	466	1
GR182	Witsukahi no Muraji	Tenmu	13/12/2	367	466	1
	Witsukahi no Muraji Kobito	Tenmu	13/12/6	367	467	1
GR183	Ama no Inukahi no Muraji	Tenmu	13/12/2	367	466	1
	Ama no Inukahi no Muraji Katsumaro	Kōgyoku	4/6/12	191	262	1
GR184	Hashihito no Muraji	Tenmu	13/12/2	367	466	1
	Hashihito no Muraji Miumaya	Saimei	3/0/0	252	330	1
	Hashihito no Muraji Ohofuta	Tenchi	2/3/0	278-9	357	1
		Tenmu	4/4/10	328	418	1
	Hashihito no Muraji Shihofuta	Suiko	18/10/9	141	194	1
GR185	Tsukiyone no Muraji	Tenmu	13/12/2	367	466	1
GR186	Mino no Yatsume no Muraji	Tenmu	13/12/2	367	466	1
GR187	Moroahi no Omi	Tenmu	13/12/2	367	466	1
GR188	Furu no Muraji	Tenmu	13/12/2	367	466	1
	Mononobe no Obito	Tenmu	12/9/23	361	458	1
	Mononobe no Obito Himuka	Tenmu	1/6/26	308	390	1
			1/6/29	311	396	1
GR189	Yamato no Atahi	Tenmu	12/9/23	361	458	1
	Yamato no Atahi Tatsumaro	Tenmu	10/4/12	351	446	1
	Yamato no Kuni no Miyatsuko Tehiko	Kinmei	23/7/0	84	123	1
	Yamato no Muraji	Tenmu	14/6/20	369	470	1
GR190	Kazuraki no Atahi	Kinmei	22/0/0	79	118	1
		Tenmu	12/9/23	361	458	1

	Kazuraki no Atahi Ihamura	Yōmei	1/1/1	107	156	1
	Kazuraki no Atahi Naniha	Kinmei	31/4/0	88	128	1
	Kazuraki no Yamada no Atahi Mitsuko	Kinmei	17/7/6	78	117	1
	Kazuraki no Muraji	Tenmu	14/6/20	369	470	1
GR191	Ohoshi Kafuchi no Atahi	Tenmu	12/9/23	361	458	1
	Ohoshi Kafuchi no Atahi Ajihari	Ankan	1/7/1 1/12/4	28 30	50 52	1 1
	Ohoshi Kafuchi no Atahi Arate	Suiko	16/6/15	137	190	1
	Ohoshi Kafuchi no Atahi Yafushi	Kinmei	4/10/4	166	230	1
	Ohoshi Kafuchi no Muraji	Tenmu	14/6/20	370	470	1
GR192	Yamashiro no Atahi	Tenmu	12/9/23	361	458	1
	Yamashiro no Atahi Momotari	Tenmu	5/10/10	335	426	1
	Yamashiro no Atahi Wobayashi	Tenmu	1/6/24	305	387	1
	Yamashiro no Muraji	Tenmu	14/6/20	370	470	1
GR193	[Naniha no]/Kusakabe no Kishi	Tenmu	12/10/5	361	459	1
	[Naniha no]/Kusakabe no Kishi Ihakane	Kōgyoku	1/2/2	172	237	1
	[Naniha no]/Kusakabe no Kishi Mato	Kōgyoku	1/2/22	173	238	1
	[Naniha no]/Kusakabe no Kishi Ohokata	Tenmu	10/1/7	349	444	1
	Naniha no Kishi	Ankan	2/9/3	32	55	1
	Naniha no Kishi Agura	Hakuchi	1/0/0	240	316	1
	[Naniha no] Hitaka no Kishi	Keitai	6/12/0	9	28	1
	Naniha no Kishi Ihakane	Suiko	6/4/0	124	175	1
	[Naniha no] Kishi no Ihakane	Suiko	5/11/22 31/0/0	124 151	175 206	1 2
	Naniha no Kishi Itabi	Bidatsu Suiko	13/2/8 8/0/0	101 125	147 176	1 1
	[Naniha no] Kishi no Itabi	Bidatsu Sushun	4/4/6 4/11/4	94 119	138 170	1 1
	[Naniha no] Kishi no Kane	Bidatsu	4/4/6	94	138	1
	[Naniha no] Kishi no Kane	Sushun	4/11/4	119	170	1
	Naniha no Kishi Kunikatsu	Saimei	2/0/0	251	329	1
	[Naniha no] Kunikatsu no Kishi Kuhina	Kōgyoku	1/2/22	173	238	1
	Naniha no Kishi Mitsuna	Tenmu	1/6/26	307	390	1

	Naniha no Kishi Miwa	Suiko	8/0/0	125	176	1
	Naniha no Kishi Muzashi	Jomei	BA/9/0	158	218	1
	Naniha no Kishi Tokomaro	Suiko	17/4/4	140	193	1
	Naniha no Kishi Wohito	Saimei	5/7/3	263	340	1
	Naniha no Kishi Wonari	Suiko	16/4/0	136	190	1
	[Naniha no] Kishi no Wonari	Suiko	16/9/11	139	192	1
	Naniha no Kishi Wotsuki	Jomei	4/10/4	166	230	1
	Naniha no Kishi Yatsushi	Jomei	4/10/4	166	230	1
	Naniha no Muraji	Tenmu	10/1/7	349	444	1
			14/6/20	370	470	1
	Naniha no Muraji Ohokata	Tenmu	10/3/17	350	446	1
GR194	Ki no Sakahito no Atahi	Tenmu	12/10/5	361	459	1
	Ki no Sakahito no Muraji	Tenmu	14/6/20	370	470	1
GR195 (a)	Yamato no Aya no Atahi					
	Yamato no Aya no Atahi	Tenmu	6/6/0	336	428	1
			11/5/12	355	452	1
			11/5/27	355	452	1
	[Yamato no] Aya no Atahi	Kōgyoku	3/11/0	190	260	1
			4/6/12	192-3	264	2
		Tenmu	1/6/29	310	394	1
			6/6/0	337	428	1
	Yamato no Aya no Atahi Fukuin	Suiko	16/9/11	139	192	1
	Yamato no Aya no Atahi Ihawi	Sushun	5/11/3	119	170	1
	Yamato no Aya no Atahi Koma	Sushun	5/11/3	119	170	2
			5/11/0	120	171	1
	Yamato no Aya no Muraji	Tenmu	14/6/20	370	470	1
GR195 (b)	Yamato no Aya no Aratawi					
	Yamato no Aya no Atahi Aratawi no Hirabu	Taika	3/0/0	228	302	1
	Yamato no Aya no Atahi [Aratawi] Hirabu	Taika	1/7/14	199	272	1
	[Yamato no Aya no] Aratawi no Atahi Hirabu	Hakuchi	1/10/0	240	316	1
GR195 (c)	Yamato no Aya no Fumi					
	Yamato no Aya no Fumi no Atahi Agata	Kōgyoku	1/2/2	172	237	1
	[Yamato no Aya] Fumi no Atahi Agata	Jomei	11/7/0	169	234	1
	Yamato no Aya no [Fumi no] Atahi Agata	Hakuchi	1/0/0	240	316	1
	[Yamato no Aya no] Fumi no Atahi Chitoko	Tenmu	1/6/24	305	387	1
			10/12/29	353-4	450	2

Appendix I

	[Yamato no Aya no] Fumi no Atahi Kusuri	Tenmu	1/6/26 1/6/27	308 309	390 393	1 1
	Yamato no Aya no Fumi no Atahi Maro	Taika	1/9/3	204	277	1
	[Yamato no Aya] Fumi no Atahi Maro	Hakuchi	5/2/0	245	322	2
	[Yamato no Aya no] Fumi no Imiki Chitoko	Jitō	6/5/20	408	515	1
GR195 (d)	Yamato no Aya no Kaya					
	[Yamato no Aya no] Kaya no Imiki Konoma	Jitō	7/9/16	413	522	1
	Yamato no Aya no Kaya no Atahi Tarishima	Saimei	7/5/23	272	350	1
GR195 (e)	Yamato no Aya no Kurakaki					
	[Yamato no Aya no] Kurakaki no Atahi Maro	Tenmu	1/7/23	315	401	1
GR195 (f)	Yamato no Aya no Ohokura					
	[Yamato no Aya no] Ohokura no Atahi Hirosumi	Tenmu	1/6/25	306	388	1
GR195 (g)	Yamato no Aya no Michi					
	[Yamato no Aya no] Michi Atahi Masuhito	Tenmu	1/6/24	307	389	1
GR195 (h)	Yamato no Aya no Naga					
	[Yamato no Aya no] Naga no Atahi	Kōgyoku	3/11/0	189	260	1
	Yamato no Aya no Naga no Atahi Arima	Saimei	5/7/3	261	338	1
GR195 (i)	Yamato no Aya no Oshisaka					
	[Yamato no Aya no] Oshisaka no Atahi	Kōgyoku	3/3/0	186	256	3
	[Yamato no Aya no] Oshisaka no Atahi Ohomaro	Tenmu	1/6/26 1/6/27	308 309	390 393	1 1
GR195 (j)	Yamato no Aya no Sakanouhe					
	Yamato no Aya no Sakanouhe no Atahi	Suiko	28/10/0	148	203	1
	Yamato no Aya no Sakanouhe no Atahi Komaro	Kinmei Bidatsu	31/7/0 1/6/0	88 92	129 134	1 1
	[Yamato no Aya no] Sakanouhe no Atahi Kumake	Tenmu	1/6/29	310	394	1
	[Yamato no Aya no] Sakanouhe no Atahi Kunimaro	Tenmu	1/6/25	306	388	1
	[Yamato no Aya no Sakanouhe] Ohohashira no Atahi	Suiko	28/10/0	148	203	1
	[Yamato no Aya no] Sakanouhe no Atahi Okina	Tenmu	1/6/29	311	396	1

GR195 (k)	Yamato no Aya no Tami					
	[Yamato no Aya no] Kahara no Tami no Atahi Miya	Kinmei	7/7/0	61	94	2
	Yamato no Aya no Uji [Tami?] no Atahi Arako	Kinmei	31/4/0	88	128	1
	[Yamato no Aya no] Tami no Atahi Ohohi	Tenmu	1/6/25	306	388	1
	[Yamato no Aya no] Tami no Atahi Woshibi	Tenmu	1/7/23	315	401	1
GR195 (l)	Yamato no Aya no Tani					
	[Yamato no Aya no] Tani no Atahi Nemaro	Tenmu	1/7/23	315	401	1
	[Yamato no Aya no] Tani no Atahi Shihote	Tenmu	1/7/23	315	400	1
GR195 (m)	Yamato no Aya no Tsuki					
	[Yamato no Aya no] Tsuki no Imiki Okina	Jitō	3/6/2	392	498	1
GR195 (n)	Yamato no Aya no Yamaguchi					
	[Yamato no] Aya no Yamaguchi no Atahi Ohokuchi	Hakuchi	1/0/0	240	316	1
GR196	Kafuchi no Aya no Atahi	Tenmu	12/9/23	361	458	1
	Kafuchi no Aya no Atahi Nihe	Suiko	18/10/17	141	195	1
	Kafuchi no Aya no Muraji	Tenmu	14/6/20	370	470	1
	Kafuchi no Imiki Tsura	Jitō	6/11/8	410	518	1
GR197	Hada no Miyatsuko	Tenmu	12/9/23	361	458	1
	Hada no Tomo no Miyatsuko	Kinmei	1/8/0	39	65	1
	Kadono no Hada no Miyatsuko Kahakatsu	Kōgyoku	3/7/0	189	258	1
	Hada no Miyatsuko Kahakatsu	Suiko	11/11/1 18/10/9	127 141	180 194	1 1
	Hada no Miyatsuko Kuma	Tenmu	1/6/29	311	395	1
	Hada no Ohokura no Miyatsuko Maro	Saimei	4/10/15	255	334	1
	Echi no Hada no Miyatsuko Takutsu	Taika	1/9/3	204	277-8	1
	Hada no Miyatsuko Takutsu	Tenchi	BA/8/0 BA/9/0	275 275	352 353	1 1
	Hada no Miyatsuko Tsunade	Tenmu Jitō	9/5/21 10/5/3	346 420	441 530	1 1
	Hada no Muraji	Tenmu	14/6/20	370	470	1
	Hada no Imiki Ihakatsu	Shuchō	1/8/13	379	480	1
GR198	Ohosumi no Atahi	Tenmu	14/6/20	370	470	1
GR199	Kafuchi no Fumi no Obito	Saimei	2/9/0	250	328	1

Appendix I 187

[Kafuchi no] Fumi no Obito	Tenmu	12/9/23	361	459	1
[Kafuchi no] Fumi no Obito Nemaro	Tenmu	1/6/24 1/7/2	305 312	387 396	1 1
[Kafuchi no] Fumi no Muraji	Tenmu	14/6/20	370	470	1
[Kafuchi no] Fumi no Imiki Akamaro	Jitō	9/4/17	418	528	1
[Kafuchi no] Fumi no Imiki Hakase	Jitō	9/3/23	418	527-8	1
GR200 Kuhahara no Suguri Katsu	Shuchō	1/4/8	375	476	1
Kuhahara no Muraji Hitotari	Tenmu	13/5/28	364	463	1
GR201 Tsukinomoto no Suguri Kachimaro	Shuchō	1/6/1	377	477	1
GR202 Hada no Miyatsuko Tsunade (Cf. GR197)					

Appendix II
INVENTORY AND DISTRIBUTION OF KABANE LISTED IN THE SHINSEN SHŌJIROKU

A. Table of Contents of SSJR

	No. of Uji	SSJR I	SSJR II
Presentation		p. 1	P. 141
Preface		p. 9	p. 144
Book I: Uji of Imperial Lineage (Kōbetsu)			
1. Left Capital (Sakyō)	30	p. 59	p. 149
2. Right Capital (Ukyō)	11	p. 92	p. 153
3. Yamashiro no Kuni	1	p. 108	p. 155
4. Yamato no Kuni	1	p. 108	p. 155
5. Settsu no Kuni	1	p. 109	p. 156
6. Left Capital, Upper	42	p. 111	p. 156
7. Left Capital, Lower	32	p. 219	p. 165
8. Right Capital, Upper	33	p. 293	p. 172
9. Right Capital, Lower	34	p. 331	p. 178
10. Yamashiro no Kuni	24	p. 433	p. 185
11. Yamato no Kuni	18	p. 451	p. 189
12. Settsu no Kuni	29	p. 475	p. 192
13. Kafuchi no Kuni	46	p. 491	p. 197
14. Izumi no Kuni	33	p. 516	p. 205
Book II: Uji of Deity Lineage (Shinbetsu)			
15. Left Capital, Upper	38	p. 537	p. 211
16. Left Capital, Middle	23	p. 617	p. 217
17. Left Capital, Lower	21	p. 677	p. 221
18. Right Capital, Upper	36	p. 722	p. 225
19. Right Capital, Lower	29	p. 799	p. 232
20. Yamashiro no Kuni	45	p. 849	p. 237
21. Yamato no Kuni	44	p. 897	p. 244
22. Settsu no Kuni	45	p. 987	p. 252

23. Kafuchi no Kuni	63	p. 1017	p. 259
24. Izumi no Kuni	60	p. 1061	p. 268

Book III: <u>Uji</u> of Non-Japanese Lineage (Shoban)

25. Left Capital, Upper	35	p. 1089	p. 279
26. Left Capital, Lower	37	p. 1125	p. 285
27. Right Capital, Upper	39	p. 1169	p. 291
28. Right Capital, Lower	63	p. 1210	p. 297
29. Yamashiro no Kuni	22	p. 1273	p. 306
30. Yamato no Kuni	26	p. 1290	p. 311
31. Settsu no Kuni	29	p. 1301	p. 315
32. Kafuchi no Kuni	55	p. 1314	p. 320
33. Izumi no Kuni	20	p. 1339	p. 329

Book III: Miscellaneous Names of Unauthenticated Lineage

34. Left Capital	11	p. 1349	p. 332
35. Right Capital	23	p. 1353	p. 334
36. Yamashiro no Kuni	11	p. 1364	p. 338
37. Yamato no Kuni	11	p. 1367	p. 340
38. Settsu no Kuni	14	p. 1371	p. 341
39. Kafuchi no Kuni	31	p. 1377	p. 343
40. Izumi no Kuni	16	p. 1394	p. 348

B. Distribution of <u>Uji</u> by <u>Kabane</u>* in the <u>SSJR</u>

Kabane	Book I Kōbetsu	Book II Shinbetsu	Book III Shoban	Book III Unauthenticated Lineages	Totals
1. mahito	44			4	48
2. asomi	79	19	10		108
3. sukune	12	55	25		92
4. imiki	1	6	41	2	50
5. omi**	47	12		4	63
6. kimi (kō)	41	3	9	9	62
7. zero	45	62	42	41	190
8. muraji	19	154	74	11	258
9. obito	24	29	18	22	93

*Listed in the order of their first appearance in the <u>SSJR</u>.

** 臣

10.	fubito	3		23	2	28
11.	abiko	1		2		3
12.	suguri (katsu)+	1	1	4	1	7
13.	agata-nushi	5	6		1	12
14.	kimi (kun)	3	1			4
15.	atahi	3	27	7	5	42
16.	miyatsuko	6	25	41	8	80
17.	hafuri	1	1		2	4
18.	kan-nushi		2			2
19.	omi***		1	4		5
20.	suguri++			17	5	22
21.	ohokimi			2		2
22.	wosa			4		4
23.	eshi			1		1
24.	kusushi				2	2
	Totals	335	404	326	117	1182

*** 使主
+ 勝
++ 村主

C. Distribution of Uji by Geographic Area in the SSJR

	Kōbetsu Book I	Shinbetsu Book II	Shoban Book III	Unauthenticated Lineage Book III	Totals
Left Capital (Sakyō)	104	82	72	11	269
Right Capital (Ukyō)	78	65	102	23	268
Yamashiro no Kuni	25	45	22	11	103
Yamato no Kuni	19	44	26	11	100
Settsu no Kuni	30	45	29	14	118
Kafuchi no Kuni	46	63	55	31	195
Izumi no Kuni	33	60	20	16	129
Totals	335	404	326	117	1182

Appendix II

TABLE I: CHRONOLOGICAL LISTING OF THE KABANE-RECIPIENT UJI
AND INDIVIDUALS DURING THE REIGN OF TENMU*

PART A: GRANTS OF MURAJI TO EIGHTEEN INDIVIDUALS
IN A.D. 680-681

Grant Number (GR)	Uji	Prior Kabane	Personal Name	Type of Lineage	NSK Reference Frequency	Kabane Later Granted to Uji Muraji	Sukune	Imiki
GR1	Imibe	Obito	Kobito	shinbetsu	Cf.		GR142	
GR2	Kusakabe	Kishi	Ohokata	shoban	Cf.	GR59		GR193
GR3	Nishikori	Miyatsuko	Wokida	shoban	Cf.	GR34		
GR4	Tawi	Atahi	Yoshimaro	shoban	1			
GR5	Sukita	Kurahito	Mukatari	shinbetsu	2			
GR6	[Sukita	Kurahito]	Ishikatsu	shinbetsu				
GR7	Kafuchi	Atahi	Agata	shoban	13			
GR8	Oshinumi	Miyatsuko	Kagami	shinbetsu				
GR9	[Oshinumi	Miyatsuko]	Arata	shinbetsu	Cf.	GR52		
GR10	[Oshinumi	Miyatsuko]	Yoshimaro	shinbetsu				
GR11	Ohokoma	Miyatsuko	Momoe	shoban	Cf.	GR39		
GR12	[Ohokoma	Miyatsuko]	Ashitsuki	shoban				
GR13	Yamato	Atahi	Tatsumaro	shinbetsu	Cf.	GR20		GR189
GR14	Kadobe	Atahi	Ohoshima	shinbetsu	Cf.	GR33		
GR15	Shishihito	Miyatsuko	Okina	lacking	1			
GR16	Yamashiro no Koma	Zero	Ikamaro	shoban	1			
GR17	Toneri	Miyatsuko	Nukamushi	shoban(?)	3			
GR18	Fumi	Atahi	Chitoko	shoban	Cf.	GR19		GR195

*Listed in sequence in which grants are noted in NSK.

PART B: GRANTS OF MURAJI TO FIFTY-FIVE UJI IN A.D. 682-684

Grant No.	Uji	Prior Kabane	Type of Lineage*	NSK Reference Frequency	Prior Kabane Grants	Kabane Later Granted Sukune	Imiki
GR19	Yamato no Aya	atahi	shoban	Cf.	GR18		GR195
GR20	Yamato	atahi	shinbetsu	Cf.	GR13		GR189
GR21	Kurukuma	obito	lacking	2			
GR22	Mohitori	miyatsuko	shinbetsu	1			
GR23	Yatabe	miyatsuko	shinbetsu	3			
GR24	Fujiharabe	miyatsuko	lacking	1			
GR25	Osakabe	miyatsuko	shinbetsu	Cf.		GR152	
GR26	Sakikusabe	miyatsuko	shinbetsu	1			
GR27	Ohoshi Kafuchi	atahi	shinbetsu	Cf.			GR191

GR28	Kafuchi no Aya	atahi	shoban	Cf.			GR196
GR29	Mononobe	obito	kōbetsu	Cf.		GR188	
GR30	Yamashiro	atahi	shinbetsu	Cf.			GR192
GR31	Kazuraki	atahi	shinbetsu	Cf.			GR190
GR32	Tonohatori	miyatsuko	lacking	1			
GR33	Kadobe	atahi	shinbetsu	2	GR14		
GR34	Nishikori	miyatsuko	shoban	5	GR3		
GR35	Kazura	miyatsuko	shoban	2			
GR36	Totori	miyatsuko	shinbetsu	1			
GR37	Kume no Toneri	miyatsuko	lacking	1			
GR38	Hinokuma no Toneri	miyatsuko	shinbetsu	1			
GR39	Ohokoma	miyatsuko	shoban	4	{ GR11		
GR40	Hada	miyatsuko	shoban	Cf.	GR12		GR197
GR41	Kahase no Toneri	miyatsuko	lacking	1			
GR42	Yamato no Umakahi	miyatsuko	lacking	4			
GR43	Kafuchi no Umakahi	miyatsuko	lacking	10			
GR44	Kifumi	miyatsuko	shoban	6			
GR45	Komotsume	miyatsuko	shinbetsu	1			
GR46	Magari no Hakozukuri	miyatsuko	lacking	1			
GR47	Isonokamibe	miyatsuko	lacking	1			
GR48	Takara no Himatsuri	miyatsuko	lacking	1			
GR49	Hazukashibe	miyatsuko	kōbetsu?	1			
GR50	Anahobe	miyatsuko	lacking	1			
GR51	Shirakabe	miyatsuko	shinbetsu	2	{ GR8		
GR52	Oshinumi	miyatsuko	shinbetsu	7	GR9		
GR53	Hatsukashi	miyatsuko	lacking	1	GR10		
GR54	Fumi	obito	shoban	Cf.			GR199
GR55	Wohatsuse	miyatsuko	kōbetsu	1			
GR56	Kudara	miyatsuko	shoban	1			
GR57	Katari	miyatsuko	shinbetsu	1			
GR58	Miyake	kishi	shoban	Cf.		GR154	
GR59	Kusakabe	kishi	shoban	Cf.	GR2		GR193
GR60	Hahaki	miyatsuko	lacking	1			
GR61	Fune	fubito	shoban	8			

Appendix II

GR62	Iki	fubito	shoban	13		
GR63	Sarara no Umakahi	miyatsuko	lacking	1		
GR64	Uno no Umakahi	miyatsuko	lacking	1		
GR65	Yoshino	obito	shinbetsu	1		
GR66	Ki no Sakahito	atahi	kōbetsu	Cf.		GR194
GR67	Uneme	miyatsuko	shinbetsu	1		
GR68	Atoki	fubito	shoban	1		
GR69	Takechi	agatanushi	shinbetsu	2		
GR70	Shiki	agatanushi	shinbetsu	1		
GR71	Kagami Tsukuri	miyatsuko	shinbetsu	1		
GR72	Mino	agatanushi	shinbetsu	1		
GR73	Kura no Kinunuhi	miyatsuko	lacking	2		

*Lineage per Ōta, Nihon jōdai shakai soshiki no kenkyū, p. 565-566.

PART C: GRANTS OF **MAHITO** TO THIRTEEN UJI IN A.D. 684

Grant No.	Uji	Prior Kabane	NSK Reference Frequency	Type of Lineage	Ancestor
GR74	Moriyama	kimi (kō)	1	kōbetsu	Bidatsu
GR75	Michi	kimi (kō)	4	kōbetsu	Bidatsu
GR76	Takahashi	kimi (kō)	1	kōbetsu	lacking
GR77	Mikuni	kimi (kō)	7	kōbetsu	Keitai
GR78	Tagima	kimi (kō)	12	kōbetsu	Yōmei
GR79	Umaraki	kimi (kō)	1	kōbetsu	lacking
GR80	Tajihi	kimi (kō)	13	kōbetsu	Senka
GR81	Wina	kimi (kō)	6	kōbetsu	Senka
GR82	Sakata	kimi (kō)	3	kōbetsu	Keitai
GR83	Hata	kimi (kō)	6	kōbetsu	Ōjin
GR84	Okinaga	kimi (kō)	4	kōbetsu	Ōjin
GR85	Sakahito	kimi (kō)	2	kōbetsu	Keitai
GR86	Yamaji	kimi (kō)	1	kōbetsu	Ōjin

PART D: GRANTS OF **ASOMI** TO FIFTY-TWO UJI IN A.D. 684

Grant No.	Uji	Prior Kabane	NSK Reference Frequency	Type of Lineage	Ancestor
GR87	Ohomiwa	kimi (kun)	32	shinbetsu	Susanowo

194   Ancient Japanese Nobility

GR88	Ohokasuga	omi	5	kōbetsu	Kōshō
GR89	Ahe	omi	56	kōbetsu	Kōgen
GR90	Kose	omi	44	kōbetsu	Kōgen
GR91	Kashihade	omi	16	kōbetsu	Kōgen
GR92	Ki	omi	28	kōbetsu	Kōgen
GR93	Hata	omi	4	kōbetsu	Kōgen
GR94	Mononobe	muraji	53	shinbetsu	Nigi Haya Hi no Mikoto
GR95	Heguri	omi	5	kōbetsu	Kōgen
GR96	Sazakibe	omi	1	kōbetsu	Kōgen
GR97	Nakatomi	muraji	60	shinbetsu	Ama no Koyane no Mikoto
GR98	Ohoyake	omi	5	kōbetsu	Kōshō
GR99	Ahata	omi	8	kōbetsu	Kōshō
GR100	Ishikaha	omi	3	kōbetsu	Kōgen
GR101	Sakurawi	omi	8	kōbetsu	Kōgen
GR102	Uneme	omi	8	shinbetsu	same as GR94
GR103	Tanaka	omi	11	kōbetsu	Kōgen
GR104	Woharida	omi	4	kōbetsu	Kōgen
GR105	Hozumi	omi	22	shinbetsu	same as GR94
GR106	Yamashiro	omi	2	lacking	lacking
GR107	Kamo	kimi (kun)	4	shinbetsu	same as GR87
GR108	Wono	omi	10	kōbetsu	Kōshō
GR109	Kahahe	omi	26	kōbetsu	Kōgen
GR110	Ichiwi	omi	1	kōbetsu	Kōshō
GR111	Kakinomoto	omi	2	kōbetsu	Kōshō
GR112	Karube	omi	2	kōbetsu	Kōgen
GR113	Wakasakurabe	omi	4	kōbetsu	Kōgen
GR114	Kishita	omi	3	kōbetsu	Kōgen
GR115	Takamuku	omi	8	kōbetsu	Kōgen
GR116	Shishihito	omi	3	kōbetsu	Kōgen
GR117	Kume	omi	3	kōbetsu	Kōgen
GR118	Inukami	kimi (kun)	8	kōbetsu	Keikō
GR119	Kamitsukeno	kimi (kun)	7	kōbetsu	Sujin
GR120	Tsuno	omi	4	kōbetsu	Kōgen
GR121	Hoshikaha	omi	2	kōbetsu	Kōgen
GR122	Oho	omi	9	kōbetsu	Jinmu
GR123	Munakata	kimi (kun)	2	shinbetsu	same as GR87
GR124	Kurumamochi	kimi (kun)	1	kōbetsu	Sujin
GR125	Aya	kimi (kun)	1	kōbetsu	Keikō

Appendix II 195

Grant No.	Uji	Prior Kabane		NSK Reference Frequency	Type of Lineage	Ancestor
GR126	Shimotsumichi	omi		1	kōbetsu	Kōrei
GR127	Iga	omi		4	kōbetsu	Kōgen
GR128	Ahe	omi		2	kōbetsu	Kōgen
GR129	Hayashi	omi		1	kōbetsu	Kōgen
GR130	Hami	omi		1	kōbetsu	Kōgen
GR131	Shimotsukeno	kimi	(kun)	2	kōbetsu	Sujin
GR132	Sami	kimi	(kun)	5	kōbetsu	Sujin
GR133	Chimori	omi		2	kōbetsu	Kaika
GR134	Ohono	kimi	(kun)	2	kōbetsu	Sujin
GR135	Sakamoto	omi		9	kōbetsu	Kōgen
GR136	Ikeda	kimi	(kun)	1	kōbetsu	Sujin
GR137	Tamate	omi		1	kōbetsu	Kōgen
GR138	Kasa	omi		2	kōbetsu	Kōrei

PART E: GRANTS OF <u>SUKUNE</u> TO FIFTY <u>UJI</u> IN A.D. 684

Grant No.	Uji	Prior Kabane	Original Kabane if Different	NSK Reference Frequency	Type of Lineage	Ancestor
GR139	Ohotomo	muraji		83	shinbetsu	Ame no Oshi Hi no Mikoto
GR140	Saheki	muraji		20	shinbetsu	same as GR139
GR141	Azumi	muraji		15	shinbetsu	Wata no Kami Wata Tsumi no Toyo Tama Hiko no Mikoto
GR142	Imibe	muraji	obito Cf. GR1	6	shinbetsu	Futo Tama no Mikoto
GR143	Wohari	muraji		4	shinbetsu	Ho Akari no Mikoto
GR144	Kura	muraji		1	shinbetsu	same as GR143
GR145	Nakatomi no Sakahito	muraji		1	shinbetsu	same as GR97
GR146	Haji	muraji		21	shinbetsu	Ame no Ho Hi no Mikoto
GR147	Kanimori	muraji		3	shinbetsu	Furu Tama no Mikoto
GR148	Sakahibe	muraji		16	shinbetsu	same as GR143
GR149	Sakurawi no Tabe	muraji		3	lacking	lacking
GR150	Ihokibe	muraji		2	shinbetsu	same as GR143
GR151	Kamunakibe	muraji		1	shinbetsu	same as GR94
GR152	Osakabe	muraji	miyatsuko Cf. GR25	3	shinbetsu	uncertain

GR153	Kusakabe	muraji		3	kōbetsu	Kaika
GR154	Miyake	muraji	kishi Cf. GR58	5	shoban	Silla ancestry
GR155	Kobe	muraji		1	shinbetsu	same as GR143
GR156	Tasuki no Tajihi	muraji		1	shinbetsu	same as GR143
GR157	Yuki no Tajihi	muraji		1	shinbetsu	same as GR143
GR158	Nuribe	muraji		2	shinbetsu	same as GR94
GR159	Ohoyuwe	muraji		1	lacking	lacking
GR160	Wakayuwe	muraji		1	shinbetsu	same as GR94
GR161	Yuge	muraji		1	shinbetsu	same as GR94
GR162	Kamuhatori	muraji		1	shinbetsu	uncertain
GR163	Nukatabe	muraji		7	shinbetsu	uncertain
GR164	Tsumori	muraji		14	shinbetsu	same as GR143
GR165	Agata no Inukahi	muraji		8	shinbetsu	Kamu Musubi no Mikoto
GR166	Wakainukahi	muraji		5	shinbetsu	same as GR143
GR167	Tamanoya	muraji		1	shinbetsu	same as GR139
GR168	Nihitabe	muraji		3	kōbetsu	Annei
GR169	Shitsuori	muraji		1	shinbetsu	same as GR165
GR170	Hi	muraji		4	shinbetsu	same as GR94
GR171	Ohoshiama	muraji		2	shinbetsu	same as GR141
GR172	Yamabe	muraji		1	lacking	lacking
GR173	Yatsume	muraji		1	shinbetsu	same as GR94
GR174	Sawi	muraji		4	shinbetsu	same as GR94
GR175	Hatakumi	muraji		1	shinbetsu	same as GR165
GR176	Ato	muraji		4	shinbetsu	same as GR94
GR177	Mamuta	muraji		2	kōbetsu	Jinmu
GR178	Tame	muraji		2	shinbetsu	same as GR165
GR179	Chihisakobe	muraji		3	kōbetsu	Jinmu
GR180	Uji	muraji		1	shinbetsu	same as GR94
GR181	Woharida	muraji		1	shinbetsu	same as GR94
GR182	Witsukahi	muraji		2	kōbetsu	Annei
GR183	Ama no Inukahi	muraji		2	shinbetsu	same as GR141
GR184	Hashihito	muraji		5	kōbetsu	Chūai
GR185	Tsukiyone	muraji		1	shinbetsu	same as GR94
GR186	Mino no Yatsume	muraji		1	lacking	lacking
GR187	Moroahi	omi		1	lacking	lacking
GR188	Furu	muraji	obito Cf. GR29	4	kōbetsu	Kōshō

Appendix II 197

PART F: GRANTS OF <u>IMIKI</u> TO ELEVEN <u>UJI</u> IN A.D. 685

Grant No.	Uji	Prior Kabane	Original Kabane if Different	Cf. Prior Grants	NSK Reference Frequency	Type of Lineage
GR189	Yamato	muraji	atahi	GR13, GR20	4	shinbetsu
GR190	Kazuraki	muraji	atahi	GR31	6	shinbetsu
GR191	Ohoshi Kafuchi	muraji	atahi	GR27	6	shinbetsu
GR192	Yamashiro	muraji	atahi	GR30	4	shinbetsu
GR193	Naniha	muraji	kishi	GR2, GR59	31	shoban*
GR194	Ki no Sakahito	muraji	atahi	GR66	2	lacking
GR195	Yamato no Aya	muraji	atahi	GR18, GR19	57	shoban
GR196	Kafuchi no Aya	muraji	atahi	GR28	4	shoban
GR197	Hada	muraji	miyatsuko	GR40	14	shoban
GR198	Ohosumi	atahi			1	shinbetsu**
GR199	Fumi	muraji	obito	GR54	7	shoban

*May also be <u>kōbetsu</u>. SSJR lists a Naniha no Muraji as <u>shoban</u> and a Naniha no Imiki as <u>kōbetsu</u>.
**Uncertain.

TABLE II: ALPHABETICAL LISTING OF THE <u>KABANE</u>-RECIPIENT <u>UJI</u>
AND INDIVIDUALS DURING TENMU'S AND JITO'S REIGNS

Uji and Grant Number (GR)	Grant Numbers under which references listed in Appendix I, Part B	
Agata no Inukahi no Muraji (GR165)	GR165	縣犬養連
Ahata no Omi (GR99)	GR99	粟田臣
Ahe no Omi (GR89)	GR89	阿倍臣
Ahe no Omi (GR128)	GR128	阿閇臣
Ama no Inukahi no Muraji (GR183)	GR183	海犬養連
Anahobe no Miyatsuko (GR50)	GR50	穴穗部造
Ato no Muraji (GR176)	GR176	阿刀連
Atoki no Fubito (GR68)	GR68	阿直史
Aya no Kimi (GR125)	GR125	綾君
Azumi no Muraji (GR141)	GR141	阿曇連
Chihisakobe no Muraji (GR179)	GR179	少子部連
Chimori no Omi (GR133)	GR133	道守臣

Fujiharabe no Miyatsuko (GR24)	GR24	藤原部造
Fumi no Atahi Chitoko (GR18)	GR195	書直智徳
Fumi no Muraji (GR199)	GR199	書連
Fumi no Obito (GR54)	GR199	文首
Fune no Fubito (GR61)	GR61	船史
Furu no Muraji (GR188)	GR188	布留連
Hada no Miyatsuko (GR40)	GR197	秦造
Hada no Miyatsuko Tsunade (GR202)	GR197	秦造綱手
Hada no Muraji (GR197)	GR197	秦連
Hahaki no Miyatsuko (GR60)	GR60	伯耆造
Haji no Muraji (GR146)	GR146	土師連
Hami no Omi (GR130)	GR130	波彌臣
Hashihito no Muraji (GR184)	GR184	間人連
Hata no Kimi (GR83)	GR83	羽田君
Hata no Omi (GR93)	GR93	波多臣
Hatakumi no Muraji (GR175)	GR175	爪工連
Hatsukashi no Miyatsuko (GR53)	GR53	羽束造
Hayashi no Omi (GR129)	GR129	林臣
Hazukashibe no Miyatsuko (GR49)	GR49	泥部造
Heguri no Omi (GR95)	GR95	平群臣
Hi no Muraji (GR170)	GR170	氷連
Hinokuma no Toneri no Miyatsuko (GR38)	GR38	檜隈舎人造
Hoshikaha no Omi (GR121)	GR121	星川臣
Hozumi no Omi (GR105)	GR105	穂積臣
Ichiwi no Omi (GR110)	GR110	櫟井臣
Iga no Omi (GR127)	GR127	伊賀臣
Ihokibe no Muraji (GR150)	GR150	伊福部連
Ikeda no Kimi (GR136)	GR136	池田君
Iki no Fubito (GR62)	GR62	壹伎史
Imibe no Muraji (GR142)	GR142	忌部連

Imibe no Obito Kobito (GR1)	GR142	忌部首首
Inukami no Kimi (GR118)	GR118	犬上君
Ishikaha no Omi (GR100)	GR100	石川臣
Isonokamibe no Miyatsuko (GR47)	GR47	石上部造
Kadobe no Atahi (GR33)	GR33	門部直
Kadobe no Atahi Ohoshima (GR14)	GR33	門部直大嶋
Kafuchi no Atahi Agata (GR7)	GR7	川内直縣
Kafuchi no Aya no Atahi (GR28)	GR196	川内漢直
Kafuchi no Aya no Muraji (GR196)	GR196	河内漢連
Kafuchi no Umakahi no Miyatsuko (GR43)	GR43	川内馬飼造
Kagami Tsukuri no Miyatsuko (GR71)	GR71	鏡作造
Kahahe no Omi (GR109)	GR109	川邊臣
Kahase no Toneri no Miyatsuko (GR41)	GR41	川瀬舎人造
Kakinomoto no Omi (GR111)	GR111	柿本臣
Kamitsukeno no Kimi (GR119)	GR119	上毛野君
Kamo no Kimi (GR107)	GR107	鴨君
Kamuhatori no Muraji (GR162)	GR162	神服部連
Kamunakibe no Muraji (GR151)	GR151	巫部連
Kanimori no Muraji (GR147)	GR147	掃部連
Karube no Omi (GR112)	GR112	輕部臣
Kasa no Omi (GR138)	GR138	笠臣
Kashihade no Omi (GR91)	GR91	膳臣
Katari no Miyatsuko (GR57)	GR57	語造
Kazura no Miyatsuko (GR35)	GR35	縵造
Kazuraki no Atahi (GR31)	GR190	葛城直
Kazuraki no Muraji (GR190)	GR190	葛城連
Ki no Omi (GR92)	GR92	紀臣
Ki no Sakahito no Atahi (GR66)	GR194	紀酒人直
Ki no Sakahito no Muraji (GR194)	GR194	紀酒人連
Kifumi no Miyatsuko (GR44)	GR44	黄文造

Kishita no Omi (GR114)	GR114	岸田臣
Kobe no Muraji (GR155)	GR155	兒部連
Komotsume no Miyatsuko (GR45)	GR45	薦集造
Kose no Omi (GR90)	GR90	巨勢臣
Kudara no Miyatsuko (GR56)	GR56	百濟造
Kuhahara no Suguri Katsu (GR200)	GR200	桑原村主訶都
Kume no Omi (GR117)	GR117	來目臣
Kume no Toneri no Miyatsuko (GR37)	GR37	來目舍人造
Kura no Kinunuhi no Miyatsuko (GR73)	GR73	内藏衣縫造
Kura no Muraji (GR144)	GR144	倉連
Kurukuma no Obito (GR21)	GR21	粟隈首
Kurumamochi no Kimi (GR124)	GR124	車持君
Kusakabe no Kishi (GR59)	GR193	草壁吉士
Kusakabe no Kishi Ohokata (GR2)	GR193	草香部吉士大形
Kusakabe no Muraji (GR153)	GR153	草壁連
Magari no Hakozukuri no Miyatsuko (GR46)	GR46	勾筥作造
Mamuta no Muraji (GR177)	GR177	茨田連
Michi no Kimi (GR75)	GR75	路公
Mikuni no Kimi (GR77)	GR77	三國公
Mino no Agatanushi (GR72)	GR72	三野縣主
Mino no Yatsume no Muraji (GR186)	GR186	美濃矢集連
Miyake no Kishi (GR58)	GR154	三宅吉士
Miyake no Muraji (GR154)	GR154	三宅連
Mohitori no Miyatsuko (GR22)	GR22	水取造
Mononobe no Muraji (GR94)	GR94	物部連
Mononobe no Obito (GR29)	GR188	物部首
Moriyama no Kimi (GR74)	GR74	守山公
Moroahi no Omi (GR187)	GR187	諸會臣
Munakata no Kimi (GR123)	GR123	胸方君
Nakatomi no Muraji (GR97)	GR97	中臣連

Appendix II

Nakatomi no Sakahito no Muraji (GR145)	GR145	中臣酒人連
Naniha no Muraji (GR193)	GR193	難波連
Nishikori no Miyatsuko (GR34)	GR34	錦織造
Nishikori no Miyatsuko no Wokida (GR3)	GR34	錦織造小分
Nihitabe no Muraji (GR168)	GR168	新田部連
Nukatabe no Muraji (GR163)	GR163	額田部連
Nuribe no Muraji (GR158)	GR158	漆部連
Oho no Omi (GR122)	GR122	多臣
Ohokasuga no Omi (GR88)	GR88	大春日臣
Ohokoma no Miyatsuko (GR39)	GR39	大狛造
[Ohokoma no Miyatsuko] Ashitsuki (GR12)	GR39	(大狛造)足圷
Ohokoma no Miyatsuko Momoe (GR11)	GR39	大狛造百枝
Ohomiwa no Kimi (GR87)	GR87	大三輪君
Ohono no Kimi (GR134)	GR134	大野君
Ohoshiama no Muraji (GR171)	GR171	凡海連
Ohoshi Kafuchi no Atahi (GR27)	GR191	凡河内直
Ohoshi Kafuchi no Muraji (GR191)	GR191	凡川内連
Ohosumi no Atahi (GR198)	GR198	大隅直
Ohotomo no Muraji (GR139)	GR139	大伴連
Ohoyake no Omi (GR98)	GR98	大宅臣
Ohoyuwe no Muraji (GR159)	GR159	大湯人連
Okinaga no Kimi (GR84)	GR84	息長公
Osakabe no Miyatsuko (GR25)	GR152	刑部造
Osakabe no Muraji (GR152)	GR152	忍壁連
Oshinumi no Miyatsuko (GR52)	GR52	忍海造
[Oshinumi no Miyatsuko] Arata (GR9)	GR52	(忍海造)荒田
Oshinumi no Miyatsuko Kagami (GR8)	GR52	忍海造鏡
[Oshinumi no Miyatsuko] Yoshimaro (GR10)	GR52	(忍海造)能麻呂
Saheki no Muraji (GR140)	GR140	佐伯連
Sakahibe no Muraji (GR148)	GR148	境部連

Sakahito no Kimi (GR85)	GR85	酒人公
Sakamoto no Omi (GR135)	GR135	坂本臣
Sakata no Kimi (GR82)	GR82	坂田公
Sakikusabe no Miyatsuko (GR26)	GR26	福草部造
Sakurawi no Omi (GR101)	GR101	櫻井臣
Sakurawi no Tabe no Muraji (GR149)	GR149	櫻井田部連
Sami no Kimi (GR132)	GR132	佐味君
Sarara no Umakahi no Miyatsuko (GR63)	GR63	沙羅羅馬飼造
Sawi no Muraji (GR174)	GR174	狹井連
Sazakibe no Omi (GR96)	GR96	雀部臣
Shiki no Agatanushi (GR70)	GR70	磯城縣主
Shimotsukeno no Kimi (GR131)	GR131	下毛野君
Shimotsumichi no Omi (GR126)	GR126	下道臣
Shirakabe no Miyatsuko (GR51)	GR51	白髮部造
Shishihito no Miyatsuko Okina (GR15)	GR15	宍人造老
Shishihito no Omi (GR116)	GR116	宍人臣
Shitsuori no Muraji (GR169)	GR169	倭文連
[Sukita no Kurahito] Ishikatsu (GR6)	GR6	(次田倉人)石勝
Sukita no Kurahito Mukutari (GR5)	GR5	次田倉人椹足
Tagima no Kimi (GR78)	GR78	當麻公
Tajihi no Kimi (GR80)	GR80	丹比公
Takahashi no Kimi (GR76)	GR76	高橋公
Takamuku no Omi (GR115)	GR115	高向臣
Takara no Himatsuri no Miyatsuko (GR48)	GR48	財日奉造
Takechi no Agatanushi (GR69)	GR69	高市縣主
Tamanoya no Muraji (GR167)	GR167	玉祖連
Tamate no Omi (GR137)	GR137	玉手臣
Tame no Muraji (GR178)	GR178	田目連
Tanaka no Omi (GR103)	GR103	田中臣
Tasuki no Tajihi no Muraji (GR156)	GR156	手繦丹比連

Appendix II

Tawi no Atahi Yoshimaro (GR4)	GR4	田井直吉摩呂
Toneri no Miyatsuko Nukamushi (GR17)	GR17	舍人造糠蟲
Tonohatori no Miyatsuko (GR32)	GR32	殿服部造
Totori no Miyatsuko (GR36)	GR36	鳥取造
Tsukinomoto no Suguri Kachimaro (GR201)	GR201	槻本村主勝麻呂
Tsukiyone no Muraji (GR185)	GR185	舂米連
Tsumori no Muraji (GR164)	GR164	津守連
Tsuno no Omi (GR120)	GR120	角臣
Uji no Muraji (GR180)	GR180	菟道連
Umaraki no Kimi (GR79)	GR79	茨城公
Uneme no Miyatsuko (GR67)	GR67	采女造
Uneme no Omi (GR102)	GR102	采女臣
Uno no Umakahi no Miyatsuko (GR64)	GR64	菟野馬飼造
Wakainukahi no Muraji (GR166)	GR166	稚犬養連
Wakasakurabe no Omi (GR113)	GR113	若櫻部臣
Wakayuwe no Muraji (GR160)	GR160	若湯人連
Wina no Kimi (GR81)	GR81	猪名公
Witsukahi no Muraji (GR182)	GR182	猪使連
Wohari no Muraji (GR143)	GR143	尾張連
Woharida no Muraji (GR181)	GR181	小治田連
Woharida no Omi (GR104)	GR104	小墾田臣
Wohatsuse no Miyatsuko (GR55)	GR55	小泊瀬造
Wono no Omi (GR108)	GR108	小野臣
Yamabe no Muraji (GR172)	GR172	山部連
Yamaji no Kimi (GR86)	GR86	山道公
Yamashiro no Atahi (GR30)	GR192	山背直
Yamashiro no Koma no Ikamaro (GR16)	GR16	山背狛烏賊麻呂
Yamashiro no Muraji (GR192)	GR192	山背連
Yamashiro no Omi (GR106)	GR106	山背臣
Yamato no Atahi (GR20)	GR189	倭直

Yamato no Atahi Tatsumaro (GR13)	GR189	倭直龍麻呂
Yamato no Muraji (GR189)	GR189	大倭連
Yamato no Aya no Atahi (GR19)	GR195	倭漢直
Yamato no Aya no Muraji (GR195)	GR195	倭漢連
Yamato no Umakahi no Miyatsuko (GR42)	GR42	倭馬飼造
Yatabe no Miyatsuko (GR23)	GR23	矢田部造
Yatsume no Muraji (GR173)	GR173	矢集連
Yoshino no Obito (GR65)	GR65	吉野首
Yuge no Muraji (GR161)	GR161	弓削連
Yuki no Tajihi no Muraji (GR157)	GR157	靫丹比連

Bibliography*

A. PRIMARY SOURCES
(Texts, Commentaries and Translations)

Kojiki:

Chamberlain, Basil Hall. *Translation of "Ko-ji-ki" or "Records of Ancient Matters."* 1932.

Kurano Kenji, Takeda Yūkichi, annotators. *Nihon koten bungaku taikei*, vol. 1, Kojiki-Norito. 1969.

Motoori Norinaga. *Kojiki-den*, 2 vols. 1930.

Philippi, Donald L., tr. *Kojiki*. 1968.

Nihon Shoki:

Aston, W.G., tr. *Nihongi, Chronicles of Japan from Earliest Times to A.D. 697*, 2 vols. London, 1956.

Iida Takesato. *Nihon Shoki Tsūshaku*, 5 vols. 1926-27.

Kuroita Katsumi, ed. *Shintei zōho kokushi taikei*, vol. 1 (in 2 parts), Nihon Shoki. 1966.

Maruyama Rinpei. *Teihon Nihon Shoki*, 3 vols. and index. 1966.

Sakamoto Tarō, Ienaga Saburō, Inoue Mitsusada, Ōno Susumu, annotators. *Nihon koten bungaku taikei*, vols. 67-68, Nihon Shoki. 1967.

Shoku Nihongi:

Saeki Ariyoshi, ed. *Zōho rikkokushi*, vols. 3-4, Shoku Nihongi. 1939.

Snellen, J.B., tr. "Shoku Nihongi, Chronicles of Japan, Continued from 697-791 A.D.," *Transactions of the Asiatic Society of Japan*, second series, vol. 11, 1934, pp. 151-239; vol. 14, 1937, pp. 209-278.

Shinsen Shōjiroku:

Kurita Hiroshi. *Shinsen Shōjiroku kōshō*, 12 vols. and index. 1900.

Saeki Arikiyo. *Shinsen Shōjiroku no kenkyū, honbunhen*. 1966.

Kogoshūi:

Ikebe Mahari. *Kogoshūi shinchū*. 1928.

Katō Genchi and Hoshino Hikoshiro, tr. *Kogoshūi: Gleanings from Ancient Stories*. 1926.

Mizoguchi Komazō. *Kogoshūi seigi*. 1935.

B. REFERENCE WORKS

A Dictionary of Japanese History. Joseph M. Goedertier, comp. 1968.

Daigenkai. Ōtsuki Fumihiko, comp. 4 vols. and index. 1937.

*All works published in Tokyo unless otherwise indicated.

Dai Nihon chimei jisho. Yoshida Tōgo, comp. 6 vols and index. 1911.

Dai Nihon jinmei jisho. Dai Nihon jinmei jisho kankōkai, comp. 5 vols. 1937.

Historical and Geographical Dictionary of Japan. E. Papinot, comp. Ann Arbor, 1948.

Kokushi jiten. Tsuji Zennosuke, 4 vols. 1940-43.

Nihon kodai jinmei jiten. Takeuchi Rizō, Yamada Hideo, and Hirano Kunio, eds. 5 vols. to date. 1968-69.

Nihon rekishi daijiten. Kawade Shobō. 10 vols. 1968-70.

Nihonshi jiten. Kyōto Daigaku Bungakubu, Kokushi Kenkyū-shitsu, comp. Osaka, 1955.

Nihon shiryō shūsei. Shimonaka Yasaburō, ed. 1956.

Nihon Shoki sōsakuin. Nakamura Keishin, comp. 4 vols. 1964-68.

Rikkokushi sakuin. Ōno Tatsunosuke, comp. 4 vols. 1963-69.

Seishi kakei daijiten. Ōta Akira, comp. 3 vols. 1934-36.

Shinsen Shōjiroku sōsakuin. Seki Arikiyo, ed. Osaka? (mimeographed), 1957.

C. BOOKS AND ARTICLES IN JAPANESE

Abe Takehiko. "Kuni no miyatsuko no kabane to keifu." Shigaku zasshi, vol. 59 (November 1950), pp. 57-68.

―――. "Tomo no miyatsuko, tomobe kō." In Sakamoto Tarō Hakase Kanreki Kinenkai, Nihon kodaishi ronshū, vol. 1 (1962), pp. 105-132.

―――. Uji-Kabane. 1966.

Akimoto Kichirō, annotator. Nihon koten bungaku taikei, vol. 2, Fudoki. 1967.

Egami Namio. Kiba minzoku kokka: Nihon kodai shi e no apurōchi. 1967.

Fujii Kanji. "Jōdai kika shizoku no shakai kōzō: Yamashiro ni okeru Hada uji o chūshin toshite." Ritsumeikan Daigaku ronsō, vol. 73-74 (November 1949), pp. 101-111.

Fukuda Hisamichi. Kojiki-den no kenkyū. 1941.

Handa Yasuo. "Hada uji to sono kami." Rekishi chiri, vol. 82 (September 1953), pp. 2-13.

Hayashiya Tatsusaburō. Kodai kokka no kaitai. 1966.

Higo Kazuo. "Dajōdaijin ni tsuite." Shigaku zasshi, vol. 48 (August 1937), pp. 1045-1085.

Hirano Kunio. "Hada uji no kenkyū." Shigaku zasshi, vol. 70 (March 1961), pp. 25-46; (April 1961), pp. 42-74.

―――. "Kodai shisei jinmei ni arawareta kaikyū kankei: toku ni kikakei shizoku ni tsuite." In Sakamoto Tarō Hakase Kanreki Kinenkai, Nihon kodaishi ronshū. vol. 1 (1962), pp. 1-46.

―――. "Taika zendai no shakai kōzō." In Iwanami kōza, vol. 2, Nihon rekishi (1964), pp. 81-122.

Ienaga Saburō. "Asuka Hakuhō bunka." Iwanami kōza, vol. 2, Nihon rekishi (1964), pp. 315-346.

Inoue Hideo. "Shiragi no koppin seido." Rekishigaku kenkyū, 304 (September 1965), pp. 40-51.

Inoue Mitsusada. "Futatsu no shizoku riron." Nihon rekishi, vol. 12 (April 1948), pp. 37-44.

_____. Nihon kodaishi no shomondai. 1949.

_____. "Kuni no miyatsuko no seiritsu." Shigaku zasshi, vol. 60 (November 1951), pp. 1-42.

_____. ed. Shin Nihonshi taikei, vol. 2, Kodai shakai. 1954.

_____. Nihon kokka no kigen. 1960.

_____. "Jinshin no ran, toku ni chihō gōzoku no kōdō ni tsuite." Kodaishi kōza, vol. 11 (1966), pp. 264-298.

_____. Nihon kodai kokka no kenkyū. 1967.

Ishii Ryōsuke. Nihon hōsei shi gaisetsu. 1950.

_____. "Uji to kabane." In Nihon hōsei shi (1954), pp. 221-230.

Ishimoda Tadashi. "Kodai no mibun chitsujo, Nihon no baai ni tsuite no oboegaki." Kodaishi kōza, vol. 7 (1966), pp. 242-288.

_____. "Nihon kodai ni okeru bungyō no mondai." Kodaishi kōza, vol. 9 (1966), pp. 312-345.

Iwahashi Koyata. Jōdai kanshoku seido no kenkyū. 1962.

Kawakami Tasuke. Nihon kodai shakai shi no kenkyū. 1947.

Kawasaki Tsuneyuki. Tenmu Tennō, 1966.

Kida Shinroku. Reiseika ni okeru kunshin jōge no chitsujo ni tsuite. Ise-shi, 1972.

Kishi Toshio. Nihon kodai seiji shi kenkyū. 1969.

Kitamura Bunji. "Kabane no seido ni kansuru shinkenkyū josetsu." Jinbun kagaku ronshū, Hokkaido University, vol. 3 (1964), pp. 90-137.

Kitayama Shigeo. Asuka Chō. In Kokumin no Rekishi, vol. 3 (1968).

Kōno Shōzō. "The Hitachi-Fudoki, or Records of Customs and Land of Hitachi." Sakai Atsuharu, tr. Cultural Nippon, vol. 8, no. 1 (1940), pp. 145-181; vol. 8, no. 2 (1940), pp. 109-156; vol. 8, no. 3 (1940), pp. 137-186.

_____. "The Izumo-Fudoki, or The Records of Customs and Land of Izumo," Sakai Atsuharu, tr. Cultural Nippon, vol. 9, no. 1 (1941), pp. 141-195; vol. 9, no. 2 (1941), pp. 119-183; vol. 9, no. 3 (1941), pp. 108-149.

Kuroita Katsumi. Kokushi no kenkyū. 3 vols. 1939.

Maekawa Akihisa. "5, 6 seiki no shisei-sei to bemin-sei." Rekishigaku kenkyū, 304 (September 1965), pp. 33-40.

Maruyama Jirō. Nihon Shoki no kenkyū. 1955.

Matsumoto Shigehiko. "Kabane kō." Chūō Daigaku bungakubu kiyō, no. 1 (1955), pp. 1-12.

Mishina Shōei. "Ama-tsu-kami zoku, kuni-tsu-kami zoku to sōbun soshiki." Shirin, vol. 60, no. 6 (November 1955), pp. 1-18.

Miura Hiroyuki. Hōsei shi no kenkyū. 1924.

_____. Zoku hōsei shi no kenkyū. 1925.

Nakada Kaoru. "Kabane-kō." In his Hōsei shi ronshū (1943), pp. 1027-1049.

Naoki Kōjiro. "Kodai shizoku kenkyū no dōkō." Hisutoria, vol. 18 (1957), pp. 65-70.

———. Jinshin no ran. 1964.

———. "Ōjin ōchō-ron josetsu." Naniha no miya shi no kenkyū, vol. 5 (1964), pp. 1-20.

———. Nihon kodai kokka no kōzō. 1966.

———. "Kodai Nihon no uji." Kodaishi kōza, vol. 6 (1966), pp. 271-303.

———. Nihon kodai heisei shi no kenkyū. 1968.

Ōta Akira. Nihon jōdai ni okeru shakai soshiki no kenkyū. 1940.

———. Seishi to kakei. 1942.

———. Zentei Nihon jōdai shakai soshiki no kenkyū. 1955.

Saeki Arikiyo. Shinsen Shōjiroku no kenkyū, kenkyūhen. 1962.

———. Nihon kodai no seiji to shakai. 1970.

Sakamoto Tarō. Taika kaishi no kenkyū. 1938.

———. "Keitai-ki no shiryō hihan." Kokugakuin zasshi, vol. 62 (September 1961), pp. 43-54.

———. Nihon kodaishi no kisoteki kenkyū, vol. 1 (1964).

Seki Akira. "Yamato no Aya uji no kenkyū." Shigaku zasshi, vol. 62 (September 1953), pp. 794-835.

———. Kikajin: kodai no seiji, keizai, bunka o kataru. 1956.

———. "Nihon kodai no mibun to kaikyū." Kodaishi kōza, vol. 7 (1966), pp. 210-239.

Sogabe Shizuo. "Tenmu yakusa no kabane no yomikata." Nihon rekishi, vol. 68 (January 1954), pp. 6-7.

Takeuchi Rizō. "Tenmu 'hassei' seitei no igi." Shien, vol. 43 (1950), pp. 27-48.

Takigawa Masajirō. Nihon hōsei shi. 1941.

———. Nihon shakai shi. 1946.

Tōma Seita. Nihon kodai kokka. 1947.

Tsuboi Kiyotari and Kishi Toshio, compilers. Kodai no Nihon, vol. 5, Kinki (1970).

Tsuda Sōkichi. Kojiki oyobi Nihon Shoki no kenkyū. 1924.

———. Jōdai Nihon no shakai oyobi shisō. 1933.

———. Nihon koten no kenkyū. 2 vols. 1948 and 1950.

———. Nihon jōdai shi no kenkyū. 1949.

Ueda Masaaki. "Agata oyobi agata nushi no kenkyū." Kokugakuin zasshi, vol. 52 no. 2 (July 1953), pp. 27-42.

———. "Yamato kokka no kōzō." In Iwanami kōza, vol. 2, Nihon rekishi, (1964), pp. 1-40.

———. Kikajin: kodai kokka no seiritsu o megutte. 1965.

———. Nihon kodai kokka seiritsu shi no kenkyū. 1966.

———. "Yamato kokka no seiritsu katei." Kodaishi kōza, vol. 4 (1966), pp. 229-265.

———. Yamato chōtei. 1967.

_____. Nihon kodai kokka ronkyū. 1968.

Umezawa Isezō. Ki-ki hihan: Kojiki oyobi Nihon Shoki no seiritsu ni kansuru kenkyū. 1962.

Yoshimura Shigeki. "Jōdai ni okeru chihō seido no ichikōsatsu, toku ni kuni-no-tsukasa to kōri-no-tsukasa to no kankei ni tsuite." Rekishi chiri, vol. 67 (January 1936), pp. 23-44.

D. BOOKS AND ARTICLES IN WESTERN LANGUAGES

Asakawa, Kan'ichi. The Early Institutional Life of Japan: A Study in the Reform of 645 A.D. New York, 1903.

Bock, Felicia G. Engi-Shiki: Procedures of the Engi Era, Books I-V. 1970.

Hall, J. Carey. "A Decade of Reform Work in Japan at the Opening of the Eighth Century." Transactions and Proceedings of the Japan Society, London, vol. 15 (1916-17), pp. 151-194.

Hall, John W. Government and Local Power in Japan, 500 to 1700: A Study Based on Bizen Province. Princeton, 1966.

_____. Japanese History, New Dimensions of Approach and Understanding. Washington, 1966.

_____. Japan from Prehistory to Modern Times. New York, 1971.

Kamstra, J.H. Encounter and Syncretism: The Initial Growth of Japanese Buddhism. Leiden, 1967.

Kiley, Cornelius J., "A Note on the Surnames of Immigrant Officials in Nara Japan." Harvard Journal of Asiatic Studies, vol. 29 (1969), pp. 177-189.

Lewin, Bruno. Aya and Hata: Bervölkerungsgruppen Altjapans Kontinentaler Herkunft. Wiesbaden, 1962.

Miller, Richard J. "An Historical Study of the Higher Administrative Officials of the Council of State in Japan in the Eighth Century A.D." M.A. thesis, Berkeley, 1947.

_____. "A Study of the Development of a Centralized State Prior to the Taika Reform (A.D. 645)." Ph.D. thesis, Berkeley, 1953.

Reischauer, Robert K. Early Japanese History (c. 40 B.C.-A.D. 1167). 2 vols. Gloucester, Mass., 1937.

Robinson, G.W. "Early Japanese Chronicles: The Six National Histories." In W.G. Beasley and E.G. Pulleyblank, eds. Historians of China and Japan, London, 1961, pp. 211-228.

Sansom, George, "Early Japanese Law and Administration," Transactions of the Asiatic Society of Japan, second series, vol. 9 (1932), pp. 67-109; vol. 11 (1934), pp. 114-149.

_____. Japan, A Short Cultural History, rev. ed. New York, 1943.

_____. A History of Japan to 1334. Stanford, California, 1958.

Tarring, C.J. "Land Provisions of the Taihō Riō." Transactions of the Asiatic Society of Japan, vol. 8 (1880), pp. 145-155.

Tsunoda, Ryūsaku, tr. Japan in the Chinese Dynastic Histories, Later Han through Ming Dynasties. South Pasadena, 1951.

_____. W.T. De Bary and D. Keene. Sources of the Japanese Tradition. New York, 1958.

ISBN: 0-520-09494-8